Other books by same author:

Guided by Your Light, 2015

Video Sessions Available:

www.Heart4Souls.com; www.SpritualServices.online

Truth Beyond

Rev. Judi Stetson Weaver

BALBOA.PRESS

A DIVISION OF HAY HOUSE

Balboa Press books may be ordered through booksellers or by contacting:

Balboa Press
A Division of Hay House
1663 Liberty Drive
Bloomington, IN 47403
www.balboapress.com
844-682-1282

www.Heart4Souls.com; www.SpiritualServices.online
Rev.Judi.Weaver@gmail.com

Print information available on the last page.

ISBN: 978-1-9822-5339-4 (sc)
ISBN: 978-1-9822-5361-5 (e)

Balboa Press rev. date: 09/11/2020

This book is dedicated to the Love of my Life,
Derek Lynn Weaver

Thank you for choosing to lead before me, so that you could shine the light on a new path for me to see...
Always My Love

EPIGRAPH

THE WORLD IN WHICH WE live is vast, complicated and chaotic. It is filled with millions of species that coexist simultaneously on a rock, one whose physicalness is still a mystery to us as it continues to float in an ever-expanding universe. We know as little as two percent about our universe. Science helps us to understand the what, how and why in the physical realm. History helps us with the where, and that just leaves - The Who. Who is that stranger on the flight that felt so familiar, like we had been friends for years? Who is that beautiful soul across the room that forces your eyes to fixate only on them, with enough energy to stop the whole room? Why do we have a feeling of dread every time we eat at a restaurant without that special someone? Energies and intuition seem to have no real rhyme or reason, when we don't stop and actually try to understand the message. Why is it making you feel the way it does?

When my mother, the author, told me she was writing her second book, I insisted on writing this forward. Growing up as her middle child, I was the socialite of my family. After fifteen years of bartending, I have spent numerous years of my life observing human behavior and have felt many different energies from all types of people. My mother's book is about what she has discovered in her second act in life, as her first was raising three boys. We have had many conversations about intuition, about complete strangers which I meet, and she has always helped me understand them and why I get the vibes that I do. As a white light healer, her focus is on energies. Energies could be anything from a gut feeling, to messages from beyond the grave, or even beyond this universe, from any and all walks of life, those that we see and those we cannot. Many things can be explained and even more cannot. This book is based on her experiences with all of these types of energies, and the tools in which she uses to decipher the extraordinary. Hers is a gift that most of us fear, or simply ignore.

Love Always,

Dustin Stetson

CONTENTS

FORWARD

AS IS SO OFTEN THE case when embarking on a spiritual path, we start to pay attention to random encounters with angels in human form who encourage us along our way. Judi and I met by chance one sunny day during the summer of 2008. My heart had been shattered, which my ego and my practiced skill set could not "fix." One of the mediums in the Cassadaga Spiritualist Camp in Florida had helped me resolve a life crisis a number of years earlier, so I returned once again for healing.

I entered the Caesar Foreman Healing Gazebo and was captured by the sparkling azure eyes of Master teacher and Healer Lorraine Peterson, who was instructing a student. I was consumed with emotional upheaval and did not notice the other person sitting on the side of the room until my session was completed. As I arose from the stool, in my altered state of peace, a brilliant hazel gaze and smile locked with my eyes and blessed me. While orienting myself to the Earth plane, I noticed a leopard print dress, an abundant mane of chestnut tresses and a sweet Chihuahua curled on her lap. We did not speak, but we acknowledged each other with a respectful nod. Still, Spirit locked this memory in my heart, as it often does with people who are or will be of significance in my life.

We continued our classes in Cassadaga separately, and periodically we would share a teacher and a few friendly words. We followed our individual learning paths, becoming comfortable in our familiarity, but living our separate lives. Judi became a Certified Healer and I became a member of the Cassadaga community following my metaphysical studies.

My discovery of Judi's healing ability occurred at the People's Church of Divine Prophesy in Daytona Beach in 2011. I had been invited there by Wendy, a visiting healer from New York with whom I had befriended in Cassadaga. She was speaking at the service and would conduct one of her famous "Slayed in the Spirit" services later in the evening. During the morning service the call for healing was made by the pastor, Steve. I took my opportunity to sit in a chair on the side of the sanctuary. This is a common part of the Spiritualist order of service, and I prepared my heart, with head bowed, to receive the loving essence of the Holy Spirit. There was nothing particularly remarkable about receiving healing energy until a pair of hands rested on my shoulders from behind me. I was immediately transported into the starry heavens and could feel my etheric body lifting off the seat—amazing and wonderful! When the female voice whispered "Blessings" I did not want to return. As I stood, I turned around and witnessed a pair of golden eyes returning to hazel and the familiar smile. It was Judi!

Over time our experiences entwined as we continued our spiritual unfolding, eventually becoming trusted friends. We shared a teacher, Rosa, resulting in separate pilgrimages to Brazil to see the world-famous medium, John of God. This mutual experience cemented our friendship. During 2017, we agreed to travel to the Omega Institute in Rhinebeck, New York to reunite with him. I needed a couple of psychic surgeries after a car accident, and Judi wanted more surgeries from the Entities to strengthen her healing abilities.

What transpired at the Omega Institute and the Artistes Guest House forever changed the intensity of our mutual commitment. That commitment was to the mission of no longer merely receiving blessings but also to extending the wisdom teachings to others. In the kitchen of this bed and breakfast, we received a prophesy, in evidentiary form, by Judi's dramatic and unexpected channeling of a Lenape Chief. Julie and Peter, the innkeepers, clarified some of the omissions and confusion of the channeled message, as well as contributed historical information about the turn-of-the-century Rectory. My purpose in being present was to witness the actual event as truth. The verbatim transcript of this prophesy is found in the next chapter, but the following excerpt expresses the forthcoming of this book:

> *Each path is filled with many twists and turns and different destinations; however, we all go to the great **beyond**...**Beyond** within and around...You choose to look beyond the physical of what is for what **truly** is...You are an energy source...to gather the wisdom and knowledge of **beyond** that will come to and through the world...through you!*

My gratitude is extended to the dedicated ladies who put their earthly lives on hold to meet on a regular basis, faithfully seated in the meditation circle, to raise the energy vibration and to support the completion of this important work. The teachings are presented in the actual words of the Entities who incorporated into Judi and used her voice to communicate their messages. Know that the channeling sessions are recorded, available for review and witnessed. Comments from members of the meditation circle can be found in the last chapter entitled "As for the Others."

It has been my personal honor to be a part of this process as the earthly oracle. As I review the mechanics of this manuscript, I polish my own heart, lending my expertise to ensure authenticity and advocating for my friend and colleague, Judi, who is on her special mission from God Source. I can attest, having experienced many gifted spiritual teachers, that Judi is ready to change the world, Heart to Souls.

Whether you are placing your first foot on your spiritual quest, seeking "something more," that is calling from **beyond** your mind, or are well on your way to connecting with the Divine, you will find **Truth Beyond** extremely valuable to your progress. Take these words into your heart and grow with the angels who surround YOU!

Namaste...the Light in me sees the Light in you!

SU

PREFACE

THIS BOOK IS A CULMINATION of channeled messages and guidance that has been provided from the God Source and Universal Light Beings.

I spent several months in a place of semi-isolation where there was minimal exposure to books, classes and electronic communication to ensure that the information that was being relayed remained as clear and not influenced by other writers or channeled guidance.

I clearly received guidance and instruction of how this beautiful project would unfold for mankind.

God Source about Channeling and energy exchange

The early morning hours are the most precious time. It is the time when the veil is upon its thinnest. It is the time of the day when the energies are allowed to flow back and forth and into and through one another with a much clearer communication. It is the time when the humans are allowed to be in a slower space so that they can actually coordinate with the different energies of above... Channeling is a different type of communication as you're tapping into the energy force, however you're acting as a third party. You allow yourself to step aside, so that the energy and the information of the other beings are transmitted through the physical body in which is channeling. They're allowed then to step in and to utilize the voice, hand gestures, their words or utilize any information that the human has gone through in their lifetime. Beings may utilize information of their own Essence and to be able to relay it in any way possible. Channeling is generally in a more of a monotone nature, however every single Spirit is different.

It is most important to keep your hearts pure of wanting a betterment of mankind. To keep yourself in a prayerful space. A space of honoring and a space of being honored for who you are, and for your hearts purpose. It is important to allow love. The pure essence of love to be the greatest beacon of all. Just allow that love light to lead you forward, and to allow others to come into and through that love light. You don't have to worry about where the information will go. The information will make it to the parties that it's intended to at the appropriate time. It's all about you child. It's all about your gifts, your destination and following your path. The rest of it truly doesn't matter, because it's not yours to. Just enjoy the journey my child. Enjoy the blessings my child. Enjoy the peace my child. And enjoy the opportunity to meet and to understand and to be able to have an understanding of information and beings that are far beyond what you knew before. This is what life is. Allowing yourself to become the expansion of. And to expand to and through you also. What a joyful place that is. To know and to be and to become. I want to thank you dear one for choosing. Choosing to read this. Choosing to allow yourself the opportunity to think beyond what you knew. And to allow new into you. Blessings dear one, blessings to you.

This message is but a taste of what is about to unfold before you within the pages, chapters and loving guidance that has been provided by so many. They only want what is best for us and to assist each of us into being our best. Enjoy your journey into the Truth Beyond.

Prophecy

> Daughter, your faith has made you well; go in peace.
> Mark 5:34

It was the fall of 2017 when I felt a calling to visit John of God once again. I did not travel alone but invited a dear friend Su to join me on this spiritual adventure. I had first met John of God in 2013 when I traveled to Abadiăia, Brazil. It was nearing Easter and I arrived on Maundy Thursday. I spent eight glorious and magical days experiencing a complete transformation that unlocked my mind, body, and soul to more than I ever knew was possible in this lifetime. An energetic bond had been formed to the Universal connection that was ignited within me through my spiritual experiences in Abadiănia and the Casa de Dom Inacio.

I had planned some energy work along the way, so we took a side trip to Harrisburg, PA. I worked with several wonderful people at Reiki by Ricki along with performing a soul retrieval. In life, we are never given more than we can handle and are asked to take steps of faith. We may not understand the reason, but there is always a lesson and an overall purpose to the experience. This journey was but one of those steps, not knowing the what or why, but following the where and when.

We continued our journey, staying in a lovely B & B that was in a 19th century Victorian rectory hall along with other guests who came to visit the Omega Center in Rhinebeck, New York. Each day at Omega was filled with a sea of white. Everyone coming to this prayerful place was dressed accordingly and resonated peace as well as love. Prayers would be shared from our souls and many were answered such as the lame who walk miraculously before our eyes. Most of the seekers were looking to grow and expand within, not truly having an understanding of what was being asked of us but answering the internal yearning that thirsted for more within the soul.

We had a wonderful first day and returned to our lodging to rest after our visit. I experienced a deep, pulsing headache that night and prayed for guidance as to what this throbbing pain was all about and received an answer: *You only use a small portion of your brain, both the left and the right. I am opening new areas of your brain that you will be using for your work.* During the night, I could feel both hemispheres of my cranium being squeezed into a beanie cap on the top of my head and down around the hairline. Thoughts and energies moved into and through all regions of my brain, blending the rational with the artistic, opening all channels of communication. Spirit guided me in the following quote: *Delete trying to understand what is happening to you and allow it to be what it is.*

The Full Moon reflected brightly into the Library window while I tossed and turned throughout the night. Just before 2:00 a.m., I heard the alarm clock randomly beep twice. A couple of minutes later, both Su and I were awakened by a car alarm going off in the street. "Judi, is it yours?" Su inquired. It was not, but I went outside to check the area anyway. When I returned to the room, I could feel spirits gathering and strengthening for no apparent reason and pressure built in the center of the bottom of my skull connecting to my neck. I tried to sleep again with no avail. It was now 2:12 a.m. and the alarm clock was watching and telling me to prepare.

Within seconds, the car alarm sounded outside once again. I got up and heard the guests who owned the car bound down the stairs to shut off the alarm. I waited for everyone to return to their rooms, for the house to become still and tiptoed into the kitchen and channeled the following message:

My daughter, you have come to this space for many amazing and magical experiences to take place. It is…happening with you… It is happening through you… It is happening into and through your lineage, too. Your cells are each alive! They are with life, with feelings, emotions and the physical too. My daughter, so much is going to be happening to you, far beyond what your tiny mind can possibly fathom to come forth. The energies which are happening within you are already shaking to make the cars beep, as they, too, are sensitive to the transmission and the transference of great energies. The alarm clock heard it. It is about the two o'clock, … the two's…the two-two,…the two-two-two's… Angels have followed you with the one's, but the true wisdom comes from the two's… being present with the two's and listening to all the messages which are… You have come here for healing, too…healing within your heart and soul, along with the physical. You have asked to be…be here, be open, be willing, and be ready. My daughter, I hope that you are ready, because so much is getting ready to be!

I never can gift you with more than you can handle in this life span, but there is so much more available for you than what you are ever willing to go forth to dream about…far beyond the walls of a room…far beyond the confines of the outside space… far beyond the limits of a planet and a galaxy, too! There is great transmission and energies that can be communicated to and with…all of this is from within. My child, it is not that there is just one or two that you have come to meet here in this space, but a transformation of all is getting ready to take place.

A Center is a lovely and beautiful idea that will help to heal some souls. You, my daughter, it's far beyond the walls of a single place. Your heart is open. Your spirit is willing, and your love is far beyond anything that others could imagine. The pure transmission of information, which comes through you, is such a gift to those around you, too. It provides peace. It provides healing, child… They feel the love and the sorrows within and are allowed to weep without. Just be, my child. Be that loving presence. Be the extended arms of God to go forth and to help my children…to heal my children…to love my children…and to hold them up, too. They need to understand, they are not crazy!

It is what it is, child… a beautiful journey, and amazing path that leads before each of us within this world. Each path is filled with many twists and turns and different destinations; however, we all go to the great journey beyond… beyond within and around. My child, you are surrounded by so much love…so many loving beings and so many miracles! It takes again the insight to see the miracles which happen all around you. You are blessed to be able to see because you choose to see. You choose to look beyond the physical of what is for what else truly is.

My daughter, this time you are awake to be able to start the transference of new energies. It says to awaken and spend time in meditation. This is what you shall do. This is what you are, my child. You are an energy source…to be able to gather the wisdom and knowledge of beyond that will come to and through the world…through you! …You as the channel… My daughter, great healing wisdom is coming through now…(channeled Lenape language for twenty-five seconds, and then the car alarm resumed blasting in front of the guest house, on the street, during the ending) Chi-cha!, Chi cha! Chi-cha! The energies of the car blow again. It cannot handle such transmission. It is more than what they can feel. Blessings, dear daughter. You will know what these words mean soon enough. Do not worry, my child. It is time for me to pass again, too. Amen.

I returned to my bed and noticed the clock read 2:22 a.m.; another affirmation of the reality of what had just transpired. (The Angel number 222 signifies peace and harmony. It also suggests the search of a sense of balance, and it is the best time to have faith and to keep trusting). I had had a fitful night of unrest. Su emerged after waking to the alarm at 6:30 a.m. for the final day at Omega, dressed and looked for coffee. Julie was in the kitchen. I emerged from the bedroom, groggily, and helped myself to some coffee. "Do you want to hear what I was up to in your kitchen earlier this morning?" Julie smiled and nodded her head, while finishing the scrambled eggs at the stove. Su, Julie and I listened to the recording I had made of the channeling. When it was done, Julie shared that when she and Peter purchased the church, there was much disturbance in the house. They contacted a local Shaman for a smudging and house blessing. Apparently, part of the church had been built on top of a Lenape burial ground, and most of the spirits who visited were friendly. We reveled to Julie that we were spiritualists. Julie was delighted to know, as our conversation flowed, and the visit was purely delightful.

My journey was ending – or rather just beginning. When I returned to Florida and the Church of Divine Prophesy on the following Sunday, Steve, the pastor of the church announced his resignation, naming me as the fulltime pastor. My day job had been in great flux with a major powershift and I came in second for the City Manager's position. I saw it as a death sentence in the 3D world. However, Spirit always has another plan and it sometimes just takes us a while to catch up. I have always resonated with Shamanism and indigenous spirituality, and when one is willing, Spirit provides the opportunity to grow.

Grandmother Silver Otter led the monthly Native American Talking Stick Circle gathering in Cassadaga, and shared with Su that she needed a successor, since her declining health necessitated the move to Arkansas with her family. They chatted one Sunday on the porch of the Andrew Jackson Davis Building and spoke of her imminent transition and asked if Su knew of anyone with whom she could entrust her circle family. Without hesitation, Su recommended Sun Spirit at the same time that

I was passed by for the City Manager's position. That was six years ago, and the monthly channeling with Chief White Eagle is thriving. All are welcome to this open circle to drum, eat and enjoy fellowship.

I later made my spiritual quest to Mt. Shasta, California and to the American Stonehenge in New Hampshire. Prophesy evolved into fruition and upon review of this verbiage late in the editing stages, I was completely amazed that it even included the title of the book. This story with all of its glory is revealed by the following volume.

Authors Note: Maintaining Spiritual Health includes maintaining a healthy lifestyle, preparation, grounding, a prayer of protection, highest intention for energy work, personal cleansing, appreciation, and gratitude for spiritual blessings.

ACKNOWLEDGEMENTS

I HAVE BEEN BLESSED WITH a life filled with many acquaintances, friends, and a very loving and supportive family, some by blood and others that my heart has chosen. I have traveled through many circles, states and have been touched by the countless people with whom I have shared my life with. Each sole has been a blessing of love that has added color and texture to the tapestry of my life…

This book is another amazing adventure! It has gifted me the opportunity to stretch beyond myself and allow the universe to take the lead, wherever that may be. This incredible project would never have been possible without the assistance of many Earth Angels, but I would be remiss if I did not name a few who have spent many hours of love assisting with the birthing process.

Thank you to Linda Walsh for so many hours of video recording, editing, researching, loving encouragement and amazing friendship. Thank you Su Forbes for your spiritual insight and truly tapping into the essence of each message while editing this book, thereby taking it to the next level of understanding for all of us. Thank you Nancy Jo Ricca for additional editing and our amazing creative friendship. Thank you to the brave and caring women who attended each of these circles to hold the energies and allow for this guidance to be born: Annette St. Cyr, Linda Walsh, Judy Stamper, Debbie Nunn, Karen Paradise, Ute Miklos, Joan Whittemore, Beryl Ferguson and Lorelei Holloway.

The cover image is a photo I took of Grandfather Redwing, a redwood tree that is located in Mt. Shasta, California. I do hope that each of you who reads this will see, hear, and feel a new level of understanding that truly is the **Truth Beyond** what you currently know.

INTRODUCTION

MY JOURNEY BEGINS

WELCOME TO THE CITY OF Telos. Allow me to introduce spirit guides, Jamar and Baylot. You will join me and a brave circle of women as they experience the direct imparting of spiritual wisdom from **beyond** our planet. The energy created by the weekly meditation sessions has yielded important universal **truth** channeled by me and recorded on these pages in an extremely engaging way. Read what the entities from other worlds have shared with these ladies, and now, YOU are invited to be a part of this unfolding of consciousness.

My journey begins by being shown guidance and information far beyond my wildest of dreams into new realms of reality. My life has been blessed through my faith and perseverance for more-- to see more and to be more. I listen for guidance and I watch for signs and messages that have previously been known to me in code. I strive to continually stretch my knowledge, insight, and wisdom to better understand what universal guidance has shown to me. It comes in clue format and is similar to putting together a puzzle, one piece at a time. The only challenge is that you do not ever get all the pieces at once! You could not handle it. Patience and faith that all will be revealed in God Source's time, as you need it.

I have experienced several life-altering experiences which I believe are important to share to help build the foundation of this journey.

I began understanding the call of my healing work at the age of 35, after an awakening of my father being given three months to live. I sat straight up in bed one night and was told to go and perform a healing on him. I was shocked, stunned and searched the room for a speaker. I have always been a person of faith but was pushed far beyond my comfort zone as my father was a professed atheist. Both of our lives changed through this experience. He found faith and lived another nine years. I was left thirsting to understand.

Another adventure ensued as I answered a calling and spent eight days in Abadiănia, Brazil during Easter in 2013. It took many months to coordinate the journey and I attribute the timing to the 2012 awakening. Many amazing events unfolded including a spiritual surgical transformation, where I could feel crystals being psychically inserted into the palms of my hands and crystal tubing being placed through my core center and arms. I clearly heard from God Source that I had to be inserted with this new crystal hardware to support the level of healing energy that was to take place in a few short months. Time passed and many new spiritual blessings were birthed through me and this spiritual surgery. One included the ability to channel the God Source. As time and my practice continued, so did the ability to channel higher vibrational entities such as Arch Angels, Masters and Spirit Guides.

Experience has shown me that when I feel compelled to visit a particular location, no matter how exotic, and I do so, then new information is revealed to me. I am gifted with a new piece to the puzzle. I believe this is a connection through my native roots. I have a strong relationship with Mother Earth through my Native American heritage and as a Shamanic Practitioner. I am the designated Grandmother of the Talking Stick Circle, which is hosted monthly at the Southern Cassadaga Spiritualist Camp in Cassadaga, Florida.

The past few years have been personally transformative with the loss of my husband after a debilitating illness. I know this too was part of God's plan and I was ready for my next step, whatever that may be.

Not long ago, I felt the calling to go and visit Mt. Shasta, California. I have heard talk of the power of the mountain and truly had no idea what would unfold. I made travel arrangements with an open heart and schedule leading into the unknown of what would enfold. My plan was to answer the call and audio record channeled messages from the energies and beings that needed a voice. This would provide me with guidance that would create a path for me to follow.

My first visit was to Bunny Flats, the only area that was not snow covered and I was able to walk. The mountain and its energies spoke to me.

Mt. Shasta

Ah, my Daughter,

You have come to the mountains as you have been called to do. Do you feel the power that radiates to and through you? It comes from the ancient one. Ancient as the trees, the redwoods, who are all connected far, far below… Far below the earth's surface into another dimension and time… Where all is connected to the one, the only one, the one space of love… True love. This is what emanates to and through each and every particle of life including you, my child.

There are huge changes coming, not just for you personally, but also for this earth plane that you find yourself at this time upon. There will be a call for great leaders, for strength, for deep healers to be able to hold the energy up and enlightenment up for man… For the mankind who are not of that space and place. I am calling forth all my healers to come forth to lift to hold the energy to allow for what shall come to be.

Ah, peace, enlightenment, great wisdom and grace… This is what shall be showered upon all… Ah, my darling daughter, blessings. You have such greatness that is going to happen upon this space and place.

Be gentle with self and allow it all to unfold. Blessings, dear daughter, blessings to you.

That same night before I slept, I received this next message from what previously, to me, had been but a myth, the existence of Lemurians:

Jamar First Communication

Child, we too have called you to this space. The golden energies of old are here. The light rays of all time are also centered within this space. Child, we do not look forward to what is coming forth. The love that we have tried so diligently to share is not being shared the way it needs to. We continue to press forth, to allow it to be born, to grow and to manifest to multiply in all of mankind. Mankind is stubborn. Mankind can be very loving. Mankind can be very hardheaded. We, the people, have been very patient and continue to do so; however, through the shift which is happening, it takes great energy to continue to elevate. This is why we have called in all of our light workers to help and to be able to spread this love, to hold this vibration at a higher level so that love and peace and joy truly can rule the world.

Child, the frequencies are being held within so many of the crystals. The crystals are within the mountain. The crystals are within the waters and the crystals deep within the lava tubes. All of this energy of love is what is being emanated back into the world.

There is such greed and many power-hungry people. They are the ones that hold it down. And not… mankind has learned to use different wave lengths of energies. They are using this to control people. They are using this to control weather. They are using this to control mankind. They are changing thought patterns of the people who are around and unaware of what is transpiring: for money, for greed, for power, for personal gain. All things which do not last. Such short-sightedness, because they do not understand, then this is, what is.

Child we will take you deep within. We know you have an open heart and you too will be able to share this love. Not just with the ones that you know here, but with the ones that you will be traveling to see later. They are in many forms, as you know teleportation is what you shall be coming to do. So much is ready to be opened for you, child. Just be. Be the loving presence. Be the open heart. Be the child of God.

Blessings to you. (I didn't know at the time but later learned who had spoken, Lemurian Elder "Jamar".)

I had spent several days in the Mt. Shasta, California area. Following inner guidance to visit various locations: Bunny Flats, Castle Lake, McCloud Falls, Medicine Lake (road closed by snow), Lady of the Garden, Pluto Caves and a need to visit Panthers Meadow, which was buried under deep snow. I visited where I could, took photos, channeled messages, and worked to attune my energies in alignment to the areas.

On the last day, I was guided to where I knew was a portal entry tunnel into Mt. Shasta. This included a large rock with a highly visible face known to me as the Gatekeeper. That evening going to sleep, he too provided a message.

A Gatekeeper for Telos

Yes child, now it can be revealed to you. As you have seen the gateway in. You have also seen the guardian protector of the door. You also understand that the tree is what called you to this space. This is a very sacred opening that not everyone is able to see or is ready to see. You, child, have been invited. You child have done your work by coming here to Mt. Shasta and are now being invited to go into to see the city of Telos. The city of Telos is beautiful. Within the center, an enormous green crystal stands where it illuminates all light within the city. It is a very fast and bustling city with so many lights, but it is a peaceful place with a peaceful people, all interacting and loving one another. Child, when you go to sleep this eve, you will be greeted by three. Three of our greeters will come and they will invite you in, order for you to come and see for yourself. You will only remember pieces and parts and that is fine, because your consciousness is what remembers. And again, the cellular activity that is taking place within you is what is happening. You have purchased the crystals. You have gone and blessed them and opened them at Mt. Shasta. You have also opened all of your chakras above and below and created a full circle of energy, where now your chakras are in complete alignment and ready. They have to be within this level of readiness, or the energy shift is too hard for the physical being, even for the spiritual being. They have to be prepared for this adventure in order to be invited in. I am the guardian of the gateway and I am the one who called you to the gateway. Since you listened and came, now you can go in, child. Blessings to you.

I know I was very blessed and visited the City of Telos. I knew during my visit that I was gifted with my second spiritual surgery and that twelve of my chakra centers were replaced with new pure essence crystals of various minerals to align with each of my centers. I had been told that it would take forty-five days to complete the alignment of energies within my physical body.

When I returned home, I replayed the audios over and over. I needed to take some time to assimilate and come to terms intellectually with the encounters. Meeting a new species, I had to integrate the reality of my personal experience. This was extremely difficult, even though I already knew of and about other species. It was vastly different to have a firsthand account that included irrevocable memories that I could not rationalize away. The other challenge was ego thought and the anticipation of being ostracized by community members for thinking and understanding beyond what most of the population believed or is willing to admit.

I had another knowing. Once again that I was being called to write a second book. Jamar needed to have a place to be heard and therefore this was going to be specifically based on channeling. I knew Jamar was the seed that initiated this adventure for all of us. I was guided how to arrange the channeling group and specifically to the participants. Several of the participants provided testimonies of their impressions and experiences as noted later in the book.

It was particularly important to keep the meditation circle limited to a small number of open-minded and highly supportive energy human beings. As a group, we created various questions that we wanted to know, and a limited number allowed for open guidance of wisdom to come from various speakers on subjects of their choosing. I explained to the group how the process was created through channeled guidance and that we would be allowing for the process to unfold. The group participants were all seekers of a higher vibration, curious for more wisdom, knowledge and information that would assist with their personal growth and spiritual development. I believe that the right participants were specifically chosen by the God Source to ensure development and success of this project. We made arrangements for a seven-week series and later expanded to a total of nine sessions for additional information and to assist in a cohesive flow of thoughts and direction.

PROLOGUE

CHANNEL SPIRIT CIRCLE

IN PREPARATION FOR THE CHANNEL Spirit Circle, I decided to ask the entities for direction for the circles and if they wanted a specific format or ideas that should be relayed throughout the sessions.

God Source

Ahhh my Daughter,

There are many who want to choose to be able to speak through you. You have such a keen ability of allowing those to be able to be heard. A long line of energies want to be able to participate in this experiment.

This experience with mankind... We are all doing as you have asked. Baylot is your guardian (Gatekeeper), who stands fast and who stands at the Bridgeway. We are all in the line waiting our turn to be heard.

This is an opportunity so that people who can come can ask subject questions so that information can be relayed back to mankind. Be sure that you take the time to ask, who is speaking... where are they from... and what is their most important message that they would like to share... and then you go ahead and ask a question. It also could be helpful while you were working through this process, is to go ahead and do have a subject question asked and then we will talk amongst ourselves and decide who would be the best to come forth to answer the question. There are so many different entities who all have information, which would be at the highest in the best for mankind. It's not that one is better than the other, but it is different as to who and what information you will be receiving from them, and their point of view about mankind and what you are needing and asking information for.

This is a very exciting time for each of us, because we are now opening up a new channel, a new pathway of communication and of also information and education... Education for us and education for you also. So, be patient with the process. Allow time pass, because sometimes a secondary source will step in to provide their take on the same subject matter, so it may be helpful if you decide ahead of time what question or who is going to ask the question and who is going to help be the Keeper of the information to make sure that everything is kept in an organized fashion and it doesn't become too overwhelming for us or for you in the process.

You truly have to do this with another person now child. This is more than what you can really do by yourself on a regular basis. You have to have someone who is with you, who is driving you, if you're going to be driving places or you need to just plan to be at your home so you don't have to travel anywhere afterwards. You are always protected and guarded, and we will always be there to guide you; however, it just makes sense because you are going to be in such different levels, vibrations, and frequencies. It is going to become harder and harder for you to be able to stay completely settled in that in the human 3D form so that you'll be in a place of being able to drive the car safely, and to think about all of the business thing.

Now this is an overly exciting time for all of us, so please be sure that you can just change channel, which you can easily do, and we are here to help you through that. So, I think for this evening, it makes the most amount of sense if you go ahead and explain what you are planning to do with the process. Why you have come to be for this... The channeling opportunities... and then we will go ahead and start over all topics... Not just personal topics, but global topics, topics of humanity, topics of environment, or topics of universal interest, not just for personal gain.

Now that means they can talk about emotional and spiritual topics, that are experienced by each of mankind, but to try not to go into the details of *individualized questions, just for personal gain. It needs to be more for a larger entity. The information which is being gathered through these different sessions is going to be published, so we can go forth and truly have our voices heard in a different manner. I think that is enough for now. Blessings daughter, blessing.*

GATEKEEPER BAYLOT

I spoke about my Gatekeeper Spirit Guide, Baylot, and our development in building a better relationship to accommodate this opportunity. After I began to channel, the process was rather erratic in nature as I did not understand the full process and best strategies or techniques. There is very little training about channeling and mine was naturally developed through continued exploration and spiritual growth. I knew I was protected and guarded, but I was also so very curious for more. I strived to be a vessel for guiding beacons of light and hope for others here on earth. I would allow for transformations to take place at specific times and messages to come. Some of these messages were for groups or personal guidance. For others, it was cleansing, to assist in their purpose and following their life path. People often commented about the pure power and eternal love that they felt and were in awe after the experience.

After several years, I met another earth angel and he helped to organize my channeling process. I was guided to my sacred spiritual place that includes a pond and a small stream. Over the stream is an arched bridge and on the other side is a large gazebo. Baylot and I worked it out so that he stands on my side of the bridge and we allow for all other Beings and Light Entities to gather on the other side around the gazebo. When timing is coordinated, he easily monitors who can come over and incorporate within the sessions.

This has worked out very well and Baylot has grown much stronger now that he has a voice of his own. He is much less concerned about needing to keep me protected and safe and it has become a highly organized arrangement for both of us. Baylot also acts as a moderator and will ask if we want to hear from additional sources and if it is time to move onto the next question or topic. At times Baylot will ask for open topics from any entities to provide the most essential information of the highest and best to be shared. Baylot has greatly enjoyed this process, and his newly developed universal role.

As previously stated, there is not a great deal of training available for channeling. Therefore, there is a great demand from Universal Light Beings to have an opportunity to share their wisdom and guidance to a receptive participant.

During a channeling, I know I am fully protected and guarded. However, for many reasons I always continue to seek and add the power of protection around me and what I am sharing. I continue to have a strong faith and God Source connection. I walk a life path where I try to live sharing the greatest gift of all – LOVE to all with whom I come into contact – a life filled with peace and love to all of mankind. This can be a difficult task because in our culture we are taught "It's a dog eat dog world" and "You'd better get to it first or you will be left out in the cold." Competition and making oneself better than the other are a driving passion for most people. If you are not driving yourself upwards and onwards, then you are looked down upon and possibly shunned for not fitting within the invisible standards of what is expected by society. So many people run through life as if they are a hamster on a wheel running faster and faster to... do, do, do, and they never arrive, because they cannot get off. They just run themselves down into a place of complete exhaustion. Some never recover and give up and die. Others may choose to jump off after a complete burnout and begin a new search which can lead them to realize, there is something more than what they ever could have imagined possible. All they had to do was to stop, look, listen, and have enough faith in themselves, to realize, *there is a better way.*

People come to this earth with a soul level of understanding what they want to accomplish; however, through the birthing process, one forgets most of their Soul's purpose, memories, and goals. The few glimmers of remaining wisdom generally fade away within the first few years of life. A person is taught how to fit into society by the cultural and environmental teachings of their surroundings. These mind illusions include the physical, spiritual, mental, and artificial (media) intentions. You actually learn to replace love with fear, so the mind can distract you from your Divine Purpose.

I want to speak about the density of human souls. We move through many different lifetimes, and elevation is based on cycles of age, experiences, and development. This is directly impacted by biology and the instinctual need to reproduce and provide heirs for longevity of the species. So much is driven about the need to find a partner, to be a partner and to be one with another. People spend so much time searching for what is thought in their minds as the perfect soul, but in actuality one follows their heart, words and feelings. They will often see and believe what they imagine it to be over the reality of what it is. People look to find and fulfill their self-love from the outside rather than first finding the love within. Then they can allow the light of that vibration to align with others who would then be called to join them.

Because of our physical make up and the emotions which drive our desires, goals, and ambitions, the lessons that happen throughout our lives attract many different energies and people around us. This includes ones who are alive, and oftentimes, will include other spirits who choose to attach themselves for an extension of their existence. We may not necessarily even realize the attachments are present and influencing our lives which can increase the drama.

The information that is collected within these channeled messages is for all who choose to open their minds and hearts to understand. The ability to understand spiritual truths is very different based on what each person's unique experiences have been. The transmissions which are recorded in these pages include Beings that receivers may or may not have had communication with previously.

THE STORY BEGINS

IT WAS AUTUMN, AND I found myself feeling the call to visit a cabin in Georgia. The cabin is small and located on a mountainside next to a stream and surrounded by a majestic forest filled with wildlife. This place has a magical feel and the cabin is two stories with a loft, where I found myself settling down after the long drive north from Florida.

I had been working on a project with my classes, and we all left that week with homework to reach out beyond during our sleep time. Prior to going to sleep, I had my Lemurian crystals by my bedside, and with full intention I had prayed to remain open and allow for guidance, information, and travel to be relayed to me as available. The night passed into dawn and upon waking, I began to write as my heart remembered all that had transpired.

I found myself to be standing in front of the Gateway that I was shown while I was in California. The Gatekeeper is a large granite rock that is upright along an embankment that falls quickly to fast moving waters below. There are redwood and other trees dappled along the water's edge and a well-worn walking path blanketed by soft needles and leaves. I walked to a narrow ledge along the water's cliff-side. The Gatekeeper was welcoming in a stoic type of way, as I noted his prominent facial features etched in the granite that guards the tunnel entry. He greeted me respectfully and was glad to see that I had arrived once again as truthful, honest, and sincere in my visit, along with my intentions. His large boulder mountainside presence rolled aside and allowed me to enter.

Upon entering it was dark, but as my eyes adjusted, I could see that I was standing in the large lava tube cave system to begin my travels. The walls were very smooth in texture; however, they were not straight. They had curves, bumps, and areas above and below where old drips of lava had formed and hardened. Jamar, a Lemurian Elder was there to greet me.

Jamar is fairly tall, over seven feet in height and a slender, graceful build. He has a very warm and welcoming presence. His skin color is very pale but illuminates with a sparkling sheen. He has bright wide blue eyes, a firm jawline, a wide smile, and longer blond hair which gently cascades around his face and shoulders. He is wearing a white robe that ties in the center and it floats around him as he walks in smooth long strides. His presence and energy are so bright. He radiates pure love and I could see and feel his joyful delight to see me once again.

Jamar did not bring anyone else to meet me on this visit as he had other plans arranged for us. He was pleased that I arrived so quickly and easily to join him for our adventure. As we walked through the tubular pathways there was darkness, but also plenty of light that illuminated the side walls. Light emulated from the wall areas with beams shinning upwards and fanning out for great distances ahead of us. We walked for quite a while as Jamar spoke of our joint project and inquired about my process. I was enthusiastically sharing with him about having the opportunity to meet other people of like mind who are ready to expand themselves and their knowledge. He began speaking of the various attendees who are a part of the channeling circles and commented on information about each of their spirit guides and his impression of them. He was very excited about this experiment.

He told me that he wanted to take me to meet some of his fellow Lemurians, so we continued on the path until the tunnel ended along with other cave entrances where we found ourselves standing on the edge of the community. We had entered into the City of Telos. There were buildings, roadways, gardens, and bustling noises of being within an actual civilization. I could not see a sky as I looked up, but neither did I see a roof, and there was plenty of light, the same as if outside on an overcast day, and no ending to the space that was all around. It was huge and vast. We were in a fully functioning and operational city, where I could see for blocks ahead, and peaks from taller structures. We continued to stroll along until we came to this large building with white pillars in the front. It was grand in stature and resembled a combination of Roman and gothic architectural style. A very large and ornately carved triangle was located on the front fascia of the building entry. There were at least six large columns supporting the entry and we climbed twenty steps to arrive at the entry landing. The stairs were wide, finely polished, and the triangular roofline protruded over the landing and the grand entry doors. The building appeared to be made of marble. It was smooth, primarily white with swirls of other colors intertwined. It was not just the gray tone swirls but included other colors. The other colors were finely crushed muted crystals that added depth, strength, and character to the building. I believe the combined mineral composition provided increased levels of vibration for communication to travel through, in an expansive from, such as an antenna built into the structure.

The entry doors were wooden and enormous, made of Redwood I believe, with an arched top. There were large brass rings as handles. The door opened easily as we stepped through the threshold. The entry was very inviting, and the ceiling must have been two stories in height. The hallway was wide, and the floors glistened from the same white marble crystal colors which reflected the lighting. Lighting was of a white nature in here and everything was very large, white, shiny and bright. It did not feel cold or overwhelming, but actually very warm and welcoming. I could hear the echo of my feet as we walked ahead. There were several doors that aligned both sides of the hallway. They had different geometric symbols designed on each of the doors as identification markers.

Jamar told me that we were visiting the college and he was taking me to meet his colleagues. We came to the end of the hallway and there was a double door ahead that was made of an opaque essence of green and pink swirled glass welcoming us in. Jamar opened the door for me, and we entered. There was a large oval table in the center of the room with approximately thirty chairs around it. The room was rectangular in shape and along both of the long walls were three rows of elevated stadium-type seating. The room was buzzing with activity and many Lemurians were present. When we entered, the noise level hushed rather quickly, and everyone gave a respectful bow towards Jamar. The level of regard and prestige he holds as a highly valued Elder among his people was obvious. He too gave a slight bow to return the respected greeting gesture.

The Lemurians are a much taller species and incredibly beautiful people. Their skin was nearly iridescent, white, shimmering, and translucent all at the same time. Most of them had blonde hair in many lengths and hairstyles. Their eight-foot frames were lean, with willow arms and they wore mostly white etheric attire. The women wore flowing garments that were layered, wrapped, and elegantly draping their bodies. They were adorned with various large gemstones, jewels and gold as necklaces, wrist and arm bracelets, belts, and hair jewelry. The men also wore elegant formal robes in the Greece-Roman, style with Egyptian shaped jewels in their belts and broach clasps.

Everyone was so very welcoming and warm in their presence. This was a fairly large gathering, and everyone knew and regarded the importance of this visit. The side row seating was designed for the students and they began to quietly filter into the room as led by their elder teacher. The rows were slightly terraced upwards to allow for perfect viewing. Once everyone had arrived and were settled, there must have been more than a hundred in attendance.

The feeling in the room was curious. There was excitement, joy and such a level of respect for who I was along with acceptance of our differences. Physically, I looked quite different from them because of my shorter statue, darker hair, body build, shape, skin coloring and dress. I looked down and saw that I too was wearing formal whites for this auspicious event. Those in attendance had all come by personal invitation from Jamar. The point of this gathering was to explain how Jamar and I are conducting our Channel Circle sessions. They too had many questions for me, and I quickly realized that this was the same situation, only reversed. Jamar had invited me into this circle to assist in their education and allow for a sharing of information and guidance. It is so remarkably interesting and humbling to reflect that I had become a representative of our species and planet.

Selected dignitary settled into the chairs around the large oval stone table. Communication was not really with voices, but with mind energy and knowing. I heard in my mind's eye a slight buzz with many communicating at once and as it settled, the energy shifted and became quiet and peaceful. Lemurians generally choose to use their voices in times of making a speech or when it is an important event. Jamar moved to the end of the table and gestured for me to be seated next to him. I knew that the beings who filled the table were all elders, teachers, and leaders of the Telos community and all the students were the ones seated around in outside edges. Everyone settled quickly and we began. It was curious in many ways. I do not remember Jamar asking if I would be interested in this type of a gathering or if I would be comfortable meeting so many of his colleagues. This was an extremely exciting opportunity for all of us, and he knew I would be fine with it. I too, am a teacher in his mind and we are both doing the same type of work only from different locations. We are both building a stronger alliance between our species and allowing for greater communication of information and guidance that can help both of us strengthen our communities.

The room fell silent and Jamar began to speak using his voice and speaking in English. Jamar welcomed everyone and began by introducing himself and me. He related our story. He filled in our history by speaking of my first visit to California, my finding the gateway and coming to Telos for the first visit. As I looked around the table, I could see the other two guides who had met me at my first visit, smiling graciously at me, sending love and joy to ensure that I felt comfortable. I gazed around the table and at the students. I was so warmly appreciated for being there. They were grateful for my wiliness to share and learn from them as well as provide my information and knowledge. I was not intimidated at al. I only felt joy, peace, and I was completely honored to be the guest invited to such an auspicious event. Jamar continued speaking about Telos and how it is such a great mystery to the humans. He stated that so many humans have no idea of their existence and others are seeking more. Some people with impure intentions are in want of greed, jewels, and fame, while yet others are working on self-expansion and universal wisdom. Humans are like many other races that they meet only with exception that we have free will, choices and the capacity to allow for growth beyond our current dimensions with greater intelligence and universal love. As Jamar spoke, everyone was so respectful and highly attentive to every word. It was very evident he was admired. Everyone showed great respect for his time, wisdom, and knowledge. He instructed about the process that a human must travel through to receive an invitation to visit the city of Telos. He then introduced the two guides who had joined my previous visit.

He gave a long and beautiful accounting of how both of our species had to focus beyond surviving into thriving, as well as the importance of our building better relationships and creating stronger communication. Jamar spoke about how each of our species is protected from one-another because of the variations in our dimensions. Yet, the personal, first-hand knowledge of each is essential for our people's growth and development. After he spoke for quite a while, he introduced me so I could tell my story. Jamar had been speaking in English and the audience all could understand him. Lemurians have the ability to understand telepathically all languages at will. I too had the ability to understand their mental thoughts, but English was also chosen for the presence of the students in the room to become more familiar with our language firsthand and as respect for me as their guest.

I sincerely thanked the group assembled so very much for this incredible opportunity, and Jamar personally for this invitation. I spoke for quite a while about my spiritual journey and then feeling and knowing the callings in my life. They were all attentive and curious as to why I actually followed these callings into the unknown. A great difference in our species is that they know beforehand and then act upon this knowing. They don't have internal urgings for more and don't have feelings as if something is missing. I spoke first of having great faith and then how my healing energies began to develop. Later, I recounted my journey to Brazil and the spiritual surgery that I had received. I told them of the crystals which were inserted into the palms of my hands and the crystal tubing that was inserted through my center core and down my arms to allow for the greater healing energies. I spoke of the changes that occurred afterwards, and many years of my growth path as it continues to unfold. I confessed my personal challenges with my jobs, family, home, and the passing of my husband. They were all highly interested and amazed at the strength and level of changes that transpired in such a short life. They were enthralled by the emotions and my will to live and grow beyond my past in preparation for the next life that was unknown and unfolding before me.

Had I been chosen to be an ambassador for the human race? I was astonished by this overwhelming and incredible honor. I stopped a moment and surveyed the room. Everyone was fully attentive to my speaking, completely engrossed in garnering new information and again sending such love energies back encouraging me to continue. It was a flash of elation of what things could be if the situation were reversed. If I were invited into a room such as this on my earth plane with mankind and Jamar or another was the speaker – how receptive would I be for this information exchange? Would I be as open, willing to listen, respectful, able to understand beyond our differences? I had only hoped I would respond the same without fear. I knew our general culture would not be very welcoming and certainly not as loving. I hoped our circle would provide that to Jamar in return.

I studied the faces of the youth that were in attendance. They were each so very interested and respectful. I never saw or felt any kind of judgement for our differences, just curiosity. I could internally feel questioning thoughts and would try to respond to them as I could during the process. I also admired their teaching methods of allowing the youth and the elders to all be in the room listening to the same information at once and learning together as a group. The meeting was for the elders and peers for full discussion and decisions, but the youth were allowed to learn about the process of how their culture operates, along with the opportunity to meet me also.

As I continued, I spoke of my trip to California, the calling from the Redwood trees that led me nearby and finding the Gateway on my initial visit to Telos. I explained the channelings from the Gatekeeper and how Jamar had reached out to me to build this relationship and our channeled communication as noted below:

Jamar's first communication is shared within the introduction and I was gifted with brief guidance to prepare me for the journey which laid ahead.

Jamar Second Communication

Child, it has been so wonderful that you have come to the mountains to see and experience firsthand the energies of activation. Love, Child is all there is! Never allow fear or stress to conflict with the greatest strength, LOVE. Be at peace, Child.

You walked through the large opening being on each side and in front. Jamar, Alevia, Rochelle were their names. Jamar was the leader of the group. Alevia knew facts and operations and Rochelle was the teacher, gardener and also spoke of family life.

They are very proud of their lifestyle and what they have been able to provide to Earth. They work diligently to be the peacekeepers. The local military monitor them often and know of their existence. They can only reveal themselves to those who have heard the individual calling and found an entry point on their own. The world is beautiful and full of abundance, peace, and pure love.

They too, are children of God and are loved for who they are. Now that you have visited, you can return as you choose through teleportation. We always have gatekeepers available to welcome guests. We love to be able to showcase our home and way of life.

You were brought to the center in front of the large green selenite crystal and asked to sit. This was a total cleansing of mind, body, and spirit. Memories are not necessary as the cells were fully charged and have individual memories now of the experience.

Jamar lead the way and spoke softly but with authority that was highly regarded by the others. It was unusual for Jamar to be a greeter, but he knew you were a very special guest.

Alevia, a male, explained the infrastructure of the city and how things operate. The water they drink was from the waterfall as it is fully charged. Telos charges the Mt. Shasta water that is fed to the people below. There are many tunnels throughout the city, and we saw only but a few. Everyone who saw us was warm, welcoming, and regarded us with respect.

Rochelle, a female, was very warm, open and the most loving of all. She showcased the community as her babies. All were a joy and peace to be proud of. I saw the gardens, homes, park areas, play areas and schools. I was able to see and feel the true beauty of the place and its people.

We asked many questions about your life and what you want. We find it so interesting when humans choose to walk a different lifestyle and dedicate their hearts to mankind and the betterment of... The love, healing ability and work to clear any residue and blockages, allowed for greater clarity and become a purer channel. We are excited that we will be partnering, as we move forward. We inserted twelve pure crystals into each of your chakra centers to allow for a more cohesive function. Your headaches have cleared now, and your digestion will improve as all are assimilated. Allow your body to rest, and in forty-five days. The next shift will take place.

Prepare Child, and continue to prepare, Child, as all is about to flourish. Thank you for your efforts. Good-bye. Our spirits have met we are permanently bonded. If you have questions, you only have to ask, and the answers will be provided.

Peace and love always, Child

My visit to California was an amazing experience and I am very humbled by having had not one, but two spiritual surgeries along with the gift of strong faith and protection. I believe that the crystals have been added to allow for a purer transmission. They allow the transmission to be emitted at a higher frequency as well as serve as a beacon for others to find. They also always allow my physical body to consistently stay in a much higher vibrational status, which is not conducive to spiritual attachments. I may not have full memories of what has transpired as I am the channel for the information; however, my soul has full understanding and can continually grow, increase my personal knowledge and global insight with each new experience.

Now, here is the twist of interest! I was able to sit once again at the table surrounded by everyone where a large screen of sorts was shown on the opposite side of the room from me. Everyone was still in complete silence and then a film of some type began to play. It was the video recordings of each of our channeling sessions. They were somehow able to connect into my memory bank and find the same frequency to view each experience. This was extremely curious, because they could retrieve the channeling and feel the internal transmissions of what I was thinking and feeling directly through each question and visitation both at the same time. Each participant in the room had a full perspective and personal experience of the channeling sessions. I spent this time watching the others. I could feel their thoughts and see their emotions. They had the opportunity to empathize with my feelings, which was a unique gift for them to experience. They also had the ability to actually experience the presence of the group participants and the ability to connect with them during these sessions.

CIRCLE WORK BEGINS

I WAS GUIDED TO CREATE a meditation circle format, which would allow for the highest support for the energy exchange during the channel session process. It was important when working with new and strong energies to have others of like minds and compatible healing energies around to support the energy flow and manage the transference of information.

I advertised for attendance to the Spirit Circles and approved invitations by individuals of interest. I planned for a maximum of ten participants that we will call "sitters" and chose people of varying levels of spiritual knowledge. This would allow for questions of all interest and depth to support a broad audience. I was careful to monitor the sitters and their energies throughout the process. Some sitters visited a few sessions, while others attended all nine sessions. All members were female, and we sat in circle to balance the feminine energy flow.

I worked with a key partner, Linda Walsh, who is a certified healer. Linda video recorded the sessions and monitored my health during trance state along with what transpired within the group.

Telepathically I received the protocol for how to prepare for the sessions. At our first gathering we chose a scribe, Deb, who would ask the group questions and take general notes of the various visiting entities. We asked each visitor: What is your Name? Where are you from? Do you have a specific message for us?

We began each circle with an opening prayer and a short-guided meditation to clearly align our energies and pure intentions. After the second week, we added a singing bowl to start each session and vibrationally tune our energies before the opening prayer.

As previously discussed, I had a Gatekeeper Spirit Guide named Baylot, who acted as a spiritual moderator for all the visitations. We completed each session with open discussion about topics and information provided, which in turn helped to create new questions and then sealed each session with a prayer.

Please enjoy these written excerpts of the channeling sessions which were transcribed from the videotaped sessions. You may find difficulty reading and understanding all the information. The grammar and phonetics are not proper English. It takes great effort for the entities to lower their vibrations, and me elevating mine, so that we can find a frequency balance for the trance communication.

The entities had completely different communication styles; however, they used the words that I have in my memory bank and sometimes had difficulty finding the correct words or ways to properly express their intended message. Often there was humming, laughing, vocal noises and physical body adjustments during the incorporation so that the entities could manage the physical visitation.

For some of the visitors, this was the first time that they had ever incorporated, therefore that transition required more time and patience through the process. Generally speaking, the transitions were fairly smooth and made rather quickly within a minute or so. Most of them genuinely enjoyed the opportunity to incorporate but found the body to be a very heavy vessel to work through. I believe each entity enjoyed feeling the emotions of the sitters in each of the sessions.

The questions are highlighted throughout, and each session is divided for easy reference. We began with prearranged questions and later allowed an open forum. Whoever had the most important message would come through and provided their guidance and we might ask additional questions based on their topic of discussion.

Questions from sitters and my communication have been written in regular text. The channeled guidance and quotes are italicized. The information was written as received. If an entity spoke in another language, I did not include it to ensure in integrity of the message and referenced communication.

Copies of the videos are available through my website: www. Heart4Souls.com; www.SpiritualServices.online.

Session 1

Opening Prayer

Heavenly Father, Thank You. Thank you for this opportunity to come together. We join together with open hearts, open minds, with open ideas and we are opening ourselves to the Universe, to the love, to the light, to the Grace, to the peace, to the wisdom, to the knowledge and to the guidance that will be coming forth to each of us. Walk with us. Keep us protected and guarded through this entire process.

We ask this in Your precious name. Amen.

Introduction

THIS FIRST SESSION BEGAN WITH an explanation of how the series came to be and introduce what was anticipated for the series of sessions. I spent some time explaining my background and energy work to allow everyone the opportunity to become familiar with me and what they may see and experience during the sessions.

The plan was for the group to discuss ideas and create questions for the entities to answer as requested. We anticipated that more than one entity would provide guidance about each question and this is what transpired. It was amazing to hear the diversity in answers and different angles of information that were provided through the same question.

It was clearly explained that this was an experiment and a new format beyond what I had previously channeled.

Question

What do we need to do to prepare for the ability to clearly receive and coordinate the information to be able to move through the changes that are occurring?

FIRST INCORPORATION: JEOORGE

The first male entity made a fairly quick incorporation after several rapid breaths. He appeared to fill the room, sat very straight in the chair, and had a presence of wisdom and confidence. Jeoorge stated that he was from Atlantis.

Ahhh, and here we are! Is this not such a good eve? I am delighted and honored that we finally come to this time and space and place. Human time takes so much longer other time. You have to wait and chat and schedule and arrange for and La-la-la-la-la-lah! Deep breathe *Humph!* Okay, *I am here.*

May I ask who is speaking please? Certainly, *this is Jeoorge.* Where are you from Jeoorge? *Ahhh, Atlantis.* Did you have many lives on Atlantis? *I had many lives, not just me, everyone on Atlantis has had many lives and we are very excited and delighted that speckles and sparks of Atlantians have traveled to and threw it into most of each of you. You do not feel the resonation with my voice and my energy?* Audience, I do, I did.

Wonderful, then you are becoming enlightened being there is hope upon this world! I keep telling them there is hope! Okay, Jeoorge do you have a message for us? *I do, I do, I do. I have been waiting so long. I can't believe I actually got to the front of the line! I had to trick a few in order to do so, but it was worth it to be able to be here at this time.*

I want you to know about all the shifts in water and the energies, which have been happening. I know you are all very... um, experienced, you're in the Florida State and therefore Dorian just came through. Did you not see the power of that one that came through? Yes. *It was exciting, but it was scary too for many of the humankind too. Do you know why there is such strength in the storms that are happening now?* Why? No. *It is because of all of the climate changes, along with the pollution. Do you know what mankind is putting into the oceans? Can you imagine? There are floating islands of garbage!* Seen pictures. *Amazing! It is amazing for us in other spaces and places to see the changes which are being allowed to happen to the Earth planet that you find yourself on. It is the same with the smoke and the smog. It is the same with the EMTs, those electo-magnetic transmissions that are happening. The zapping, zapping, zapping.*

All of that that is happening is changing the atmosphere. It is changing the temperatures. It is changing the climate. It is changing the stability of the planet's surface. It is also affecting down deep into the Mother Earth, into the core where the tectonic plates are shifting and allowing for seepage. When the seepage happens, then greater energy is shifted and added into the storms, which makes it much harder for the universe to control or of mankind or the people along the coastline and other places, too... Knew of, heard of, saw and felt the changes that were happening of this storm. And what did they do, the mankinds? They came together with solid heart and they prayed. They prayed... Not just on one God, to all Gods to all energy sources. It became a universe such as a tsunami of energy feeding back into the energy that was happening of the storm of Dorian. It was therefore pushing it off, but the poor people of the Bahamas! They felt they received the brunt of it. I do have to say this too, though. The Bahamas are a loving people and because they are such loving people, they will be warmly accepted into the United States and in into other countries and into other islands. It will take decades to be able to heal what has happened on their lands; however, what has been extremely visible through this experience is the power of the prayer. The tsunami prayer of being able to change, but it also was to be able to see the effects. Whenever has there been a Category two hurricane that hit Canada?

These are the massive climate changes that are taking place. My message to each of you is this. The power of prayer works; however, my children, it is up to each of you. To guard our Earth, our Mother Earth to keep her waters cool, to not overload it with pollutants, to try to stop all of the different smog that is going in. Try not to have so much garbage and to try to stop living with stuff, stuff, stuff, stuff, stuff! Go back to honoring our earth. Honor our water. You have no idea the power of prayer and how it will heal the molecules of the water... Not just the water that is involved in the ocean, but the rivers and the lakes, and yes, my children that air and what is in your bodies too. Healing all waters as they are all connected as a single... As a single unit of life. You each feel the changes which happen around you.

Blessings of peace to each of you. Okay. Thank you.

Jeoorge was very busy providing his message and we all forgot to remind him of the subject topic question. Therefore, he did not answer the question. Jeoorge was emphatic in speaking, using a great deal of hand gestures. He spoke clearly with authority; intent and his great wisdom was palatable within the room. Upon leaving, he too bowed in gratitude for the opportunity to speak before this group.

SECOND INCORPORATION: ADRIAN

Question

What do we need to do to prepare for the ability to clearly receive and coordinate the information to be able to move through the changes that are occurring?

There was a deep breathing between entity incorporations and low vibrational throat clearing. Lots of body movement while shifting torso weight and deep breathing. A low grumble, accompanied by a bold energy male booming voice, Adrian felt fairly large in stature and was wearing a long emerald green robe with gold braded trim. He had a full beard a broad smile and twinkling green eyes. When asked, he stated that he was from the Archaea Star System.

My turn, my turn, my turn my turn, my turn, my turn, my turn! Golly gosh, we have to wait turns. Adrian! I am Adrian... and I am from the Archaea's. Deep cleaning breath. Archaea's is that a star system? *Archaea's yes, it is a star system, not of this galaxy, of the Galexion Orphomysis system is where I come from. I don't even think you have a clue that it exists; however, it does, I do and am here and I am at the front of the line so here we go. Okay, the question is again please? I'm sorry I was working to get here and missed part of what you said.* Okay, we would like to know what it is that we need to do to prepare for the ability to clearly receive and coordinate the information coming to us, to be able to move through all these changes that are occurring.

Well, that's a funny one. How many more things could you fit in a single question? Boisterous group laughs. Adrian really enjoying the laugh and slapping leg with pure delight. *Humans are so funny, they are so impatient, they have to have it all and they have to have it all right now!* Adrian is very emphatic, snapping fingers to show examples of right now mentality. He continues to laugh through this part of answering.

You know what the funniest thing is about that they don't even know what they already have. Belly laughing once again, clapping hands with joy and delight. *They have so much already. They just don't know, but you know that's part of where they are. The human race is made of many different particles and seeds and all kinds of energies and souls and the souls that have gone through rebirth process over and over again. So, do you know that the soul over here when it comes back the next time it needs a whole new amount of information and a different vibration in order to be able to get the same information back to it. Does that make sense to you?* Yes. Yes.

So, I want to go ahead and to talk about preparing. Now, first of all I will say there are many different teachers who are out there. Already working in the energy world such as the one you have before you, but there's many that are out there and we need every single one of them, because every single person does not see, hear, and understand the exact same experience the same way. It is because they can only understand that which they have already previously experienced so that they have an understanding for. Does that make sense? Yes. *Okay so I'm going to continue.*

So, as you are on your learned path, we are going to go ahead and talk about it as a path and we're going forward and do, you know, what it's daytime. Its nighttime and sometimes you're walking through the city and sometimes you're going through the forest. You're going different places. All kinds of things come along in your path and there are obstacles, but they are not necessarily challenges. They are choices. They are choices that happen in your life as with different seasons.

I did hear conversations prior to my incorporation, and I heard the woman who was speaking about having a family and having a child and being in that space. That is a beautiful time in the life of a person is to choose to become a mother. To be honored with the opportunity to have children. Do you know how humans learn from their children…? A long pause, Adrian looks around the room smiling allowing for the question to sink in. *Their children or grandchildren.* Adrian turns to a person to his right and continues to speak. *Such as the little fairy one that we talked of earlier.* Adrian is very emphatic about what is being said and continues using hand gestures to emphasize his points. *Every experience that you have in your life allows you to be able to become and to learn and to do and to become more of who and what you want to be. The best part is there's not a specific beginning and a final ending. All the way along you can change your mind. It's kind of like you're going along the path and there's a left and there's a right and maybe take the left. You take the left a little while and then you decide no I don't want to go left anymore so I'm going to go back over here to this path and then you're going to go right and then you know what you decide, oh, I think I really did like that left. So, you back up again, you go over to the left and then you continue and then your main path shifts. It is not that the other one was right or wrong it is just that it was a different way of getting there. Did you hear what I say?* Yes. *It is a different way to getting to the same end destination, but it's with having different experiences.*

Wiping face. *This one has hair in my mouth. It's annoying sometimes. It is so important when you're going along and you're getting the messages, because people now have come into your life as the teachers, as the students. They say that you know. When the student is ready the teacher will come. The same as when the teacher is ready the students will come. Do you understand that?* Yes. *And there are always teachers and there are always students and that is the part that is so beautiful, because it is all a part of the same circle of life. So yes, each of you are on like this spinning top wheel. Now I'm going to call it a spinning top wheel. Change that!* Adrian is slapping and cleaning hands to reiterate the change. *Forget that one. I am going to go ahead and talk about your chakra centers, okay? This is a really good thing to think about at this point. It is a good… what did they call that? Metaphor, metaphor, that's the word.*

So, we are going to start down by your feet. Okay, so under your feet you actually have chakras. Do you know that? Yes. *Some do. Some don't.* Giggling once again. *Anyhow, you do and so as you start to work on your spiritual life and you're starting to get things together. Well you know what, I need to change my start place. Now I gotta change my start place, cause people don't ever know about the ones under their feet first. The only ones they know first of all are their root chakra… And again, passion and drive… and… emotion and all of that.* Large hand gestures in the center of body, then hands clasped tightly. *That is where people are truly seated at and they're going out and they are reaction driven and they are driven not just by the passion but by… um… by they have to reproduce and power… Because, they have to be seen! They have to be known! That is instinctual of the man's… And then as they grow, and they develop, and they get that chakra moving.* Hands moving in circular motions around the front of body and then moving upwards. *You know what they are going to move up to the next one. They are going to go up to the orange one and you are going to go into other developments and that is kind of like your spiritual path. So, for each of you in this room and for those who are going to be watching this at home, that is exactly what it is. You are moving up your own pattern of your chakras as you're developing and you're coming to a higher place of Consciousness.*

It's the same as what the Earth Master Woman talks about with her building. And being at a particular address in on the ground floor it's noisy if

21

you're in the city and smelly and you can go up to the third floor and then things looked nice. She looked out and you see the tree tops moving back and forth and moving along, and you go up higher and maybe the seventh floor and maybe you don't even hear all the racket of the construction down there and you are feeling a cool breeze. You make it up to the penthouse. By the time you get to the penthouse you think you are nearly in heaven. You see all the stars above at nighttime. You don't even have issues with all of the different streetlights' cuz they're far below. You have a whole different view, because you're seeing through a different level of consciousness, because you have worked through the different layers of where are.

You have come through your root, and your sacral, and your heart, and your throat chakra… The throat chakra of communication. What an important chakra that is. Every single chakra is very important. Living through your heart… giving through your heart… Being one with your heart. What a beautiful way to learn lessons in life. Is that not true? Yes. It is because humans came to this Earth, plane to experience to be one with, so that they could grow their souls Consciousness to the next level. And while you are here in this time and space, the love that you feel that you experience and that you gift to others. That is what you carry with you, forever. Through every lifetime not just this one.

The communication, oh, to be able to communicate! Not anger and hate but the love and the joy and the education and the sharing and the training with those around you. What a beautiful thing to be. To be able to ask for help and then to be able to accept the help that's being offered to you. This is where the head gets in the way. This is always where the head gets in the way, not just the head but the ego. The ego thinking, oh, I don't need, I don't need… I can. I can. I can. I can. No one can alone. You didn't get here alone! What makes you think you could possibly exist alone? You all need one another because your hearts are all connected to the same light grid of existence. Each of you has that same light star seed within you which comes from the highest love God Source, energy source. I don't care who you call it. You call it whatever you want to call it but from that same Center Source of only the highest in the best. I don't know, did I answer the question? Or did I get lost? Sometimes I travel on. Laughing once again. *Yes. Okay I'm going to let another one come.*

Adrian had such a loving and educational presence. He was working diligently to allow each of us the opportunity to feel what he was speaking as truth so that we could understand the messages and teachings more clearly. His energy was fatherly, safe, boisterous, loving and he was incredibly grateful to have had time with us.

THIRD INCORPORATION: ARCH ANGEL ARIEL

Question

What do we need to do to prepare for the ability to clearly receive and coordinate the information to be able to move through the changes that are occurring?

There were many short deep breathing bursts during transition, and within the first several minutes of arrival. Ariel has a high pitched, young sounding female voice. She has an exceptionally light, fun loving energy and is joyful, with a very playful nature to her presence.

Ahhh, I have been waiting too. Deep breathing and several sighs. Can you tell us your name please? *I'm Ariel. I'm from the angelic realm and I've had the opportunity to come and speak on this matter. And I'm coming to speak from the Light Being Ones about consciousness.* Pause. *The question again, I,... I,... I,... I'm sorry... I need to hear it once again.* Deep breathing once again. What do we need to do to prepare for the ability to clearly receive and coordinate the information coming to use so that we are able to move through the changes that are occurring? Ariel is using hand gestures throughout her incorporation especially during the numbering process.

Number one. Ask! She sits back and leaves a lengthy pause. *Did you hear me?* Yes. *Number one. Ask. How many humans ask?* Pause once again and now showing a frown upon her face. *Can you tell me that? How many ask and then the second thing is wait for an answer.* Holding up both pointer and middle finger of her right hand and drawing out verbiage along with tone variation to accentuate meaning to wait for an answer.

She then begins to giggle, very happy with her thoughts. *And number three, acknowledge the answer was given and pay attention.* Very joyful and childlike in her mannerisms. *I know I like doing this. I really do, it's such a fun thing to be able to do.* Gleeful, and giggling continues.

So, number one, most important thing for humans is to ask. Ask... Ask... ask, ask... You don't have to just ask a single entity you can go ahead and say Angels, Masters, Universe, God Source... ah, Spirit Guides, loved ones who have passed before... any and all light beings... entities... Please, help me to be able to hear, to understand and to acknowledge... And then, the key is to pay attention to signs! Ariel is continuing with vibrant body language. Moving her head, shoulders, torso forward and back, along with hand gestures, and is pointing her fingers to accentuate her words. She clearly is adjusting to the incorporation.

We do not talk the same way as you do. We cannot communicate. We work really hard to be able to come through in dreams. We work really hard to be able to find you and give you lines... Lines in a book, lines on the TV station or you're hearing something and all of a sudden it goes – ahah! Ariel speaks very quickly and is excited throughout her dialog accentuated with hand, body, face and voice tone gestures to passionately provide her guidance. *We gift you those lines, because what we are able to do is to do like an exclamation point! Ah, that's it! That's it!*

Pause and voice softens. *That's it. That is the answer; however, sometimes you are to so busy you don't hear it. And, so then we have to find another way to go ahead and give you that answer once again. And, so sometimes we will go ahead and say... oh, oh, oh let's go ahead and send a spirit. Let's send a spirit animal. We'll have a bird fly by and the bird flies by and it lands almost on your car!* So emphatically spoken. *And then you know what they do? They shoo it away.* Somber and disappointed in stature, then she takes a pause. *I go like, are you kidding me?* She bursts out laughing once again and works to gain composure once again with a few deep breaths. *I know, that's a funny isn't it?* Everyone giggles. *It is a funny. So, then we have to go ahead and do other things, and so then sometimes a butterfly will come by.* Softly spoken. *And sometimes when that butterfly is coming by a thought will come into your mind.*

Sometimes you will get the little piece of paper when you go into the Chinese restaurant. Vocals building excitedly and fast once again. *And we work really, really hard to get you the exact little piece of paper that you are supposed to have with the message that you are supposed to have. And then ... sometimes, they don't even open the cookie.* Everyone laughs. *Can you believe it? I work that hard to get the cookie to them ...* High pitched squeal. *Who doesn't like a cookie? Everybody likes a cookie! Why would you not like a cookie!* Calmer now. *I know in moderation, I get it, I do understand. I do like it though when they invite me into the body, and we have a cookie together. Ohhh... it's so delicious!* High-pitched squeal, hands clapping and so very excited about discussing the joy of sharing a cookie. Her personality is adorable and infectious with joy.

Oh! Anyway, back to the question. Okay, so for listening for the answers... Listening for the answers. The one that sits before you, one time we had her at the beach, and she was holding the sand, and trying to hold the sand and trying to hold the sand. She kept picking it up and it kept falling through, and falling through, and falling through. At that time, she understood in her heart, that there was a big change that was coming that was no way in her control to be able to hold. She just had to be in the space of allowing it to flow through her. Do you understand this? Yes.

Has that not happened to each of you at a different space and place in time in your life? Yes. *Maybe it's an emotion. Maybe it's an event. Maybe it's an activity. Maybe it is a joyful moment. Maybe it's a painful moment. Sometimes you just can't control. It you just have to allow to be in there and to allow it to flow away and to flow through. Then the number three is then once the message has been given to you and I know your monkey mind goes around in circles over and over and over and over again. Is it real? Is it real? I want another one. I want another one... Want another... You know who is that? It is the ego. The ego gets in the way... All the time... Messing with things. It just likes to put... like you know spitballs. I think is a good thing to do.* Ariel is now using her fingers like flinging spit balls across the room. *Spit balls... throwing a spitball onto where you are and what's at. So, if you're ever in a place that you really don't know if they are really talking to you or not, wait. We'll come again. We don't have to do it just one time, because you know what, there are so many of us that are working on it, so it's ok. We don't mind coming back over and over again. As long as you actually get it, but then when you get it, accept it, my children! Why don't you accept it? You think you're not worthy. You think you are not enough. You think, oh well, that couldn't have been just for me. It really was just for you! And you! And you! And you! And you, because we love you so much!*

Do you realize that each of your lives, we all get to have an extension of it? It is so exciting that we get to have an extension of it. You are over there writing; you don't have to write everything. I'm not. *Ok, because they are doing that. That taping thing. I like electronics and I like to mess with electronics.* Belly laugh, everyone chuckles. *You think that it's not a problem. It's a problem!* She gleefully claps hands again and laughs. *We spitball electronics and we laugh at you.* More joyful laughter. *So, back to actually accepting… accepting the messages that come to you. And you know what else? When you're there and you're accepting it. You know it's so funny with a human being. They don't just stay where they are. They always want more, more, more, more, more! So, they never get a chance to appreciate where they are. Do you understand that?* Yes. *We work so hard to get you to a place of where you want to be and as soon as you get there, boop, you're not even there! You don't even care that you made it there as you are already worried about someplace else that you want to be.* Pause, shaking head and smiling. *I know, aren't you guys just so funny.* Giggling once again and smiling. *You can't help but laugh at yourselves, because it's just so funny.*

So, you have taken time to be in that space and yes, I know I hear you over there, Miss Judi. Running and running and running and running and then you get there and again you are running, running and running… but do you want to know what the key is? And you each know this, already. It is the ability to let other things go. And you know what else? You don't have to be so emotionally bound to anything anymore. It's not going to change anything. Do you not think that you were the most precious thing that there is in the world? Ariel speech slows and becomes very compassionate and loving. *Because each of you are. I'm here to tell you that.*

That is my message. You are the most precious thing in the entire world! Deep inhale. *Do you feel that love coming into you right now? You are the most precious thing in the entire world!* Ariel is so very loving at this time, opens her eyes and looks at each person along with the camera. Pausing after each statement. *You are, you are, you are, you are, and you are! The most precious thing in the entire world. And we love you so much! So, very, very much!*

You've never done anything wrong, ever done anything wrong. There are other choices you could have made. That's okay. You're perfect exactly the way that you are! Her presence is so warm and loving – palatable for the audience. Ariel takes in a deep breath. *Oh, others are waiting... I gotta go... I gotta go.* Thank you, thank you. *I gotta go... I gotta go.*

Ariel was such a pleasure to channel! Her love and pure joy for life and each of us was transformative not just to me as the channel, but for everyone in the room. She was pure light, emphatic and overwhelming by showering each of us with genuine affection for exactly who we are, for mankind and everyone this message touches. Ariel's energy is a soft pink essence. I envision bouncing blonde curly hair with flowers in it. Her dress is primarily white with pink flowers embroidered throughout. The dress is shorter about knee length and bounces wide as she hops and skips about. In her pockets she carries seeds of love to nourish all plants and animals.

FOURTH INCORPORATION: GABRIEL

Question

What do we need to do to prepare for the ability to clearly receive and coordinate the information to be able to move through the changes that are occurring?

Energy shifted greatly with Gabriel, a large male presence stepping in. It was more domineering and matter of factual in his speaking pattern. He arched back in his seating to get fully incorporated.

Gabriel was articulate, rhythmed, and methodical in knowledge and information. Gabriel entered wearing a uniform that was pristine in appearance. He was clipped in his speech and stated clearly that he was from Kryon and did not want to be confused with the Angel Gabriel.

Well I guess I have to ask the time. What's the time? Are we good with time?... 7:50. We said 8:00. Is that alright? We are good. *Are we good? We're good, we're good. Humans and your time... Time, time, time, time!* There was a tone of impatience, almost frustration, and lots of body adjustments, as this being continued to get settled into a physical body.

Do you want to know why it's a complete farce -- time? It's in your mind. It's on the box that you have on the wall. You think you run your lives around it, but ahhh! Have you not noticed it changing? Confidently chuckling. May I ask who you are please? *Gabriel.* Pause. Thank you. *Not the Angel either... They mistake us often, but I'm not he and he's not me.* Where are you from? *Ahhh...* big sigh. *Where am I from — h-m-m. I don't know if I'm going to tell you right now...* Laugh, *cause I don't think I'm going to.* Okay. *I am going to let you guess about it... Maybe later, we will discuss it. I don't have much time; you've already said that! And the question is? I've got to ask again. We all do what we have to be here front and center to truly understand it.* Okay.

What do we need to do to prepare ourselves for the ability to clearly receive and coordinate the information we're receiving to be able to move through all of these changes that are occurring? *Okay, I'm going to talk about the physical aspect of the human body. As you all understand you each are made of many different organisms, microorganisms, all kinds of cells and atoms and everything operates in a particular way. When people are in good health, everything is operating, and do you realize though that the human body will absolutely heal itself from any other issues and function? However, when you're making these energetic changes into your body, physical changes are also happening at the same time, and this means that sometimes people become more tired, they become more irritable, they're sleeping a whole lot, or not sleeping at all. They've got all kinds of shifts and they don't know where they are going because they are feeling very scattered. Thoughts become scattered. Emotions become scattered. They become hot flashes because of all of the different energy surges that are happening into and through within the physical systems. So, it is very... very... very, are you hearing me yet, very, very... very... important that you are mindful of your physical body while you're going through these different spiritual changes.*

So, it's very, very important to be sure to get plenty of sleep and this means you need to have quiet dark rest. The telephone should not be in the room. You should not have a lot of background noise. You need to be in a quiet dark place, because your mental and your emotional and your physical body need to go into a complete shutdown space. So that, guess what? Your spirit can continue to travel during your nighttime hours to learning and to receive additional information, which you will be bringing back in and utilizing. You understand? Yes.

Ok, now we're going to go ahead and we're going to talk about the other pieces and parts that people don't want to - diet and exercise. Those nasty little words that people laugh about. Could you imagine how many souls are up there fighting for one single physical body and you complain about going to the gym or going for a walk and eating proper foods with green stuff. I cannot believe it! It just boggles my mind that the humans get into such! But do you realize what it comes down to? I bet you do. Three letters. E.G.O. You think you know better. You do not. Your physical body must be able to maintain the changes which are happening. That means your chakras are moving so that they are free flowing. That means and continues to be with all of the different shifts and energy. You need to be able to walk. You need to have some cardiac exercise so that you get your body moving to a higher level so that it helps to prepare your blood flow systems and your nervous system and your electromagnetic system to be able to deal with the different energetic shifts that are happening in the body.

Then it comes down to the nutrition. Because you are doing all of these different energy shifts that are happening, your body is burning calories, but it cannot tolerate the heavy, heavy dense food and the fats, heavy fats. It needs to have lighter foods. You need to be able to process your foods more quickly, because you need that fast energy that's going to be able to burn more quickly, to be able to support what is needed for your energy shifts. Do you understand what I'm saying? Yes.

That is the same with the water. Being able to drink healthy water... lots of healthy water. Do you realize that water alone will heal a cell? A good quality water, good for you for getting a new system, as discussed earlier. A good bubble of water can go ahead and allow impurities to break off. Did you know that? Yes. *Absolutely, not everybody does, I'll tell you that. So, it's very important to have lots of water.*

It's also just as important to be able to listen to your body. I'm going to ask you a question. I want you to go ahead and to answer me. Have you ever walked through the grocery store and let your body choose what foods it wants? Yes, chuckles. *So that means you're walking and I'm not talking about the frozen pizza section and the ice cream. Alright. I'm talking about walking through the vegetable aisles and you walk up and down, and you know what? You feel which ones are calling to you. And then you go home, and you know what? You mix up these crazy concoctions. It doesn't matter. It tastes pretty good, because you're listening to what your body is telling you that it wants at that time... Very, very, very, very important! How do you think you are going to be able to move to the next space and place if you physically are not in a position to be able to deal with the energetic changes? Answer me that? Doesn't happen, does it?* No. Head shaking no, also.

So, my message, my main message to you is to be able to take care of your physical body! That means eat, drink, exercise and stress. You have got to be able to deal with the stress levels and you want to know what some of the things going on are. The key to most stress is to disengage. If you're not intimately, passionately absorbed in the mix of the chaos, your stress level goes from here to, boop! Hands up high and then low to dissipate. *Let them deal with it. But you deal with the aftereffects. Allow yourself permission to hit pause. To take a break and to take care of yourself... To take care of yourself. I'm from Kryon by the way.* Laughter and smiling. *Alright, I'm out of here.* Thank you.

Gabriel had a presence of authority and great knowledge of anatomy and the functionality of the human body. He was well versed in physical changes caused by outside influences and their direct impacts both negatively and positive. Gabriel holds a medical role of importance on Kryon and it was a great honor to receive this visitation.

FIFTH INCORPORATION: GATEKEEPER BAYLOT

My hands are rubbing together and breathing changes once again while Baylot stepped in. Baylot had waited and was the very last entity to step in. He was a bit hesitant, but his presence was gentle and loving as he took a moment to introduce himself to the circle.

Have enough of your questions been answered? Yes, yes. *Have enough of your questions been answered? Okay, I just want to go ahead and say thank you. We are very excited, and we are very honored to be a part of this. Thank you for allowing and offering your time to be able to come together as one. As one we are going to make some major changes. You know this is going to happen, do you not?* Yes, I do too. I do too. *And, um… and, um…*

I am Baylot. I don't ever have a chance to speak. I am so excited that I have a chance to speak! Thank you for honoring me and allowing me this time too. And to be able to be organized because it was really difficult before with that one. So, thank you all and we will see you again next week. Okay, Bye. Bye, Thank you.

Baylot has always held a noticeably quiet voice within me. His presence has been mostly unknown throughout my life. As of the last few years, he has awakened, or rather I have to a point where he is gaining strength as our communication expands. He is especially thrilled with this channeling circle and having an opportunity to independently speak his thoughts and impressions, too. He holds a particularly important role in my life and within the circle to coordinate and balance the messages and speakers who provide guidance.

I have intentionally not offered a description of Baylot so that each of you can look and listen within to hear and understand impressions that are provided by your guides. Ask for a visual description then allow the energies and your mind to craft his image.

After Discussion

We reviewed the various incorporations and a quick synopsis of the messages. It was determined that we received question guidance that supported the power of prayer, physical body, spiritual, educational and communication. A key point to remember is to "Ask", "Acknowledge" and then "Accept" what was offered. Discussion included the importance of taking care of Mother Earth. This thought was carried forward as a question for the next session.

Closing Prayer

Heavenly Father, Thank You. Thank you for the blessings of this day. Thank You for the blessings of this circle. Thank You for the power, the guidance, and the information. Thank You for your loved ones. Thank You for each of the souls that have gathered here to be able to grow together as one to learn to and through. Heavenly Father, help us to be able to send your loving energy into the center core of Mother Earth, to heal her from pollution, to heal her breakages, to be able to clear the water, to clear the air and to protect Her lands. Heavenly Father help mankind become better stewards of nature and of life and of other men. Be with those who are so challenged by disasters and catastrophes. Help to shower your loving light and peace and grace upon them. We ask this in Your precious name. Amen.

Session 2

Opening Prayer

Heavenly Father, Thank You. Thank You for the blessings of this day. Thank You for the opportunity to be able to gather together as one. Help us to invite in the highest and the best entities. Help us to be open channels. Help us to be able to allow creativity to flow into and through. Help us to be able to allow the love of the universe to shower down to and through and into each of us and we welcome you into this circle. Amen.

Introduction

THIS SESSION BEGAN WITH A discussion of my personal impressions and feelings of being specifically guided for this project to come to fruition. The discussion continued as I shared the overwhelming humbleness that I feel, and incredibly blessed, by the amazing guidance, that is being offered and shared through this Spirit Circle. We again discussed the importance and the increased energetic support that manifests through group work as compared to individual meditation. The plan for the evening included two questions that were created from emailed ideas of the sitters along with follow-up discussions from the previous session.

First Question

What can we do to help our Mother Earth?

FIRST INCORPORATION: JEROME

The male presence incorporated very quickly. He was articulate in his speech pattern; however, he did spend some time rearranging my body such as shoulder shaking and twisting to support his transition. There was a deep inhale then exhale. There was significant fluctuation from his entry tone of a baritone low pitch and then a moving up of several octaves until his volume and pitch found balance. He had a straight, ridged posture and told us that he was from the land of Archaea.

Ahhh... Ahhh, let me get in... and get settled in this body here. Um, one more time please? Thank you. Okay, what can we do to help Mother Earth? What can we do to help our Mother Earth? My name is Jerome. I am from the land of Archaea and it is lovely to be here.

What can you do to help Mother Earth? First of all, daughters, you are doing it as one, because you're choosing to come together and to ask the question. This is a critical part of what is not being done by so many of mankind. People find themselves upon this planet and they decide the planet belongs to them. Is that not just a foolish thing? How could something that's been here for eons of years before them and long after them in any shape, way or form, be expected to belong to buy someone in between? And then when they have ownership of the property what they do? They go ahead and they rip it apart. They tear down the trees, they build buildings, they go ahead, and they pollute the properties. There are so many things I've seen traveling across the lands, where the man's will actually move an entire mountain. They go ahead and chew it down into tiny bits so that they can get the flakes of gold which are locked deep inside the... the... all kinds of different minerals. They crush all of them to get the tiny little flecks out and then they move the entire mountain to the other side. Now this is what I know each of you who are asking the question, you feel like those chewed-up grains of Earth. Just one of those tiny little grains being upon this large mountain what could you possibly do as a single in order to make a change.

This is a very good question; however, as if each of you do not already know, it is with the power of intention. It is also getting involved. It is taking time to send energy out into the world. It is about making changes in the attitudes of what is already going on. It is helping to bring what others are doing, which you're not in the highest, in the best for Mother Earth, and allowing everyone to able to see it. You may not know all of what is going on. You are not running around Washington and making the decisions as others are in the land of America. You're certainly not in England and Ireland,... and in Russia and all of the other countries, as their leaders are making decisions and choices, which affect each of their physical spaces; however, each of you are linked to all of them through the same Light Grid... Through the same energetic field of connectivity. Therefore, when you are sending energy out into... healing energy, specifically directed towards Mother Earth, it helps to go ahead and to ignite... to help that process move forward in a healing manor. It also is not just about the healing, but it helps to open doorways of communication, and it allows for things that are hidden to be seen. Do you understand what I'm saying? Yes.

That's the key. When people come together as one and or in group format and send that healing energy as a whole, it shifts what is being done and it allows for more to be born from. Do you understand what I'm saying? Yes. *Do you understand the importance of each one of you and the value that you have, too? Do not ever think that what you say and the seeds you plant is not enough, because it is! Then there's the point of each of you taking the time to try to do something of your own. That means try to eliminate the things that are throwing away, waste, garbage that goes back into the landfills. Try to gift things so that they will continue to be used if they're not of your use anymore. It's the same with the recycling of things, reusing of things in different ways and allowing more to be come from.*

It is also about taking the time to pray for... Pray for your flowers... Pray to your trees. Allow your trees that are working so hard to change the air quality. Your prayers and blessings help encourage them to do more and to be stronger through. This is such an incredible blessing in value that is a contribution from each of you.

Do you have a specific message that you would like to share with us? *I do, my favorite color is blue. I love the color blue. Do you know why?*

Because it makes me feel happy too. When I look up into the sky and I see the color blue. It's a clear sky that allows me to... So, when you think of me, I want you to think of the color blue! Blessings and blessings to you.

Jerome's energy shifted throughout the message. He started very stoic and instructional. As time passed, he became much softer and loving. He just wanted each of us to first see our personal value and worth in the world, then to understand the opportunities and responsibilities that we have and how we can make improvements to our Mother Earth. Jerome had a very round presence that was blue in color.

SECOND INCORPORATION: GRANDFATHER REDWING

While Grandfather Redwing was incorporating, it was a slow process. He began with a low guttural toning vibration of my vocal cords. His speech had a deep, slow accent and was methodical in pattern, as he took deep breaths within a single thought or sentence. He had an exceptionally large, tall and ancient presence filled with great wisdom of our Mother Earth. I knew Grandfather Redwing, as I had previously channeled him. His energy lives within a large Redwood Tree that is located in Northern California.

Question

What can we do to help Mother Earth?

Hello. Hello. *Hello.* Who are we speaking with please? *I... am Grandfather Redwing.* Pause. *I am a redwood tree.* Pause. *I have stood upon this land for centuries.* This speech is very long and drawn out, slowly articulated for each syllable. *First, as a seedling, and then I've allowed myself to grow... and to become large.* Pause. *I have seen much... as I have stood upon our Mother Earth, through the m-a-a-n-n-n-y, m-a-a-n-n-n-y generations.* Pause. *My roots carry deep within to Mother Earth...,* Pause. *so far below that I tap into center core.* Whispering. *I feel the warmth of the flowing lava f-a-a-a-a-r-r-r beneath. Pause. I have felt the raging fires which have traveled through the center, too. Pause. I have felt the cool winds travel through my branches, too. Pause. Many animals have lived with in and amongst my branches... Pause. And disease has affected me too... not just disease by bugs and bacteria's, but the d-i-s-s-e-e-a-s-s-s-e of mankind. Pause. I live up on the California coast, but I cry with what is happened in the Amazon. S-o-o-o-o-o much destruction! How do you think enough air is going to be made... to feed mankind without the rainforest? Not just the air... but all kinds of life which comes to and through. As a large Redwood, I stand strong, but I also understand the powerful winds that push through each of you. Pause.*

As a man person, you sometimes feel as if you're that seedling being tossed about in the wind, pushed by so many different things, waves of energy, waves of activity... that are happening through man... Pause. Through situations far beyond what you know them to be... Pause. or what you feel that you have power to stop them through... Pause. Daughters, do you not know that all the treed ones are connected too? The same as the people are connected through the heart centers. All life is connected through the same energetic web. Pause. Have you heard of the web and how it lies over and each of the cross-sections? They are electronic? There are... light entities at each of the crosshairs upon this fabric. This fabric that travels into and through all particles of energy that is in existence. This is not just in a single format. It is 3D and beyond 3D. It is beyond what you can see... but it is the same energetic field of all. Pause. Now, when you find yourself being but one particle... but look around the room. Are you but one particle? There are many others who sit beside you who also are wanting to have improvements. Pause. It is the same way within that electronic web world. Pause.

There are so many ways that people communicate with others that they do not know. The Facebook postings are but one. The same shifts as the wind flows through the trees is the communication as it flows through the internet... and it gains strength as with a breaking wave upon the shore with the more that get involved. Pause. It is taking the time to share those posts. It is taking time to create those posts. It is taking time to share your thoughts. It is taking time to go to the city meetings or the different clubs and groups and organizations and allowing your voice to be heard... Pause. Speaking up and saying, "No More!" Pause.

"Stop." Pause. *Be where you are and allow what is, to come to fruition without always having to destroy additional things ahead.* Pause. *Do we need? Do you need, all of the oil that's being produced?* Pause. *Are there ways to change the energy consumption?* Pause. *How can you help have a voice in allowing that to change?* Pause. *Do you have to have your air conditioning set to 65? Do you have to have your heat set to 85?* Pause. *You live amongst the world in the areas that you are because you choose.* Pause. *Try to blend into the climate of where you are. I understand in the State of Florida it is warm...* Pause. *but people do not have to live in a refrigerator.* Pause. *Do they?* Pause. *No. Do you not understand that if you plant but a few more trees the change in the temperature that naturally occurs? That is what happens. The tree people can change the climate and they can allow for the cooling. It is the same when things are freezing cold. The trees help protect to keep it warmer from the frost hitting the ground. It is just the same with the embankments... of the rocks and the mountains. There are so many natural barriers that can be used, because you've already been gifted with them upon your planet... but people come in and they tear them all down and start anew.* Pause.

Why cannot they use what they already have? Pause. *This is my question back to you?* Pause. *So, for each of you, I challenge you to be the voices... to be the voices of the treed ones, and of the rock people...* Pause, *and encourage others to use what already is, instead of just starting anew.* Pause. Several deep breaths.

I do have a message, too. I ask that each of you plant a tree in memory of me... Just one tree and bless it as I will be within it.

Blessings, daughter's blessings. Hands clapping and exits.

Grandfather Redwing was such a large presence and so incredibly wise, knowledgeable and respected. His wisdom was ancient, and I knew from previous channelings, his roots and leaf energies were interconnected to all other trees and micro-organisms along and through the Earth's surface, by the millennia of life cycles.

In retrospect, it seemed out to character that a great Tree Spirit would be current with technological communication advancements;

however, oftentimes it is difficult to understand the "how" and "why" concepts in our minds, as compared to the channeled guidance.

THIRD INCORPORATION: GREGORY

This incorporation occurred with Gregory taking several deep breaths and body adjustments. He fastened the front of the shirt, as if looking for a collar. A very commanding male voice boomed that was curt and forthright. He had a formal stance as he sat straight up in the chair. He had a military and ridged feel. He was no nonsense, and straight to the point. Gregory had a difficult time telling us his location. Jelelpia was what finally told us.

Question *please?* Yes sir. What can we do to help our Mother Earth?

Well, I'm glad you're asking the question. There's a lot of them out there that don't even bother to get around to it, do they now? They're just out there do-do-do-do… doing and not even thinking about the consequences of where is going on and where is happening. Voice is clipped, matter of fact, authoritative with a tone of disrespect.

It is amazing. It truly is amazing… Each and every day what is transpiring? You know. Just look around you, right where you are… across the street… right across the road there, all kinds of trees just mown down… mowed down, just… mowed down. Yup, yup, yup, yup, yup… got solar panels across the street for what's going to be going in over there. Yup… Gonna have some gas! Gotta, gotta… have some gas and y'all need your coffee. Y'all need your coffee and donuts and all that other shenanigans… Yep, yep, yep!

May I ask who is speaking to us please? *Oh, sure, sure, sure, sure, yeah… Yup, yup, yup… Ummmm…* Low tone vibrational vocalization tuning for several seconds. *Gregory,* Gregory, *Gregory, Gregory, Gregory, Gregory, Gregory… Yup, ummmm… let's see…* Where are you from Gregory? *I know, where am I from? Humph! Humph… um… um…* Pause, and while paused was connecting and unconnected index and thumb fingers. *I'm not able to find the word. She doesn't have the word in there. I have to be able to find it from in there and I can't find it in there, so we may have to come back to that later. I'm not sure… where maybe we can find it maybe we can pull it together. Maybe we can make it happen. Good Lord, it's hard to work from in the body.*

You know there are limits in these things. No, but you know you guys have limits too. I get that. We all have limits. We all have limits. You know I've waited a really long time to be able to come through and be able to even give any kind of advice and this is the question that they send me to. That's alright. I'm good. I've got this one. Don't you worry none about it, I've got this one.

Alright, so the first thing you can get out of this is, you know that I've got myself some confidence… and that's the part that needs to go out there. I need to have soldiers out there who are willing to have a strong voice, so that people will go ahead and listen to… um. I want you to pay attention to the candidates that are out there. I know it's that time again, one more time they all have a lot of hot air that they are gibbering and jabbering about. Question them! Question them about what is their thought process on the global warming? Don't think it isn't happening because by golly gosh, it is, as you all know.

You missed a good one again, you know. You just missed a good one. Pause. There's a reason for that too. Yeah, anyway. Alright, so what can you do in order to help our Earth? We need to stop fracking. Why on Earth do you want to shake it up like that? You think you're not going to make huge changes? You think you're not going to change the climate by cracking the Mother Earth in half? Who on Earth had that thought? Exactly! Some man with a big fat ego. And you know what, it's not just the one that's in America, they are all over. And it's not just a man, it can be a woman too. It doesn't matter what sex they are, but they all are out there thinking they know more than, and you know what it's about? It's about chasing a piece of paper that's green. Or maybe it's a block of gold. Who knows? It doesn't matter. They're not taking it with them! They're really not taking it with them. Pause. But what they're leaving behind is devastation for decades and decades and decades to come!

I want to talk to you a quick minute about nuclear power. Okay. The

40

power plants. Let's talk about Hiroshima over there over... Over there, where everything is melted down and the pollution... and they can't even... What is going to happen? How many people have died through the process? And continue? People think they need to have more... More, more, more, more, more! Why? What do you really need to live? You need a place that has some kind of a roof over your head. You need to have food for sustainability. You need to be able to feed your children; I understand that. And, you want to have a good quality of life... But having an 8,000 square foot house for two people. Is that not just a little above and beyond? And why do they need to have six and seven? They don't need to have that many homes. Nobody needs to have that many homes.

So, what's happening right now in this Earth? You're experiencing a major collapse, and you know it! You see it. You're experiencing it. You feel it. The chaos is going to continue to grow and to blow! And that's what's happening, because it has to be cleaned up and it needs to be brought back into an alignment. It's too far out of balance!

You have islands floating in the ocean of garbage. You got some surfer dudes who are out there making a difference. They're choosing to make a difference. How many people are buying those bracelets? How many people are choosing to jump on a band wagon of just a couple of people who said no more! And they're using that social media, to get people back in behind them, and doing more... And that's what it's about. It's about each of you taking the time and energy to tap into, to support, and to send healing love and prayers! George is speaking very forcefully. Instructional finger pointing and gesturing to go and do.

Your prayers are beyond the power than you could possibly imagine! You send the good forces out there and it can only manifest more. When you're sending love to the beings who are making a difference more of a difference will be made! Do you understand that? Yes. *There's not one of you here who doesn't make a difference each and every day. Because you have the hearts and you choose to, and you ask the question. Just as you have right now. But I do challenge each of you, to go out and to have a voice too. Take time to explore a little more, even around where you are.*

The garbage dump that's down there in Volusia, they just plain plow over it. Why don't they recycle anything? They could set up a store. They could go ahead and give things away. There are plenty of people who need things. They could sell them for a couple of bucks. Is that such a big deal? Why doesn't that idea come back and challenge the county? It takes but a person with an idea and somebody who pokes at them enough to make it happen. It's a voice. It's an idea. It's an action step. You understand? A voice, an idea and an action step! And that's all it is. And there are many voices right here around this room. Can you imagine the action that each of you could do? And I challenge you to! Blessings.

Do you remember where you are from now Gregory? Several short inhaling breaths. Long pause. His head is shaking no. *Where from Jel-el-pia, Jel-el-pia. I can't get it right. I can't get it right. I can't get it right. I can't get it right. She can't do it. Jel-el-pia is all I can get and that's not even right.*

Do you have a message for us that you'd like to share? *I do, when you go into one of those meetings, I want you to know I'm with you! You're not representing you; you're representing me! And so, many other thousands and hundreds of thousands of entities far above and beyond who you are. Do you understand that? Your voice is enough, because it's not just your voice! Blessings*

Gregory was tall, slender and wore a pristine and fully pressed dark colored uniform. I could see many markings or jeweled pieces precisely placed on the jacket that surely signified a long prestigious career. He seemed a bit uncomfortable that my attire didn't match his. Several times throughout this incorporation Gregory used a frequency synchronization technique, where he would create a humming sound so that he could clearly attune both our vibrations to provide a better answer. At times Gregory hardly even made time to breath as his speech was clipping along and reminded me of an old typewriter working to its fullest potential.

Gregory was so very confident and powerful, and you could feel his support along with his command to go out into our world, to have a voice and take action!

INCORPORATION: GATEKEEPER BAYLOT

Baylot wants to know if that's enough. Is that enough for that question or do you want more for that question? No, that is fine. Thank you. *That's enough, okay... Next question, please.*

Second Question

What can we do to establish clear communication with Spirit Masters?

Just the Master Spirits? ... All Spirits, Source, Master Spirits, Angels, everything... all Spirits? Yes. *Okay. Hold on one second.*

FORTH INCORPORATION: ARCH ANGEL ARIEL

The energy shifted, while I rubbed my hands, and then she started clapping. A remarkably high pitched and excited female presence steps in. She is speaking quickly and such an adorable and loving energy. Arch Angel Ariel has returned once again to answer this question. She is just so lighthearted and delightful along with thrilled to have the opportunity to incorporate.

I get this one, I get this one, I get this one! Hands are clapping, with huge smiles and pure joy and delight. *I'm back again! I'm back again! I'm back again! Ariel. I like this! I like this game. It feels like a game. I'm sorry... the question, one more time please? How to talk to us? How to talk to us? I got it, I got it. Hey, you know what? This kind of sounds like last week too. You gotta ask. Ya gotta listen and ya gotta act. Right? It almost sounds like last week.* Her hands are still clapping, very animated, using finger to accurate first, second and third. *Okay.*

So, the first thing that you need to do, that you want to communicate, is that you have to ask. Okay, because um... you have to be ready to ask. People go and they do, do, do, do, do, do, do — but you have to stop. Pause...

doing enough to think that want to ask to be able to communicate more. Okay? Yeah. Ya got that? Okay, and then when you're in that quiet place, you have to stay there a minute. And there's many, many ways that we communicate with people. Okay. So first of all, a lot of times you'll feel things. Okay. You'll feel little sensations. You might feel somebody on the back of your head. You might feel, um... you might see light and, and you might see lights, and you might see colors and you might smell things too. So different ways that each of you can communicate better is to go ahead and to find yourself in a quiet place. And this means that you have to practice. Finger snapping. *It's not something that just happens like this...*finger snapping continues. *It means you have to practice.*

So, taking time to meditate is a really, really good thing that you can go ahead and do. And um... some people will do it by listening to a guided meditation and that will help them to practice, if they really have not practiced much into the meditation. But you should be able to get to a place where... after you... know you, you get up. And it's good to do it first thing in the morning when you're... before you get carried away with things. So, that means that it is like you need to go ahead and to schedule a plan for. So that um... this is going to be something you want to do and you're going to commit to doing it and maybe it's not every day but maybe you go ahead and you commit to it three times a week. Maybe it's Monday, Wednesday, and Friday and you know you have such a busy schedule so you have to get up, at like 5:30 in the morning, so that you can spend fifteen minutes to do this. But when you go ahead, and you sit down you need to find yourself into a quiet space.

So, the first thing that you do is you breathe deep, and then you quiet yourself. And, I know sometimes the monkey mind goes, and goes and goes... Making hand gestures of circles around the head and lots of overall hand and body gestures. *But you just go ahead and allow it to flow and you can have thoughts come through... but you don't have to hold on to the thoughts. See the thing is that the thoughts come through like this and like this...* now hand passing over forehead with the pointer finger moving across in front of the brow area from one side to the other like a wavelength. *And you can choose to allow to let them to continue to travel out. So, if you don't stop to keep them to go around in circles...* Hand now moving in vertical circles in front of face. Ariel speaks quickly and excitedly throughout her message. *Then they'll just continue to travel through. So, then what you're doing is you're quiet in yourself, so that you just find a pause. A space of pause and you can start off by praying and saying, you know. Please let me to be able to hear clearly the guidance of what I need to today, and you can ask for specifics to come in if you want that may not or you may not know how to understand how they're communicating with you yet. Do you understand that?* Yes.

Because entities have different ways of communicating too. Because each one is vibrating at different frequencies and different levels and different speeds. And... um... Grandfather Redwing, he is slower than me. You notice that? Yes. *Yeah, he's slower than me. It's not a bad thing, it's a different thing.* Right. *That's with everything in life. It's not a good or a bad, thing it's just a different thing. And you know what? In different stages in your life you're going to be in a different place where you're going to be able to hear and to understand that communication level. If you're up fifty times during the night feeding a crying baby you don't have time to hear as much, as you do if you are living alone, because you have more quiet available to be able to allow yourself to hear.*

The other thing that's really, really important is when you get those thoughts that come in, write them down. Take a note. Audio record them... Something. Grasp that thought. And even if you just take one, hang onto the one. There is a whole bunch which will continue to come, but if you hold onto the one and you practice the one. And when you get that thought, I want you to think about what that message is. And you can think about it not just for a couple minutes but go back to that thought and that message many times throughout the day and maybe that's the same thought for the entire week. It's really important to go ahead and to ponder what the full meaning of each message that's communicated to you is, because it's not just a single message! Do you understand that? Yes.

Sometimes, we're tricky. And we like to go ahead and play games, too, just to mess with you a little bit... but it allows you to be able to tap into different levels of what you're seeing, feeling and understanding... To be able to see a whole other side of it. You understand that? Yes. *Okay... um... Is that pretty good for the question?* Yes Ma'am, do you have a message for us that you would like to share? *I do. First thing I just want to go ahead and say again is that I am just really, really, really, excited that you guys are doing this. And, um...*

you know what? I have to say my same message that I did. This is my message. I want you to k-n-o-w that you're perfectly loved exactly the way that you are. I want you to f-e-e-l that you're perfectly loved exactly the way that you are. You are a perfect spark of God in the center of Self and you are everything! There's nothing more that you could be or do, that we could ever be any more proud of you. That's the most important message of all because you're loved. You're truly loved for the perfectness of who you are. So that's my message to you. Thank you. *Thank you.*

Arch Angel Ariel was so very personal. She took the time to truly connect with the sitters in the room. She paused and looked at each or pointed her finger and faced them as an intimate personal connection. Her presence and exuberance were palatable. She just oozes compassion, joy and adoration for all of mankind and was so content to be working with us on this exploration journey. She was such a beautiful Angel who waited to be asked for help.

FIFTH INCORPORATION: JELLY BELLY

This incorporation began with deep inhale and then an extended very low grunt hum vibration over the exhale. He continued making humming noises that began at a low pitch and continued to elevate the tone higher until it found an appropriate vibrational level in which to begin to vocalize. This entity named itself Jelly Belly as it was not familiar with having a name and could not identify where he originated from. It took quite a while for him to complete the incorporation process and he vocalized the humming for about thirty seconds. Jelly Belly was a male essence and felt younger.

I learned throughout the channeling process that not all Beings have names as they primarily communicate telepathically and are generally recognized by their light vibration, color and tone. Sometimes, they may choose a name such as Jelly Belly did for us.

Hello, hello, *hello,* hello, *hello,* hello, *hello…* Trying the voice. *Wow!*

I made it. I made it I made it. I made it. His presence is very satisfied to have made it through the incorporation process. Male tone, but younger feeling. *I didn't think this was ever going to happen. I've been waiting a really long time for this one.* May I ask, what you name is? *Sure, sure, sure, sure... Um, I don't know if ya'll have that name. Ah, I'm going to call myself Jelly Belly.* Entity belly laughs and others in room chuckle. *Ya'll can't say the other one anyway. That's okay, and you know what? I'm from another place.* Pause. *I know, kind of wild... Um, and you know I might tell you real name later. Okay, what's that question?*

Question

What can we do to establish a clear two-way communication as individuals with the Master Spirits, the Angels and Divine Beings? *The first thing that's really challenging as you heard, when I was coming in, I had to change the, the voice vibration frequency. That's a really hard thing... Um and as I'm in here it's very, very heavy and in the center right here...* He is pointing to the center of my chest. *Um, and it's because, we too have to work really hard in order for that communication to be able to work one-on-one with a person. Not that you can't get communications on a regular basis; however, it really takes practice and one of the things that is really helpful for people, as they're working with it, is to really think about building that relationship with their Spirit Guides, because your Spirit Guide has been with you since the very beginning. Your Spirit Guide is very familiar with your current frequency and your vibration, as you continue to grow and to change, as you get older in life. And, so if you take the time to really build that relationship with your Spirit Guide, it gives you kind of a quick access and your Spirit Guide knows how to contact absolutely anybody and can get assistance and information that you need anywhere, um... and from anyone; however, they do have an easier time of being able to communicate because they can easily access different levels of frequency vibration then the human does. Do you understand that?* Yes.

Okay, so that's like a really quick simple easy answer, um... but it does take time to practice. So, you don't have to know who their name is; however, if you go ahead and you take the time to ask their name you, you're going to find out what their name is. Okay. *So... is that... is... does everybody in the room here know who your Spirit Guide is at least by the feeling of who they are? I'm going to ask, and just say yes or no – yes, yes, yes, no, no, no, yes. Okay, alright so, again the room is about 60/40 something like that. It gives you an opportunity to be able to learn who they are. And so, one of the first things that you need to do is to go ahead and to quiet yourself enough and to ask to get to know who your Spirit Guide is. Put yourself into a quiet space and listen for what comes, okay?*

Listen for what comes and you might want to chew it around and mull it around a bit, until you get there and so then you're feeling more confident in it; however, allow yourself the time to explore that. So that would be step one... Okay... Is to go ahead and take to become more familiar with your Spirit Guide. The second thing is... yes, you do need to take some quiet time, contemplation and to pray and to ask for, um... Asking and praying are both the same thing. You need to open yourself. You need to be willing to allow other information to come in. The other part is you gotta accept it's real. That's one thing that man really gets in trouble with, and it's because you have free will and you have the ability to think, but you also have the ability to question. And, so you're constantly questioning whether or not, what your hearing is real or if it's just one of those traveling thoughts that are on their way through. I like that way. I thought that was good. That traveling thought thing, I think that was a good thing. Whether you hold it or whether you let it pass along... That was a good definition of it. Anyway... so, um... you gotta ask and you got to listen.

The other thing is, I want you to be able to feel! When you know the truth of what you're hearing, you feel it. You get God bump chills. You get the heart palpitations. You get the rush. You know... when you have had that experiential opportunity of knowing the truth of when you've had a visitation... You've got information... you know it's come to be because you feel it. The energy that shifts within self is what is recognized. So that's what you need to understand is the truth. So then, you know how to work towards that same goal again. You understand? Yes. Does that answer the question? Yes, yes it does.

Audience Question

May I ask a question? *Yes.* Do we only have one spirit guide, or do we have more than one? *Oh, you have more than one.* Okay. *You definitely have more than one. And then people who passed away… some of them choose to stay and ancestors can go ahead and choose to um… come back and be helpers is what they are. So, um… you always have an angel that's with you. You have a Spirit Guide. So, you have several that are around you, but then there's others that come and go. And they come and go at different times in your life. Based on different events or where you are in your life and what is getting ready to unfold.*

So, um… when you were a child and you're growing, you may have you know a real playful one… Someone who's keeping you company, because you know what maybe you're growing up in a place that isn't really that nice. And maybe people don't treat you very nice. Maybe you have some really wonderful Spirit Guides that play with you, that show you how loved and special that you are… But later on, when you're you know you're an adult and you have your own family and you have your own children and you and they are just their blossoming. Then you've got somebody else who's in there. But then when you're in a place and you're really spiraling and you're making a difference in the world. You know what? You've got somebody else who's there, because that's their strength. So that's when they're going to come in. But your main Spirit Guide, and you do have an assigned angel. They will stay with you from beginning to end, because that's what they chose to do. Okay. They chose to be with you. So, others come and go but, two main ones, *two main ones are always there.* Okay, thank you. *Sometimes more depending on the person. So, depending on the person.*

Do you have a special message for us? *I'm still kinda chuckling of the name, it's a fake-out name.* There's a belly laugh once again, pause, deep breathing, pause, trying to find information. *I can't, I can't do the name. I can't do the name. Um… the message. Okay, hold on. I think the message was what it was. The question was a good answer for the message. That you've got two that are always with you. From beginning to end, so remember that and take the time to get to know them.* Okay.

Jelly Belly was informative, and he was very knowledgeable about Spirit Guides and helping us to understand ourselves, our loved ones and ancestors. He had a great sense of humor and really enjoyed the incorporation. Throughout the channeling, his energy continued to strengthen, becoming more confident and he became more animated with body gestures as he continued to align with my energy and the frequency transmission process.

SIXTH INCORPORATION: GOD SOURCE

Question

What can we do to establish clear two-way communication Masters – all spirits, source?

A huge, omnipotent, and most beloved presence transitioned in, the God Source. I generally reference the God Source as a "He" as the voice tone is male; however, I know neither truly apply. The room shifts as the energy greatly increases as peace and love permeated throughout. A deep inhale and the message began. The God Source spoke with a low vibrational tone accent, which reflected a formal Elizabethan period of time. His speech was slow, soothing, and methodical in pattern.

Daughters,

It is my time to speak. You, my daughters, are but the chosen ones and you are always there. I am always already within you to listen to and through. You each know who I am. I am the God Source, which lives and breathes within you. You know and you feel, and you are as we are and there is not much that you have to do… to allow it to grow through.

Take time, my children. When you feel the joy, know that I AM too. When you see the love, know that it is me showering down and upon you, too. When you look below and within the mirror see all the glory that is around and within each of thee too. When you see your children and the sparks of joy, this is me within them, too.

I need you to understand that you do not always see US in the outside but within others, too. We are in and we are around the God Sparks of all children… the old ones… the young ones… the two-legged… the four-legged… the winged ones. We are within the butterflies. We are within the flowers. We are within all life. We are within the sparkling, dancing of the light beams upon the tops of the water.

All of this is the same love energy, which is what you are searching for, for communication. It is showered around and upon you all wherever you are. You just need to see… and to be… and to accept all the love that is all around thee. We are grateful, daughters, that you have chosen to be here this day and that you have asked this question. Blessings dear ones. Blessings to each of you. Amen.

Throughout the God Source message, for each thought or phrase, he took a deep cleansing inhale and then speak through the exhale breath. I believe this allowed for more love to be expelled into the room and to each of us, through the breath, as well as the words and messages that were spoken. I always love to channel the God Source, as I personally feel so healed and overfilled with love at the conclusion.

After Discussion

It was discussed that the entities can only use the vocabulary that I have within my knowledge base. Therefore, communication can be challenging because of what I have for words and current knowledge. A profound comment followed, "That's why sometimes we don't understand the message, and we don't have it in our vocabulary to understand it". This is absolutely true as we may not have the information in our vocabulary to be able to understand what we have not experienced. This shall be a great thought and question to explore the next session.

In Gregory's message: *So, what's happening right now in this Earth? You're experiencing a major collapse, and you know it! You see it. You're experiencing it. You feel it. The chaos is going to continue to grow and to blow! And that's what's happening, because it has to be cleaned up and it needs to be brought back into an alignment. It's too far out of balance!* This was channeled in September of 2019, many months before the outbreak of the Coronavirus Pandemic that changed our world.

Closing Prayer

Heavenly Father, Thank You. Thank You for the blessings of this evening. Thank You for the blessings of these hearts who have chosen to come together. Thank You for the blessings of this energy and the information that is being downloaded and help us to be able to guide ourselves and others with this information. Heavenly Father, we are just so incredibly grateful for the blessings of your love and your life and all the lives that we're entwined with. Help us to go forth, to do your will and to walk with a loving heart always. We ask this in your precious name. Amen.

Session 3

Opening Prayer

Heavenly Father, Thank You. Thank You for the blessings of this day. Thank You for opportunity to come together. Heavenly Father we open our hearts, our minds, our thoughts, and all of our energies to the love and Light Beings which are going to come through and share their wisdom and respect with us. We ask that you stand with us and keep us protected through this time. We ask this in your precious name. Amen.

Introduction

WE BEGAN BY REVIEWING HOW everyone felt about the circle structure. The sequence of the Spirit Circle followed the order of prayer, discussion, guided meditation and incorporation for messages and the proposed questions. I explained how I had been specifically guided by Jamar, the Elder Lemurian who lived in the City of Telos, to arrange the format after visiting Mt. Shasta; however, after two weeks he had not come through as a speaker. Therefore, we decided to adjust the format slightly and would plan to ask two questions, allowing for up to three speakers to answer each. We invited Jamar to come in after the guests, so that he could provide any additional guidance that was needed. The group agreed to this pattern, and we chose our two questions.

First Question

How do we understand what we don't know when we communicate with Universal Light Beings?

FIRST INCORPORATION: ELDER JAMAR

Jamar decided to step in as the first visitor. He is an Elder Lemurian, approximately 25,000 years old, who currently lives in the City of Telos which is located inside of Mt. Shasta, California. Jamar took a deep cleansing breath and began to speak. Jamar has a formal posture and his speech pattern is fairly rhythmed and monotone.

Ahhh. This question is mine to begin with. May I ask who is speaking? *Yes, you may. I am coming early, as I am Jamar and I am coming early for this question. And I am from Lemuria.*

This is a very good question for me to start with, because this is one of the reasons that I wanted to come to be… and to have the opportunity to speak with all of those around. You are correct in that sometimes you do not know what you do not know and it does provide a barrier of being able to communicate; however, this is a wonderful opportunity for each of the humans to be able to learn and expand from what they already know. The way that Light Beings will go ahead and choose to expand a human's possibilities and the realms of understanding is by sending little secret notes, and the secret notes are emotions. They're thoughts. They are hints. They are clues of being able to communicate in a different way. It is feeling the calling as of the one before you of knowing that they needed to go out to the Mt. Shasta, and again it is following a dedicated path that you are being led to. You may not understand all of the different components of the path; however, once you get to that destination the next clue is offered to you so that you're allowed to have the next level of information.

So, I know it has been referred to you as puzzle pieces, and this truly is the best way to be able to understand it. You have to be given a puzzle piece so that you can put that before you along the path, so you'll know which way to go. So, there are many different ways of communicating, but this is what I am going to say for this one and that's all I am going to say. You will hear again from me soon. Thank you. Thank you.

Jamar felt very instructional and deeply knowledgeable, while he spoke to us, but also had a softness to his tone that was shared through his wisdom.

SECOND INCORPORATION: MELISSA

Melissa stepped in next and definitely incorporated as feminine. There were several short, deep inhales and hands rubbing together for several seconds to assist with the transition. She settled her pink presence in softly with a gentle sigh. Her tone was very refined, comforting, and tender as she told us she was from Venus.

I'll come! I'd like to answer the question, please. Can you ask it once again? Yes Ma'am. How can we understand what we don't know when we communicate with Universal Light Beings? *Yes, my name is Melissa and I am from...* Pause. *I am from Venus.* Melissa entered as a very soft and sweet female essence and shared a loving smile with us.

You didn't know you had different entities from Venus, did you? Some of you may have; however, I am within your realm... In your earthly realm, and in your universal realm of what you know... and understand of planets in your solar system. I am just but one. There are so many different light beings and universal energy beings that are all working to communicate with you. We come to communicate with you during your sleep time and also during your daydream time. And so you may not understand all of these different things, but these are opportunities for each of us to be able to come into contact with you while the veil is in a thinner place for us to be able to communicate. Sometimes what happens, is a person is given information, and they do not truly understand all of what is being said, or what is being communicated; however, if you stay in that same vibration then more information will come.

Excuse me I must shut this off. CD music was softly playing in the

background and Melissa reached over and shut it off. *I find it is distracting...
um, because it is a vibration. It is a different vibration tone than what I am,
and therefore it's creating its own interference. This is a perfect example of what
I am trying to explain. When we're coming through and providing information
of a specific and particular vibrational tone; however, if you find yourself in an
agitated place or an angry place, then this is going to change your level of being
able to hear and understand what that vibration is. Does that make sense?* Yes.
*Okay, ask the question one more time. I want to make sure that I am answering
all points on the question.*

How can we understand what we don't know when we communicate
with Universal Light Beings? *Okay. So, the other thing is, you need to be
attentive. You need to be attentive to the different clues that are coming in and
try to keep yourself in a place. Another thing, is before you go to sleep, this is a
perfect time, or if you decide to take a nap or if you decide to put yourself into
an open space of vibration and attunement... to intentionally set yourself up, so
that you can request... to understand during that time. Ask for the information
to be relayed to you in an understandable format. Does that make sense?* Okay.

*I do actually have a message for you if that is okay, too? I want to... share
a little about the planet Venus. Venus is a beautiful, beautiful planet. It's not
just with the colors blues and greens and you have all the different colors upon
your earth plane; however, Venus has more reds, and pinks and also has hues
of lavender. Those are our primary colors. We also have a different kind of an
air that is here. It is made more of a hydrogen base, rather than an oxygen base.
And, so the different Beings that are there have a different kind of air that they
have to use... to live.*

*We have many different species than what you do on your planet, because,
again, when you have a different atmosphere and a different biosphere,... you
have diversity that is different from one to the other. Does that make sense to
you?* Yes.

*I just wanted to say thank you and I hope that one day that you will be able
to come to visit my planet, too. I know people are working on it diligently upon*

your Earth in order to travel to different places and we would like to be on your radar, also. So, thank you and love and light and blessings to you. Thank You.

Melissa reminded me of a whisper type of essence. Soft, gentle, and so loving. When she spoke, it was almost like a melody as your energy was being lulled and carried along through her message. She was very enthusiastic to speak about her Venus and would truly love for us to come and visit her.

THIRD INCORPORATION: EZEKIEL

Ezekiel transitioned with several head bobs, which settled and became straight and mannerly. His voice was a monotone and stoic. I identified his essence as a male essence, but truly, he was more androgynous. He claimed that he originated from Legendary.

I'd like to speak now. Okay. *Can you ask the question once again, please?* Yes. How can we understand what we do not know when we communicate with Universal Light Beings? *Thank you.* You are welcome. *Thank you.*

So, the first thing I would like to say is you know it's kind of funny with the human mind, because you are saying that you don't know; however, realistically you know all. You have all wisdom. You have all knowledge. You have all universal information already within the heart center of self. You may not have tapped into it, but you already have that information. So, it is about quieting the mind, quieting the soul and allowing for the information to be able to bubble itself out to a higher level of consciousness, so that you can recognize what that information is being relayed. Does that make sense? Yes. *Okay, So then the key again, and I know I am repeating things which are being spoken of in previous weeks, but, the key to all of this is first recognizing it and then to be able to accept it for the truth of what it is.*

It is amazing the way the truth is spoken, and then it is not believed by the human heart, because the mind gets in the way. And it's not just the mind but the ego also, and the humanness of not being able to understand and to believe all of what the full experience is. So, I want you to go... and to... um, when you're getting some kind of an informational que and you know you are getting the informational que, because you are feeling it in the center of self. You may get the God bumps, so you may get it that way. You may also be seeing different... um, animal spirits that are coming in and messages and things like that are coming in, but you have to be able to put it all together.

But again, we are beings of energy and light. Pause. *We act upon the vibrational level which comes into tune with the humans. That means that that vibration may be through the vocals. It may be through the tones which are heard in the ears. It may be through the vibration of thought in the mind. There are many different ways. It could be electrical and nervous systems of being able to get that information in you. So, it is coming into the human body in many different formats and it comes in different tones. That's why it's important such as the woman over here who works so diligently with the crystal bowls and the tones. When you are working with a different tone levels, you are tuning in so that you are allowing the energy vibration to raise to equilibrium – an equal space of being able to hear and to be able to understand at the same time. Does that make sense? Yes.*

Audience Questions

Is there something that we can do, if we realize we are getting a message or something is being acknowledged to us, but we are not in a place where we can be completely quiet? I have this happen when I am working. I try to take time to distinguish but I have a difficult time distinguishing what the message is. Is there something I can do to assist?

Are you looking to have the information right that minute or do you want to ask them to place it on hold for a later time, when you can really evaluate and contemplate? Because you can request that they come back to you at a later time when you are in a,... in a more quiet space to be able to get the full meaning of it and you can ask for... can I have a mini clip? Fingers snapping. *Just give me the punch line. Just give me the punch line right now. When you get the punch line right now, you may not be able to remember it as well as if you ask them to come back so that you can get the full understanding of it. Does that make sense?* Yes.

Can I ask for the punch line now and fill in the blanks later? *You absolutely can ask for whatever you want to ask for, and we're here to provide you with whatever it is that you are asking for.* Sometimes I feel it's in that moment, the answer is kinda needed, and that's why I am asking. *Then please do. Please do.* Fingers snapping once again several times. *Ask for it right then. The other thing that you can do is if you are in a situation where you are looking for information and you don't think that you have the information in your physical form, you can ask for them to provide that information and to allow it to flow through you to whomever you are communicating with. Do you know that?* Okay, I did not. *Yes, you can ask for them to provide the information through you.* As Ezekiel continued to channel, he began using quite a few different hand gestures. Once he figured this out, he really enjoyed moving the body parts. Okay, thank you. *You may not remember, though, what you said. That is the only thing, but it is a wonderful way to practice because anyone can channel.*

Anyone has the ability to channel. You just have to be willing to... And know that you're protected and loved, and you are doing it in the highest and best form. That's the key that I am going to have to mention to anyone who's out in the audience anywhere. You don't just do this without protecting yourself prior to and building in resources to make sure that you are guarded through the full process.

Can we ask who you are? *Oh, did I not tell you?* No. Laugh. *Details...* Deep breathing and pause. *Legendary,... Legendary is where I am from, and my name is Ezekiel. I have to pick that name Ezekiel because I'm not,... I like that name. It's,... I don't have a name, I like that name, so Ezekiel is a good name for me, but I am from Legendary. Is that good?* Oh, that's wonderful. *Ok, I think the message was that I want to give is what already came out. Everybody has the ability to channel, ok... and I want you to know that. So, thank you. Blessings to you.* Blessings to you too.

It was fascinating to watch and feel the changes that occurred with Ezekiel through his channeling on video. As time passed, his voice tone changed and began to fluctuate as he used more octaves and became used to speaking and the capabilities of vocal cords. This was the same with his animation. He incorporated with a stoic or ridged essence and then once he tried finger snapping, he enjoyed the feel, and the ability to make additional noises with body parts. Therefore, he snapped often and added hand gestures to assist in sharing his message.

INCORPORATION: GATEKEEPER BAYLOT

How many have come through for that question? This is the third one. *This is the third one that already finished.* Yes. *Okay, then we are going to go ahead and switch questions. Did it answer all of your questions?* Yes. *Okay.*

Second Question

We need to discuss mindfulness versus individuals or society's vibrational rates and how that affects change?

FORTH INCORPORATION: JAMILLA

There was a pause, organizing the question. This allowed for the energy to build up the frequency of vibration and Jamilla was ready as soon as asked. She entered by rubbing her hands, presenting a maternal energy, sharing a huge loving smile with us. As she settled, she was posturing and you could see and feel her soft and gentle presence with her body language and pursed lips, too. Jamilla's essence glowed as she announced to us that she was from the Angelic Realm.

I'm gonna come in! I am very excited to be here. She was shrugging her shoulders and grinning ear to ear with a very joyful presence. *I am very, very excited to be here.* And you are? *I just see yellow everywhere. I can't believe all the light that's all around. It just feels so light and airy and I love the colors. I love all the colors. You each have such beautiful energies all around you.*

Um... Jamilla, Jamilla, Jamilla. I am Jamilla and... um, let's see, where am I from? Where am I from? A long time ago I was in Atlantis, a very, very, very long time ago. That was just one of my lifetimes. I guess I don't know where exactly to say where I am from, because I have had a lot of different lifetimes. So, but right now, my most recent... actually, is that I have been working very, very diligently and I have been getting some angel wings, because I come from the angelic realm, right now, and because I have worked very hard to get there.

So... um, I totally forgot the question. I am so sorry. I am so excited to be here. Thank you. We would like for you to discuss mindfulness verses individuals or society's vibrational rates and how that affects change?

Okay, so mindfulness is such an important, important key! It is because it is all about keeping your mind and your thoughts and your heart into a clean space and a vibrating higher space. If you don't keep yourself in a higher space, you are going to allow all of the other junk to pull you down, to keep you in a lower space and a slower vibration, and a lot more activity happens when you are in a higher space. That's when people notice that time is flying by... Snap, snap, snap... *much more quickly. It is because you are vibrating at a higher space, so time is moving at a faster clip. People who are stuck in the doom and gloom and woah is me, is life.* It's a much slower speech pattern. *Their life is slower, because they are feeling the pain and the drama and all of the different ups and downs of life, and the torment that is pulling and pushing you all the way through. Doesn't that make sense?* Um... aha.

I know. These things are things that we are trying to help educate the population about that they don't understand yet. So, as you are working on your mindfulness that is a key important thing; however, what is really, really difficult is when you have very large groups of people, because no one lives alone. No one can live alone. You cannot possibly thrive on your own. You need all of the others to be able to be part of a community; however, what happens is once you get a lot of people together. Again, every single human has free will, so they have the opportunity to create whatever life that they want to create. To live a life wherever and however they want and some of them are choosing to live it based on the me, me, me! And others are gifted to be able to serve, serve, serve, serve, serve. So there are very, very different kinds of lifestyles that people are choosing to participate in; however, when you are going through the process of trying to keep order with large masses of population, with people with so many different levels of their earthly pattern of where they are and what they have grown to become, and because you have them down here, you have them in the middle and you've got them in the higher. You just cannot balance all of them at once. So, there have to be laws that are put into place. There has to be some type of that somewhere along the line.

Then you have got all the people with the money and greed and feel like they have to have everything; however, the most valued people and the most valuable entities above all in the human race are the ones that are with the Mother Earth and who are caring for the Mother Earth. They are the ones that truly have the greatest power of all. Not of the people, but they are the ones who are in control of actually what is happening with the climate, and how it is shifting and taking place.

Now, because of these energies which are happening over here that will help to influence the leaders that are over here; however, it is critical that the information be given to them. And, what has to happen? The information that is over here from the Mother Earth and how it is happening has to be on the same vibrational tone. So over here the leaders must be able to tune into the radio stations to be able to hear and to understand it.

It was very good that your group came together tonight and added respect. That was a key. It is really an important thing that is not thought of nearly as often as it needs to be. People must respect, just plain respect, for another, the planet, their garbage, what they put in their bodies, how they treat their bodies, for where they live, for how they live, for who they live with, for how they treat their own selves. Think about the chain that happens with respect. It's a core component of all life. If people, the human race, chose to just live by respect... it changes all elements within the game. Does it not? Yes. Yes, it does. It absolutely does.

Ask the question one more time. I want to be sure that I have hit on all the points that I need to. We are asking for you to discuss mindfulness verses individual or society's vibrational rates, and how that effects change? *Okay, I didn't touch on the individual, but I mean its kind of a given, because if you are individually in control of your own mindfulness... Alright, and that is the key behind it. So, um... but the other thing that I am going to say... and I think this is going to be my message, is about the Law of Attraction.*

You need to be so mindful of the Law of Attraction. If you focus yourself into a place of giving of your heart, of being respectful, of loving Mother Earth, of being grateful for the opportunity to have a human life, you have no idea how amazingly honored you are to have been given this opportunity of a human existence. There are so many different spirits and entities who are just flipping out, upside down, inside out and backwards – wanting... Souls are wanting to have the opportunity to come back to the earth plane, because, they want to do it right. They want to be able to elevate themselves. They want to be able to attract more goodness into their soul-life, beyond and this is much easier, done once they are here in the human realm to be able to do that.

The key behind all of it though, is to be in a space, where you are choosing mindfulness in order to do that. That comes with time. That comes with time, love, peace and choosing to make a difference in your life. So, all I am going to say is my message to each of you is, I am very, very honored and excited to have had the opportunity to be able to speak to you, and do you know you all choose to become Angels too? It is all part of the realm, of your personal soul elevation, of what you go, and what you do and how you become... and being able to come through to cycle to the next levels.

So, I just pray that peace, love and abundance will be showered upon each of you earthly souls and that you allow that to go forth to all those around you. Blessing to you. Thank you, *Blessings to each of you.*

Jamilla was such a magnanimous and neutering presence! You could feel her love of life, and for each of us, as well as the great joy of having the opportunity to speak. Jamilla's presence was a white flowing essence. Wearing white allows one to reflect all other colors around you and to stay in a neutral and loving space throughout any visit.

FIFTH INCORPORATION: JIM DANDY

This entity began its incorporation by intentionally stretching shoulders and head and readjusted positions several times until it quieted. It then progressed by vocalizing a low murmuring hum that elevated. I sensed it was a male entity. He suddenly sat up straight and began musically pulsing, humming sounds using various octaves and tones. I could tell right from the start that this incorporation was a character, full of energy, a great sense of humor, a love for life and he was thrilled to have use of a physical body. He was curious to see what it could do, and what he could influence it to do. Jim Dandy decided to choose a name and told us that he was a Star Being from another Galaxy.

Ta-dah, I have arrived! Laughing. *I like a grand entrance!* Belly laughing. *I like music, too!* He slapped his legs and made clapping noises. *I like music too. I really like music, and that's why they sent me back for this particular question, because it's about vibrations.* Continuing a drum beat upon Judi's lap... *Changing the vibrations and becoming one with the different vibrations and being mindful of the different vibrations to make a difference and change.* He continued making many different noises to create a beat and a rhythm. He was finding great joy in being able to make both physical as well as verbal noises to assist in creating his own vibration for us to experience. *Is that not so cute?* Yes, it was. *I know. I know. I know. Jim Dandy, that's a cute little name, isn't it now.* He breaks into a full-on-out rhythm of slapping legs, clapping, dancing in the chair, squeaking the chair, whistling, smiling and very joyful to be making music? *This is really fun!* The group chuckles at him. *I don't get a chance to do this.* Continuing the rhythm. *You know I can feel it on my legs. I can hear it the noises, it's really, pretty cool!* Hands clapping, snapping fingers, whistling, popping lips. *Lots of different noises.* Continues making all types of verbal percussion sounds. *And the chair makes noises, too.* Joyfully, giggling, laughing and having a musical blast for several minutes. *Okay, okay. Alright, I'm here and I'm ready!*

Okay, you better ask that question again. I got all distracted. We would like for you to discuss mindfulness versus individuals or societies vibrational rates and how that affects change. Finger snapping continues. *It's all about the music and the tunes. Do you know what a difference it makes in life when you go and turn on a radio station and there is a nice upbeat song that you've got?* Continued chair dancing, finger snapping and shoulders moving... *And it's moving and it's grooving, and it is making you feel really good.* He stops making noise... *And that's what it is all about, becoming mindful, allowing yourself to fall into a vibration that is of a lightheartedness, will have to bring in more of that same light-heartedness vibration. Society definitely gets into the doom and gloom, and oh my God! ... and here come the hurricanes, and here comes the... this and that disaster! There is not a thing you could turn on that stupid boob-tube that by golly gosh, is not just of the deepest desp-a-i-r!* He is overly animated and exaggerating body language to clearly articulate his message.

Why do people turn those on? I do not know why they even bother! When there are so many wonderful things you could be out there doing. Fingers snapping again. *Dancing, that's another one. Doesn't that just make you move and groove and change your vibration? Yes. It does! Now, what also happens with a lot of people, when they get caught in too much of that vibrational space is that they disengage from life. They stay in the Party Zone, because they actually don't want to go ahead and connect with the real-world happenings. Now, some of those leaders, they could use a little of that party zone. I can tell you that right now. They get really stuck in the muck. I love it! I love it! Don't you love it? I know, anyway... so, it's really important to go ahead to stay in your own space and place. And you know what? If you are feeling like the gloom and dooms, go ahead and put on some nice music. Change your vibration. Change your...*

It's all about changing your clothes. Why not? You know. Change your hair. She cut her hair, you know she's looking kinda different, a little cute this week, huh? Anyway, it's all about changing. Making the changes. Why not change. Finger snapping once again. *You know what? Take the chance to make a change! Isn't that a good message? I'm giving you that one. Yeah! Take the chance to change. Step out of your comfort zone. Do something different. Be something different. Act like your something different. When you act like something different, guess what? It comes to be. Why not? Who is stopping it from coming to be? It's like you start yourself down the track, let itself open up and become what it is. Just let yourself become it! If you decide not, ah, change your* mind…whatever, whatever… *doesn't matter. So anyway, all of your vibrations… affect the change. And what you bring into your life. So, choose to put yourself into a higher, upbeat space and allow it to become a better space, for you and everybody else around you too. Alright, I'm out of here, Kiddo's!*

Who are you? *Oh, who am I?* He belly laughs and hand clapping once again. *Who am I, what did you call me a minute ago? That was a good name. Joe Shmoo.* No, Jim Dandy. *Jim Dandy, Jim Dandy, Jim Dandy, that's a good one. Jim Dandy keeping it handy. Yeah.* Fingers snapping, chair dancing once again. *Go with the flow that's me. Go with the flow! That's the way to go!* Hands slapping, clapping and chair dancing.

Mr. Dandy, can you tell us where you are from? Chair squeaking, playing rhythms. *I am a Star Being. I am a Star Being. Yes, I am. I am not even from your galaxy, but you know what? You can see me flying across the sky, every once in a while. Cause you know what? I like to hop on that comet and go. That's what I like to do!* Jim Dandy continuing to clap, squeak the chair, dance, fingers snapping and is so delighted and joyful to be making music. *Oh, I've been having such a good time, but I guess I gotta go. Be safe.* Thanks. *Bye.*

Throughout Jim's speaking it was often melodic in nature, almost like a talking song. He loved using the vocal cords and stretching them to see what they could really do. He was so very animated and made noises as often as possible with the chair, lip smacking, dancing in the chair, snapping, clapping and constantly moved throughout the visit. He was such a fun character and we all loved his robust visit.

SIXTH INCORPORATION: JEROME

A deep-pitched, mellow vibrational male voice begins to speak. It was amusing that he began by mocking and a teasing tone about the previous incorporation. Jerome was more mature, and even toned sharing great wisdom during his visit. He told us that he was from the country of Ubania, which is located within the Alkezia Star System. He spoke methodically with a steady rhythm.

Well that one was all full of himself, was he not? Group chuckles. *Come on, my oh, my! You know there's all kinds out here. Some of them choose to get all fired up and antsy, swirling and twirling. Others of us… we just sit back and watch them burn out.* Pause.

That's what happens, you know. That's okay. It's okay to put a lot of energy into something, because when you know what? When you put a lot of energy in something, you allow it to move to the next level of vibration. It's allowed to move up! It's allowed to become more than what you ever could have imagined it could be. And it is, because it's based on the energy, the vibration and it's up to the mindfulness to allow yourself to elevate up to that space and place. Does that make sense? Yes. It does. I know.

Alright, Jerome is who I am. Where are you from Jerome? *Ubania.* Thank you. Pause. *It's a Country. It's not just a City. Ubania it is an entire Country of Beings. We're Ubanian.* Where is Ubania? *It's located in another Solar System… Al-ka-za-ah, Al-ka-za-ah… system star.* He was slowly trying to articulate and sound out to pronounce. *Al-ka-za-ah… Al. Al-kezia, Alkezia, Alkezia! Ah, I got it! Alkezia. Okay… um.*

What was the question? We would like you to please discuss mindfulness versus individuals or society's vibrational rate and how that effects change? *So, society has such a broad band, they… I asked to come in because I am from an entire other country, see. So, we deal with very large masses of population and we have to deal with entities that are trying to unite and to live in unison. And to also stay of a quieter space; however, my country is a very different country in that, it is, it is very uniformed. We do not have the same diversity in the population that you do of humankind. We have a more scheduled and well, it's not scheduled. We don't have the same broad… um, choices that you do. You have free will in your countries. Therefore, you're able to have chaos to such a level that we do not have in our country. It's more… um,* pause. *I guess the word you have is regulated. I don't know if that really qualifies as an appropriate term, because it's not… it's, we just don't have the same level of discrepancies because we do not come with… um, that same wide length of variety. Does that make sense? Are you understanding that?* Yes.

Okay? So that is one thing that's a little bit different as to be able to compare to the Earth and… and your structure. Our structure is… um, we don't have the level of chaos. We don't have the bombings. We don't have the mass fighting. We don't have shooting going off in schools and killing our youth… um. We don't have that level of chaos; however, out of that level of chaos also comes great ability for creativity, because you have such diversity in one side as the other. This one is getting a headache here, because of my vibration is a much denser vibration for her physical body to deal with. Fingers pointing at the front, center of forehead to accurate the placement of pain. *So, there is a great pressure that's in the top of her head. I'm not sure how long I'm going to be able to stay because I am feeling an impacting upon her. Let me see,… let me see if I can change my tone a second.* He stopped talking, took several deep breaths and we watched his body relax more and this voice tone came back softer and less ridged.

Okay. I think that's better… um, oh, it's lighter now. It's different now. It's very different now… um, I don't know why that is. It's an adjustment in the vibration tone. Exactly as what we're discussing. I had to change my denser level. I had to be able to change it to a lighter color vibration so that it would tone more easily with her physical vibration in order to be able to communicate properly.

So, the society is a different level. Individuals, though, do need to be able to as the same with my country with your country, pay attention to the mindfulness of who and what they are. What they want to become, and what they can become. And all of this is such an easy accomplishment to move through; however, again, because you have the free will in your country and there is such craziness, but there's such growth and color and vibration that happens, too. The key is being able to find centeredness of self within the chaos that's around you. You have no idea of the power that comes from your finding the peace of centeredness in self and how that emanates out far beyond you. Does that make sense? Aha. *Did I answer the question?* Yes.

Okay, a message from me to you. My country is a beautiful country, my galaxy is beautiful galaxy, as is yours. My message to each of you is to truly look and see the beauty that's around you. To appreciate and be grateful for all that you currently have. And to know that you have the ability to manifest too. Anything that your heart desires can come into fruition before you. As long as you believe it to be.

Blessings to you. Blessings to you. *Blessings to you.*

Jerome was a wise Elder who held great authority in his country as a leader of many. He wore formal attire that resembled a uniform that was neatly pressed. He was very stoic in his presence and regarded with great respect for the use of my body. That was why he took the time and energy to readjust his vibration, so that it would align with my energy more comfortably. After he did adjust, he was taken back by how his impression and vision changed through the frequency change. It was an honor to have an incorporation of his caliber come through to help explain the differences and similarities that are required when supporting a mass population.

INCORPORATION: GATEKEEPER BAYLOT

Baylot quickly stepped in to verify that we had three message answers to the previous question and a time check. He then prepared to get Jamar for the next portion of the channeling.

SEVENTH INCORPORATION: ELDER JAMAR

Jamar is the Elder who is from Lemuria and currently lives in the city of Telos, which is located inside of Mt. Shasta, that is located in Northern California. Jamar was being invited in, so that he could speak on any subject or topic that he thought would be of interest or assistance to us. Jamar is deeply knowledgeable and articulates solid ideas, concepts and confidence when he spoke.

I am Jamar, and I am one who wanted to have the opportunity to speak. I am very honored that each of you have chosen to participate within this time and this space. I want to explain about how this came to be. The one who sits before you came out to California, and because she went to many different spaces and places, and chose to open herself, then more clues were opened before her. Once this fully transpired, then she was shown a Gateway; however, she wasn't just shown the gateway, she was shown a tree, and because she listened to the tree the Gateway was revealed to her. Once the Gateway is revealed, person is prepared energetically to be in a receptive space of being able to learn about more. This happens while they are in a sleeping state and in an altered state of consciousness.

It is extremely difficult for a human to reach that state of consciousness in the physical, in an awake place in space, nearly impossible, because humans just cannot travel to the different dimensions thereof, where we are operating. You currently find yourself in the third, fourth realms of existence. Our city of Telos is located inside the mountain of Shasta; however, it's not just in the mountain of Shasta. It is also located in a number of different countries, different universes, but we all unite on different levels and planes of existence. We are vibrating on the fifth, sixth, seventh, and eighth levels. Now, what happens with these different levels are many different things.

First of all, you're invited to go into the city of Telos, and you're invited by different guides, who will meet you, greet you, and take you in. This is to be able to explain to the humans and to cure,... curb the curiosities of your human experience. So, the child before you were welcomed by me, Jamar as an Elder, and there were also two other guides who met her, and we traveled down within. Now, let me explain about the two other guides, and who they are, what they are, and what their purposes are in order to help the process.

The first one is a female and what she does, she was actually born in the city of Telos and she was raised there and educated there and so she has spent her entire lifetime there... and I want you to know that our lifetimes and your lifetimes are very, very different. We live for thousands of years, ten thousands of years and we don't even age unless we choose to have the wrinkles upon the face. We could look in many different fashions. Mostly we have very clear skin and we have long hair and we have lighter colored skin and we're a taller species than you... and we are more angulated, because we have more,... we have a longer face and longer arms,... and we are just taller all the way around.

So, anyhow the female went ahead and showed the child about the existence of the city and how it operates. So it operates,... oh, I guess a little bit like what's your cities do, because we do have an education system; however, not everyone is allowed to just become parents. You have to be able to be chosen and approved that you're worthy to raise a child. This is something that the earthlings could learn from, and they would do well to learn from. They let anyone have children and they're not the best parents, and then all kinds of chaos ensues... but, let me not divert and go back to where I want to be.

So, I want to go ahead and talk about how we grow our food. We also grow our food mostly with waters. Hydration is how we do; however, I want you to know that we have pure plants, but we do not need to eat the same that you do. In the earthly plane you have to... and in your three-dimensional world you have to eat a lot in order, because your body is going through... all of the different... um, circulations that it needs to in order to work.

We're different. We ae at a different, higher vibration. We don't have to have food for all of those nutrient values the same that you do. We do have some, but we, we also feed upon the energies... and we feed upon the crystal energies, which we have around us and into and inside all of the different areas of... not just the Earth universe but the other universes that are around. So, we collect our energies through minerals and rocks and through sunlight and through ... um, many different vibrations of energy... is... is what we feed upon that's beyond the food level.

Now, back to the woman again and what else she does. Okay. So, she also helps with individuals with their jobs. So in order to run a system of wherever, you have a population of beings, there has to be some kind of organization and different entities have different responsibilities of what they choose to do, but everyone has a choice as to what they're going to do and they all enjoy and find peace and love in doing their service to provide a betterment of... Some of that includes... um, builders, construction and that means homes and all... and... um. We have all kinds of art and beauty too. It's very, very important to be able to provide the art and the beauty, because that provides joy and peace. Joy, peace and beauty are a wonderful thing. We have incredible flowers, and topiary gardens, and we have water and waterfalls, and we have carved structures and beauty that are all around. And that was what this child was here to see.

There was a second guide who was there. This was a gentleman spirit. Well, I don't want to call him spirit, he is another Being who was also born in the city of Telos. And now he is a gentleman who helps to understand how everything operates. So, it's facilities, and so, he went through and showed about how the water systems work, and how the transportation works. There are much different ways of transporting around, because it is again a very busy city. And not just one city, we travel from many, many places. There are many kinds of transportation, so it could be light rails. It can be teleportation. There are many, many kinds of transportation. And do you know what? We have animals here, too. We have wonderful, beautiful, loving animals. Sometimes they choose to carry us from one place to the next place, because they choose to with joy and with peace in their hearts, and we allow them to. We can communicate with them telepathically, as do sometimes you can from time to time.

So, as we travel down into the city of Telos, in order to show about what this type of an existence is. It is very light. There is no darkness, because the crystals are the lights. There is light far beneath and beyond from what you would think with your different dimensions. We can tap into the light of the sun and we can then just have it fractioned, so that it can be seen in any place, no matter where. It doesn't have to be above ground, but below ground, under the ground and out into the cosmos system. Anywhere. It doesn't matter, because when you're operating on different dimensions you have an ability to tap into the resources and then to realign those resources into a different fashion that's much more usable for you, where you are. Does that make sense? Yes. Good. I would like to be able to allow you a minute to ask a question or two from me, if any of you in the audience would like to ask something specific of me.

Audience Questions

I would. Why is your vibration affecting me the way that it is? I feel like I'm trying to be sent to a different place. *What did I say? Where am I at? What is my vibration? My vibration is different... I'm not from the 3D and the 4D vibration. I am higher, always operating in the fifth, sixth, seventh and eighth dimensions. You are a sensitive audience and therefore, you may be feeling that. I apologize. I don't mean to draw you into a different space, but when I step into this space, I can't contain myself to just the physical body of the being that I'm... I'm transmitting through, because her body is of the third and fourth dimension, but I don't fit in it. Does that make sense?* Yes. *So, I apologize and... um, you can choose to set a protection. You can choose to say, "Please stay outside of my space".*

Going forward, we can create an energy barrier, let me do that now. Pauses. Jamar breathes deeply, extending arms and pulls in energy more closely to his body. *Does that help? Does that help?* Yes, it helps. *You're okay, I'm so sorry. I didn't even think about that, but that was good that you mentioned it. Okay, so now I have created a more condensed barrier to keep the energy within me.*

Okay, is there another question? Yes. Why are you Beings living in Telos? What is the purpose and the reason that that you have these places of life and people there? Is there a reason for us on Earth? Is there a reason for your own Evolution? What is the purpose of the whole Community entails? *Well first of all, it's much easier to be there and to be separated and segregated from the human population, which can be chaotic. Okay, so you know that's number one.*

We are there because first of all, we are evolving as our own people and... so, you are evolving as your people. We have been evolving for tens of thousands of years and we continue to evolve ourselves, too. Are you Lemurians? We are Lemurians and we are... but, we can have visitation from other entities. You humans have come in and out of the city of Telos. Not all humans will admit that they have come in and out of the city of Telos, but they have. It's very difficult though, for humans to spend much time in the city of Telos, because the vibration is too strong. Just as you just experienced now. So, they can only have very short times in there and almost like there are intermediary spaces. Where we will come to one side, they will come to the other, and then there's a buffer space between, where we're able then to communicate in a better space, with that the gap-age in between. Does that make sense? Yes.

Is that how you are connected with Saint-Germain? Wasn't Saint-Germain one of the people that connected with the people in Lemuria, Telos? *Saint-Germain is... and he absolutely is another Being who has come in and out. It's not just Saint-Germain. We connect to all kinds of light beings. Included the God Source, Jesus, and Buddha. We connect with all kinds, not just Saint-Germain. Yes. Saint-Germain absolutely is known more so in that area, because it's kind of like, he liked the tag line of being connected with it. But it's not just that one.* So, you're evolving? You're all evolving? *We are all evolving. We are all evolving, only we are just evolving at a different dimension than what you are. And it's the same with the Atlanteans. The Atlanteans still exist. You know they still exist. You're going to be, you've already talked to an Atlantian a couple of weeks ago. One came through.*

Maybe that's what we'll do next week. We'll invite an Atlantean, so we can have a conversation with them to find out the difference between an Atlantean community and the Lemurian community. How about that? That would be good. *That sounds interesting. That sounds like it's a good idea. Did that answer your question?* Yes, very much. Thank you.

Is there another question? Time check 7:50... 7:50, uh... oh. It's okay, it was very good information. *Okay, well I do want to give you one last message. I want to say thank you to the one that sits before you and I want to thank each of you for taking the time to be able to ask the questions and please invite others to be a participant in this. The greater the information, the greater the energy that comes in the more that will come out of it. So, I just really want to say thank you and I'm very excited for what will come to be.*

So, blessings to each of the. Thank you.

After Discussion

After the session, the circle discussed how physically impacted that we still were after Jamar's visit. The room was buzzing, and everyone was still feeling the residual effects of the energy. We discussed and agreed that we felt as if Jamar had raised the vibration of the environmental space to another dimension to accommodate for his visitation. Deb shared her experience with the group that she could see her physical hands morphing and shifting in shape and felt a deep head buzz that was altering her presence from the proximity of his energy field. He did not incorporate into our third world dimensional space but had altered the room to at least the fifth or sixth dimension during his visit.

We also discussed the fact that the more you practice, the more sensitive you become. It is always important to monitor your own energy exchange. I planned to leave more physical space around me in the room next week. It is important to begin with intention of preparation, protection and cleansing afterwards to maintain your highest health.

Closing Prayer

Heavenly Father, Thank You. Thank You for the blessing of this day. Thank you for the blessing of all of the Light Souls that came through. Heavenly Father, walk with each of us, keep us protected, and guarded and surrounded with your love and respect. Help us to go forth and to do your will and your work each and every day. We ask this in your precious name. Amen.

Session 4

Opening Prayer

Heavenly Father, Thank You. Thank You for the blessings of this day. Thank You for the opportunity to be able to join our hearts together. We invite in all of the energies, the loved ones, the angelic realm, the masters and the universal light beings. We invite in the power of protection, Heavenly Father, to be around each of the individuals that are here and those who are participating in this circle. We pray that you continue to keep this sacred space with only the highest and the best. Allow for clear communication and understanding from all universal light beings. We ask this in your precious name. Amen.

Introduction

We briefly reviewed the previous session and the adjustments for us as participants to be mindful of, along with reminding everyone that the entities are also adjusting to this circle and channeling through me. Because of the powerful energies of each of the Entities, the circle energy must allow for an even higher level of communication to take place. It is important to be free from distraction of phones and other interruptions that may influence frequency, vibrations, and overall flow of energy. This session we again have two questions and then allow for Elder Jamar to speak as he desires.

First Question

Discuss how our DNA is changing and can we do anything to support this transition?

FIRST INCORPORATION: JARELLA

Several deep breaths were taken and then adjustments were made to clothing during the incorporation. A female presence stepped in with a fairly matter of fact speech pattern. She told us that she was remarkably busy and had things to do. I believe she was from the Intergalactic DNA Bank. She was very business-like, formal and had a rapid clipped voice tone.

I'm going to come. Okay, alright I'm going to come... um, I'm not going to say my name at exactly this moment. We'll get back to that shortly. I seem to be pressured on... on a time limit on my side. I'm not quite sure what that's about, but apparently, I need to move along with us, because, I need to get back. I really needed to step into the space so I'd have an opportunity to speak; however, it's pulling me away from my other duties and I have others waiting with needs, that I'll need to get back to rather quickly so we need to get right into this.

Can you please tell me the question one more time? Yes. Please discuss how our DNA is changing and can we do anything to support this transition? *Yes, Okay. Jarella. Jarella is my name and I actually work with more-so of the physical bodies not just the human physical bodies; however, I actually work with all kinds of different life entities and their... their DNA structures, because your human DNA structures didn't start from you. Okay. Yes, there are many different particles which make up your structure which come from all kinds of different life entities and all kinds of extraterrestrials, which are outside of the earth realm and of your galaxy that you're aware of at this time.*

We actually... um, I know this is going to sound a little far-fetched, but you asked so I'm here to tell you. We actually have DNA banks. Okay, we work together with all kinds of different life entities where we, we keep a bank of different DNA, and so when we see that a shift is changing or coming about and needs to change in a particular planet, then we go back and see what is needed in order to help them, to be able to sustain themselves and to be able to tolerate the change that's taking place, because as you are very aware you are moving up in your realm. You've been operating in the third and the fourth, and you're getting ready to move yourself up to the fifth dimensions, and some people are already operating there sometimes and some are even really and truly moving into that sixth and seventh dimension. But these are individuals who have come back with knowledge and through other lifetimes from other star systems, and so then they didn't remember when they got here; however, they are being able to. They're being awakened, such as you. Pointing to an audience member. *And dealing with the issues that you are and then all of these downloads of information are coming into them and the physical bodies are struggling in order to catch up.*

It's the same with what you were mentioning... um, to this one earlier about the tuning forks and it's all about tone and vibration, which is what we've been talking about the last few weeks, anyway, because again being energy, all of you are vibrating, and so you're moving yourself right through and along. What we were able to do was to incorporate the changes of the DNA through electrical pulses that were being emitted down to the... um, the Earth... the entire Earth. Now, the difference with these different pulses that have been coming in truly are becoming more of a voluntary acceptance of allowing this to change.

Audience member coughing. *If you're feeling uncomfortable and you're coughing, you can do what you need to do, to eliminate that, because the shift of vibration is difficult for people, and may affect each of you.*

So, back to the pulsing vibrations that are now being emitted into the mankind's. Not everyone's in a place of being able to receive them. It's all about that same as path that each of you are on and that tone of enlightenment and allowing yourself to be open to be able to receive! You're able to receive the information. You're able to receive the download and through this, you're able to receive the physical changes which are happening within your DNA's, which is also stopping the aging. I bet you weren't aware of that.

If you truly allow yourself to step into the plane… that is coming forth before you, everything's being created new… over and over and over and over and over and over and over… faster and faster. So how can all of your cells get old and die, if they're becoming new, refreshed and stronger? Just as you. You've heard a little bit about this when you heard from Jamar from the city of Telos. How old did he say to his peoples were? Tens of thousands of years old. They are. Tens of thousands of years old! Not just them. The Atlanteans, all kinds of entities, are that old. Humans have the capacity to live for hundreds of years, if they choose to believe and continue to allow that full transference of energy which then circulates through to create the perfect cells once again. You're born with the knowledge of how to create perfect cells throughout your entire bodies. And now you're being infused with the information on how to replicate that continually going forward. Again, this is choice and free will. Not everyone wants to live forever, because they've already felt like they've done enough. They have reached their level of satisfaction of their personal growth of what they came here to do. And now they feel like they're done so they allow the soul to pass, so another can come through. So, does that make sense? Yes.

Okay. I do want to say a quick little message… quick little message… quick little message. So I want each of you to spend a little time in quiet and I want you to envision this lavender light, which is specifically coming down and into and those are the rays and the vibration the violet rays of vibration which are being infused into your DNA cells. Just allow that to happen. And I want to you spend a couple of minutes, just envisioning that before you go to sleep and then let me know how it goes next week. Okay? Yes.

Alright, thank you, gotta go. Where are you from? Jerilla was gone and didn't answer.

Jarella spoke with great knowledge and authority as a scientist; however, she spoke very quickly and it was clearly evident that she didn't have much time, but wanted to be certain that we were provided with critical information about the DNA bank and the specific adjustments that are pre-calculated for humanity and our highest good.

SECOND INCORPORATION: VICTOR

Victor stepped in very quietly and said hello many times as he was exploring the use and range within the vocal cords. It was a soft, male energy with a sweet presence. He was tall, slender, gentle and told us that he was from Germania.

Hello? Hello. *Hello? Hello?* Hello. *Hello-o-o?* His voice is elevating and lowering with a big smile while repeating hello. Is there anybody out there? *There is, I'm here.* Grinning joyfully. *I have to tell you a funny, just to get started. You just have no idea what it looks like up there, over there, by that woman over at her gazebo. There is a line that goes back for miles, and they are all so excited about the opportunity that is being offered here in this room, in this space. I want to mention to you ladies, first of all, it is not by happenstance that there are all ladies who are sitting here. We need that feminine energy. It helps to feed us, and be able to work with this much easier, so I just wanted to mention that to you, right off the bat. The other thing is they are just so excited and delighted to have the option to be able to have a voice.*

Oh, my name is Victor! I forgot to mention that didn't I? I did forget to mention it. That's okay. Let's see and where am I from? I remember hearing these other questions. I've been up there for weeks waiting around you know. Every week we got more and more coming. Everybody knows and they are all so excited to come! That's okay. It's alright if only a few get to come through, because do you want to know what else we're able to do?

We're able to send our thought patterns and information while we're waiting in line. We're able to cumulatively send that information into the one who is able to incorporate before you. So, you are not just getting one entity's information. Is that not interesting, huh? Aha. *I bet you didn't know either. I know. It's very exciting! So, I even heard one of my thoughts come out two weeks ago. I just want you to know even though you didn't even see me, my thought was here.* Chuckling and giggling with joy. A very happy entity, light and loving. *Love that, love that, love that, love that, love that!* Bouncing back and forth in the chair in a dancing manner. *Um, …*

Germania, Germania is where I am from. And, … um, I don't believe that you're familiar with where it is, but that's okay, it doesn't matter. I am going to go ahead and talk about the DNA aspect, because I'm very familiar with that, because we actually went through this entire process… oh, I'm going to say, I don't know, maybe a hundred years ago. It really wasn't that long ago, because we also were a very, very dense… planet of people… um, and it's very, very hard for us to compare ourselves to your planet Earth, because your people are just so diverse. And… um, and the energy is just so diverse, and it is…. It's a different chaos, and it's different art. There is just such flamboyance, but there is such brilliance and there is such hatred and such anger. So, there's just such extremes of everything here… um, and so we actually don't have quite that same level of anything in our planet, but I will just spend a few minutes talking about what happened to our people through the process.

So, one of the things that happened on our particular planet was there was a huge shift that was happening in the environment. And… um, we would have become extinct if we did not physically change, in order to accommodate the changes, what was happening. Our sun actually was burning out, and therefore it was becoming much cooler and more dense and so, we needed to figure out how to be able to draw additional energy that we needed, not just from the sunlight. And so, we had to convert our DNA so that we were able to then draw some of our energy from the different minerals, which are provided within the planet itself.

Now it's very interesting, because I do know that people who are of… um, lighter vibration, they definitely have a higher resignation with the different crystals and different minerals that are out there. It's because they are feeling that magnetic pull; however, it's very unusual for the um… from what I have seen, that is me seeing as an outsider, not being a human being, because I certainly couldn't possibly relate to all of what you people are involved in and doing and being; however, it looks to me like and it seems like that you're just not able to tap into the resources that are readily available for you to be able to draw from, if you need to. So, for us we needed to make this change, so that we didn't have to use so much sunlight in order to survive. We had to change our DNA structure to actually tap into that bank. I know that… um, the last speaker, and I don't remember her name, who came through, she was talking about this. And it is… It's an Intergalactic Bank that is out there of all DNA life entities.

So, it's all life. It's not just humans, person, animal, plant and mineral. There are different... um, cellular samples of all life forms in this one particular place. So, what they're able to do is to look at,... the information from all light entities and galaxies and so they understand. They'll find another galaxy that's more like the one that they're on and they understand what needs to be changed, altered and adjusted, to be able to help them survive and thrive through that next transition,... and it's because your Mother Earth is alive! She's alive too, and so, because of that, she's always going to continue to grow and to shift and to change. You as a living entity upon this planet also needs to be able to grow and to change and to be able to adjust to whatever else is happening.

Again, you also know that there are great changes which are happening on your Mother Earth, which are directly related to mankind, and how it's being treated and what's happening there. There are other adjustments and thoughts that are being brought into how the physical is going to be able to breathe. Is this not a very good question? If there is such air pollution that is domineering in so many different countries of your Earth plane, how long you think it's going to take so that it doesn't pollute the entire Earth? It absolutely will! There's no way it won't, unless something dramatically stops it immediately, otherwise you're going to need to be able to shift enough so that you're still going to be able to get the sustainable Life Force air that you need. But you know what, maybe you don't need 98% anymore. Maybe you only be 94%, because you're going to allow these physical changes to transpire within yourself. I'm not saying this is right or wrong or good or bad. I'm just saying that these are what can be.

So,... um, I believe they already mentioned to you that... It's how it's being transmitted into each your physical bodies. It's, you know again, a light wave that's being pulsed in and so you can be receptive to it. Some people are absolutely finding challenges with this coming in. Okay. Some people are finding challenges with the quickening and the changing of the vibration and they're having physical impacts. The thing is, it's so critical for you as a human... Pause. You have so many different systems that are already operating and working at full capacity in order to keep you, you know, just in your plane space of where you are. You also are trying to do things to be able to survive, and so, then you have responsibilities of families and jobs and everything else. You've got to be able to find some balance somewhere.

You need to be able to allow rest. It is so amazing the amount of regeneration and transformation that happens to you, in you and with you when you allow yourself to be in a place of rest. Pause. *But this is very difficult for a lot of people, when they're working three jobs and they only allow two hours of sleep. So, they continue to wear themselves out further and further and further, and they're not allowing the recharge to happen. When they're not allowed to get the full recharge, then they're not going to be able to get the benefits of the transition which needs to take place. And so, then what's going to happen is they're going to fall away, because they haven't been able to receive what's coming into them. Do you understand that?* Um,… ha… Okay… *Um, does that answer the question?* Yes.

Let me see, a message of my own. A message of my own. Very agitated, rubbing hands together, clapping some. *I have been thinking about this for a while, what I would, might want to say if I had a chance to actually get here. I'm really excited that they let me come through.*

I just want to say I hope that you appreciate the vibrancy of where you live! You have such a spectacular opportunity in life, because you can see, feel and smell and taste. You can also sense with all of your senses so-o-o much texture and color and vibrancy that is just not in other places. So, I want to challenge each of you to go out, and to do, and to be, and to live and to experience the pure joy of everything that you can. It's such an incredible gift! And do you know what? Most of you never take the time to open it! So, blessings to each of you, blessings to each of you. Blessings.

Victor was such a bubbly entity. He was joyful and so excited to have had the opportunity to come and personally speak with each of us. As time passed, he became more animated with hand and body gestures as well and adjusting his speech patterns. His tone fluctuations through his message was palatable with flavor and delight.

INCORPORATION: GATEKEEPER BAYLOT

I feel like the question has been answered fairly well. Do you feel like the answer has been enough, or do you want more information? This is Baylot asking. I think that we have done well. *Okay, I felt that you did too, because you actually heard about a lot of this information a couple of weeks ago, when it was really talking about the physical things that you can do to be able to help with the vibrational changes… The exercise, the nutrition,… so I want you to make sure that you go back and you think about those things too, because, all of those things certainly support you in in what's happening with your physical changes and having that dark sleep too. I remember that was being discussed last week, putting yourself into a dark quiet place, so that you really allow that rest to come in.*

Okay, so we're going to go ahead and pass along to the next question.

Second Question

We would like to invite and to speak to an elder from Atlantis to discuss his or her community. How do they operate? What they do and any other general information they would like to provide.

THIRD INCORPORATION: ESMERELDA

For this incorporation we had specifically requested to speak to an entity from Atlantis. This included information about their community and how they operated. This was a quiet transition that had a stillness, and then several deep breaths were taken. The voice was fairly monotone and didn't sound male or female but held a neutral gender tone.

This is a little bit different because you're asking to have a specific one come in and I'm going to fill in for that space. I am from Atlantis. I have been around for several, the whole, I don't even know how long it's been a very, very, very, very, very long time. Esmerelda is who you're speaking to.

I just want to take a minute to explain what I'm seeing and feeling, as I'm stepping into the vibration of this room in this space. I am seeing so many different light sparkles around each of you and this entire room. Is anyone else able to see this, the sparkles that entered into the room? No. Well, they are here and don't be surprised… if the sparkles don't follow you home and… and you sparkle around at, nighttime, when you're sleeping. It's... it's a joyful opportunity that were able to send a little extra sparkle around.

So, I'm going to take some time to speak about Atlantis now. Atlantis is something which has been discussed since the beginning of time. Certainly, from when man was ever going to speak about it and it was,... and, it is still a population which is housed in many different locations, not just upon your Earth planet, but in other planets, too, but we really like to be in the sea, because there is just so much different depth within the sea and the life that is there, and we actually have been able to utilize the different seaweeds and the salts within the water to be able to capture that as our energy sources, to function at a higher level. We're also able to tap into the different crystals which are far below the Earth in the water below.

These are things that we actually have done. So, I am going to talk about the original Atlantis, that people have spoken of for so many years and what they have envisioned in their own minds. Yes, the Crystal City for sure is what is was, a vibrant and so far ahead of anything that you have had upon this Earth. Chuckling while speaking. *It really is rather ironic. Here, this was tens of thousands of years ago and we're light-years away from where you will be. I don't know when that will happen or if, but the difference is that we actually spent our time and energy together as a people working towards a single goal, which was the betterment of our entire community. We spent a lot of time with engineering and with math and calculation and creation, to be able to support the betterment of,... our people as a whole. We also spent much time with the crystals and we were able to tap into the information that is in within the crystals, along with the knowledge which is within the crystals and to be able to communicate to other entities, solar systems and galaxies through the transmissions of the crystals.*

This is something, Earthlings, you really have not been able to capture at this point, but that's something you will be able to learn and work your way through, too, but when you do find particular crystals, please take the time to acknowledge it, and to be able to commit to having a relationship with that crystal and then to be able to spend time listening to what it's trying to teach you. Do you understand that? Yes. Yes, because they too, are a living essence and they can only add more to your life and to your knowledge and to your wisdom, if you choose to listen,... but this again is up to you.

So, as for our people... our people have been... um. It's a true population such as any different countries or cities, or whatever you want to say. We've had to have a structure in order to function. We had facilities. We had water. We had education and training. We certainly had duties that people needed to do in order to maintain a civilization... um, and we had lots of joy too. We really love the Arts. We love drama and theater. We had to create our own drama and theater, but now we just watch you! She stops and smiles at everyone in the room and then chuckles.

It really is rather amusing, because you do such outlandish things that we could not even think of. We do pray for you. Chuckles continue. *I want you to know that, we do pray for you, and we do not wish you any harm, and we do not want you to harm your,... your Earth! If you harm your earth, you're harming more than just your population. There are many different civilizations that are affiliated with the Earth. Not just the Atlanteans, not just the Lemurians. Yes, there are so many others who are coming and going and having civilizations and a majority of them are actually in the oceans. They come and go. People don't even know, because they don't know what they don't know. They can't see because they're not a part of it. And then there are other populations that live under the water. The Mer-people.*

The Mer people are real. Why not? Their DNA was adjusted too. So that they could breathe and thrive in the sea. Pause. *The old fisherman knew. They saw them too. There are many, many, many, many, many, many different species. That are all a part of this Earth, and we all pray for her. We are here to help protect her too when great danger comes. When comets are crashing down towards this Earth. We have the ability to pulse light to blow it up, so it does not crash upon the Earth and make it disintegrate. This has happened many times. People in your government know about it. People... know about it, but not many really want to talk about it. They don't want to acknowledge it, because it's not on their way to get the coffee on the way to work. It's something else.*

So, yes, we got into battles too. We became power hungry. Our egos were driving us. We thought we were better than... and this created the demise of the original Atlantis, but it was not all for naught, because what we were able to do through the process of the massive explosion. We were able to send all of the crystal sparks out all over the Earth. Not just the Earth plane but into the

Universe in to many different spaces and places, as little seeds of light... of seeds of information... of seeds of knowledge and wisdom and greatness that have the opportunity to come through them; however, it takes particular souls who are walking upon the Earth plane who are in a place of being ready to listen and to communicate with to understand what that is.

I do want to mention, though, that I recognized several souls in this room, including the one before you, as they too have spent time as an Atlantean. It's a beautiful place. It's a beautiful people, but you too are beautiful people. You are just in a different space and time and evolution of where you are. I would ask each of you though, to truly take time to look within, to listen within, and to try to be better within. Be better than what you ever thought you could, and you watch, because you will become that.

Is that enough information? Okay, I think I like that as my message, too. That was a good message? Yes. Yes, I do. You said take time to look within, listen to within and? *You will become the magic of manifestation. Okay blessings.* Blessings.

Esmerelda was a very joyful presence who had such compassion and empathy not only for our human population, but for each of us too. Esmerelda was wearing a long aqua robe, tall, slender, stately posture and had sparkles all around them too. I never received a full impression of either gender. I do not think it truly matters to their species and sustaining their population.

INCORPORATION: GATEKEEPER BAYLOT

This transition took a bit of time. It was scheduled that Jamar would be the speaker after hearing from Atlantis.

I am getting Jamar; I am getting Jamar. He is really rather busy up there and is working his way through. It really is rather busy up there. Several deep breaths and body adjustments during this transitional pause. A different entity came in. *Okay, all right then.*

FORTH INCORPORATION: GEROME

Gerome entered in. He is noticeably young male presence that is sweet, joyful, and overly excited to have snuck his way in. He has a very curious nature and is not a planned visitor; however, he was very eager to have an opportunity to speak. Gerome told us he was an Angel in Training.

All right then... Nope, this is not Jamar, not Jamar. He was taking too long. I snuck on through. That's what gets to you. Oh. Shrugging shoulders, coming through very happy. *The late one the lazy one... You're going to have to run to come through now, that's what I'm talking about.* Laughing and giggling. So happy to have made it through. Child-like voice.

Oh, what am I going to talk about? Let's see I'm just going to sneak in. It would just be for a minute. He won't get too mad at me. It's all right, because I've been wanting to for a really long time too. An... an... an... an... and, I'm ready... Ummmm... Gerome, Gerome, Gerome is... is my name. I'm real... He begins to whisper. *I really... I'm not supposed to be doing this. But I was able to sneak through, cause they were all so busy doing all their other stuff.*

Oh, okay. So, what I really want to say. Speaking very fast and still in a whisper tone. *I just want to say is you know,... um. They are not all old ones up there, too. There are young ones that are here, too, and you know we really like to play, and we like jokes on people, because it's a really fun thing. And you know, sometimes we go around, and we hide your stuff that is in and around in, in and around your house.* Audience giggling. *We like to move your keys.* Everyone giggling... *and put them like under the table... And you were not even going to look... and... and... and... You know you thought you had one more piece of chocolate, you know in the bar... Laughing, and you don't... I really like chocolate! I'm not the only one, but I really like it!*

We have fun doing like little things. You know, if you're afraid of snakes, do you want to know what we do? We go find em... Laughing. And we go tell the snake... Psst! Finger calling them in. Come on, come on over here... and then we wait for you. You know why? You guys are really funny to watch jumping all over the place. It's really fun! Anyway, we don't mean to ever hurt you or anything like that, but you know sometimes we get bored, and sometimes we got to try to do something to have a little bit of fun. And you know, and ya'll are just always funny. You're always so funny. You're always so funny. Still giggling. *Funny, funny, funny!*

Where are you from Gerome? High pitched squeak – *Ahhhhhhh...* Giggling fits again. *Shhhhh...* Finger in front of mouth and whispering. *I'm, I'm an Angel in Training. But, it's okay, 'cuz we do it with love.*

We do it with love. You want to know what else we do? We... we actually like to test your patience. So, we're trying to make you better. We are... Giggles... *and sometimes when you're really looking for that thing you were supposed to have, that you're late for, because you didn't get there. We help to save you from an accident. So sometimes, it's really good. So, we're watching out for you. And um,... I just wanted to say that I was excited to be able to sneak through, 'cuz you know, they're all up there like that, and I was able to go through.* Zig zagging hand gestures... *and boop! There I am! Here I am! Okay... Alright... so, um...*

I just want to say one more thing before I go. Can I come back? Sure, yes. *I'd like to come back! Maybe you could invite me back?* Pleading voice. *You know I have a lot of friends, too. Maybe you could go ahead and invite the little ones in. Say, hey, can we hear from the ... you know 'cuz you know, I got a whole little gang.* Moved hand on hip and proudly postured. *I got a gang of Angels.* Giggling *'Cuz,... we like to go around together... to keep each other company and to really mess with ya'll, Jes' a little bit. Just a little bit... A little bit.*

So anyways, love and blessings. I'll come back if you let me come back. Hands clapping. *Okay,... Okay... bye.* Bye in unison. Chuckling filled the room.

Jerome was such a loving and young spirit filled with joy, delight and so very excited to have had a chance to visit. By the way he spoke, maturity of his voice, exuberant mannerisms and moving into baby talk at times. I estimate as a comparison to us, that he was about four years old.

FIFTH INCORPORATION: ELDER JAMAR

Elder Lemurian, Jamar stepped in from the city of Telos. He began a bit annoyed that due to the transitional time, he lost his entrance. After last session and the physical impacts that were felt in the space, Jamar was working harder to adjust his energy so that it would be more compatible with the room upon his incorporation.

There wasn't a specific topic of discussion. We were providing an open forum for any subject that was of interest.

You give them a minute and look what happens! Just one single minute, and the next one sneaks on through! All right, I'm here and I know you have been waiting for me, but you know you're not the only ones that I am working with at this time. I need to make sure that you understand that, too.

Okay, I will mention a couple of things in regard to that, because I do believe it is important for you to understand that when you were working with the different Light Beings and Elders, we do have the ability to be in many places at the same time with our energy, and it's also because we can operate on different dimensions at the same time, which I do want to go ahead and mention once again. I apologize for last week for being a bit too bold. I've pulled my energy in quite a bit, and I think that was part of the reason for the delay and allowed for that sneaky little one to come through, but are,… is… everyone comfortable in the room? Yes. All right then, I'll continue on with my conversation to begin with.

I do want to take a few minutes to talk about the different entities and their energy levels and how they affect people that are around them, and… um, you have all done what you needed to do with your power of protection which is all good,… but it's really important… um, certainly when you are in a place of exploration and expansion, that you allow yourself to get near and to commune with these different energy experiences, because then it allows that vibration to work in conjunction with your vibration and it's exercising them. Does that make sense to you? Yes. Okay, good.

So, I do want to continue talking about speaking to different people at the different time and space, because… um, physically I'm not located here. Pause.

Physically, I am currently still in the city of Telos. Pause. *You are experiencing my same energy within this Being that is before you. We have the ability to be able to fragment off of our energy centers to be able to go to other places. This can be called teleportation. This can be called... ah what is that other one they do,... soul travel. There's many different terms that they use for it; however, we don't always,... because we have lived for tens of thousands of years we've been able to develop ourselves to be in multiple functioning places at the same time. So, my physical body is still in the city of Telos and still functioning and doing things and having other conversations... where my presence before you is a completely different experience. So, does that make sense to you?* Yes. *All right 'cuz you're quiet, and I just really want to make sure that I'm articulating the way that I need to be able to articulate. The energy is different for me today here. It definitely is different here today.*

Um... I'm probably just much more conscious of trying not to impact the environment which is... um... which is probably causing a bit of friction. I want to spend a few minutes to talk about... um, one of the things the one before you were spending time meditating on this week was the crystal.... That she was brought down before this very large green crystal... and this is a centerpiece of our energy... Um, and it's about fourteen feet in diameter and it's probably two stories high and it's a very pure green crystal cut many-faceted sides upon it and it's actually made of Green Selenite... and,... um, it was not brought from the Earth plane it was brought here from another galaxy. This specific type of a crystal is known for... Selenite is known for its cleansing properties, but the green is all about the purification and the growth. The healing energy that comes from it. So, it's healing and cleansing, magnified to such a level that you just can't even possibly imagine. This is one of the energies that we feed upon.

Another energy that we feed upon besides the food factor, is when other things around die. That energy exchange is released, and we're able to absorb that energy, that's being released without taking it from them. Once it's released, we're able to absorb that energy and use that too. Is that not just an interesting fact? Yes. Yes. *I thought you might find that interesting.*

Um... I want to talk to you a little bit about the water. Water is so important on the Earth and not just on the Earth, but in the Earth and in the people and in all existence... and I know a number of different entities have spoken about the water and the importance of the water, but I need to be... I need to take the time to also accentuate that point. Please, please help to keep the water clean! Help to clean up the garbage along the coastlines and in the rivers and in the streams. Allow for the purification of the water to naturally take place. Thank you for that.

    I want to allow an opportunity for people to ask questions of me today. I know we did not prepare for this, but perhaps you have some questions for me. I do want to spend time every week coming because I wanted to come forth to this. So, I want you to be able to ask questions of me and of my... um community, and how we live and our wisdom so that you have the ability to learn from that. Is there a subject you'd like to hear about? Pause and no one spoke. *Okay, I'll pick a subject. Let's talk about ...* Pause. *Hmm-ha-hmm-ha-hmmm. You've already talked about vibration. And you've already spoken of music. And you've already talked about the environment. And you've already talked about...um...* pause.

    Let's talk about Heaven. What is your version of Heaven and what you think Heaven is? And what my interpretation of is... what Heaven is. Heaven is another dimension. Once your physical body is done and the Soul is released, then the Soul is allowed to be able to go and to do so much more than it's been able to do in its physical form. It sparks off and it elevates, but first it actually takes time to think through the different experiences in one's life. They call it... a recall of your entire life or whatever you know. But what you do is you spend time moving through your heart memories. Many things happen in a human's life. They could not possibly remember all of what happened in their life. They remember the most sacred moments: the birth of a child, a graduation, the marriage, a job, a promotion, moving somewhere, or an incredible journey that they went on. It's the things that made them feel! That's what the heart kept as the most precious memories of all, were the things that made them feel.

    It was never about what color shoes they had. Maybe it is where their house was located, but more than likely not. Very seldom did they remember a meal, or their bank account. They remembered the heart moments of joy, of love, of peace. The fear is no longer there. There is no room for anger or hate or regret. There's only joy and love is what you're carrying with you when you leave the

Earth plane. When you leave the Earth plane, and you leave your loved ones behind, you still have such joy and delight for them. Smiling widely with a pause. *And you're so excited to be able to share your new knowledge with them. They just cannot necessarily hear and understand what you're trying to share with them, though.*

This is how electronics are an easy way for new souls to be able to communicate with those left behind, because they're able to zap. They're able to zap back and forth and to change the fluctuations in the energy and to shut it on…, turn it on, and shut it off. So that it makes changes and impacts to it, but anyway, that's not Heaven. It's part of the process of dying, and I think that's what I wanted to talk about, the process of it. So many people have such fear about leaving this space, or being left behind, while others travel forward for their space. We can all celebrate when that new change comes forth and yes, it is painful for the ones who are left behind, because their hearts hurt for the love that they had, but it is such a joyful place to travel on. They're able to unite with so many other souls.

I want to explain to you at this time. It is a different space, where all the different Master's and Elders and Angels are. It is not that they don't commune with the Souls, but the Souls are always at a different space. It's all about where you live your life, too, and once you get to a specific plane and then you pass along, then you're with those Souls of like minds, and you continue to elevate and to evolve in your own soul consciousness to a higher level. So, it is not that much different than what is here upon the Earth plane, only you're doing it at a soul level. The difference is the chaos in the pulling all of the commitments and responsibilities that you're trying to manage get in the way of even choosing to work on soul elevation, while you're here on the earth plane.

Does that make sense? Yes. *Did you find that informative?* Yes. *Think about what kind of a subject you'd like to discuss perhaps next week. I don't know exactly what to talk about or what you want to learn about.*

Audience Question

Excuse me. I have a question. *Certainly.* You just talked about dying and moving on into heaven, and that's on the soul level. How can we, kind of like, die before we leave this physical plane? Does that exist in your perception?

Are you talking about the physical body dying or the soul dying? The soul can die prior to leaving the physical body. And you see these empty souled people still walking amongst the street, lost and confused. I later went back to clarify this concept with Jamar. He used the term "soul dying", but in actuality this was referencing the soul leaving the physical body prior to its physical death. *And it's not that they will not have a place to go when the physical body stops. They will just be at a lower elevation because they still have to be with like-minded souls. It would be so difficult for someone who is in such a place of deep despair that they just cannot find joy, to be in the same space with somebody who is who joyful and light all the time. It's an uncomfortableness on both of them so we always keep them with a little bit higher, so it helps them to elevate to the next level, but it's not too much of an un-comfort on anyone. Does that make sense? Did it answer your question?* No.

Then you're going to have to ask the question again, so I understand what it is. Okay, you were talking about the soul of those people who are lowered. Into lower elevation. With no Soul, with no Soul because they are still continuing to live here on Earth.

Yes. I am talking about those who are able to elevate their Soul while still in the physical body here on Earth and having a broader perspective of the whole realm before they leave this plane. *Well, that's what each of you are doing. You're choosing to be here, to learn about, to experience and to expand while you're still in your physical bodies, because you're choosing to spend your time with meditation and with other like-minded people so that you're expanding beyond, while you're still in the physical. Does that make sense?* Yes.

You don't have to die to continue to expand. That's why so many souls fight so diligently to come down to the Earth plane or to other planetary existences, because they want to be able to be provided with an opportunity to be able to work your way through… and, but you,… you're able to work through faster, but it's much harder because it's much denser, and it's much more difficult. It's very difficult to deal with all of the emotion and the pain, and the frustration, and the hurt and the... and... all of the pulling parts of the worlds along with the physical. Does that make sense? Um ha...

Can I ask a question? *You may ask a question.* I have never heard of a Soul dying before a body and I guess I wonder what causes that. And what does that mean for the body that still here and for those around it? Does that explain some of the chaos that we are experiencing? *It probably does explain some of the chaos. And yes. A Soul can die because a person becomes so traumatized in whatever it is that the person checks out.* This can also be termed as fragmenting soul parts. *They can check out with drugs. They can check out with alcohol. They can check out because they've chosen not to care anymore. And then the carcass of the physical is continuing to create more pain for those that are around it trying to save it. But they really have to just let it go.* The Soul can't come back? *The soul is generally, generally speaking I'm not going to say 100%. Generally speaking, the souls become so damaged and, and decimated there's nothing to come back to. They can't pull it back together.* Additional clarification, Soul Retrieval requires skilled assistance of a professional, such as me to gather the fragmented or splintered soul pieces and then, heal them so that the soul can function and thrive once again within same lifetime.

It is very hard for people to understand suicide. And sometimes that is a blessing for a Soul. It gives them peace, and that's the first gift they've been given in a very long time. They may not understand that, but it's a gift to not have to anymore. Does that make sense? Yes.

Okay, I think that's good for today. Is that good for today? Yes. *All right thank you. Thank you and I'll see you next week. Thank you.* Thank you.

Thank you, I'm very much enjoying this. I'm going to let Baylot speak, one more moment here. He says he wants to be able to speak. He's liking this speaking.

Jamar was very somber throughout this transmission. The energy of the room was of a slower vibration. It may have been due to his readjusting his presence or one audience member was highly distracted due to an evolving emergency family issue and text messages.

Jamar spoke of the soul dying; however, we all know that energy doesn't die as it can only be transformed. His reference was more about if the soul experiences or endures great human pain or tragedy and it may have chosen splintering, fragmenting as a self-preservation technique. There is also an option of the soul leaving the body prior to end of life for the physical body envelope.

INCORPORATION: GATEKEEPER BAYLOT

I am liking this speaking. I am liking this whole experiment and this experience very much. I will say there are definitely many more Souls and entities up here than I had ever anticipated were going to come through.

I want to make sure that everyone is good with the format and how this is going? And if there's anything else that you'd like to have changed or suggested? Pause. I think it's working. *Wonderful, wonderful, wonderful!*

Well thank you again for this opportunity and I look forward to seeing you again next week. Blessing's to you. Goodbye.

After Discussion

Every single week is very different… I love feeling the different personalities. The energies were lower on this day and it was discussed that perhaps Jamar had worked too hard to curb his energy or he was affected by the lower group vibration.

Audience question to Judi

When they come through do you also feel them, as if you're them? Or whatever they may look like? *I don't see what they look like at all. I saw colors. With the Atlantis one, I saw lots and lots of sparkles that came in right away. Did you see sparkles?* To attendee who sees auras. Not today. Another attendee. I saw the green selenite crystal. That crystal is amazing...

Do all of these entities have bodies? *No, not all of them. Some are just energy. Jamar does. He is an Elder that I met when I went to Telos. He has a physical body, but he obviously can split as he was telling us, splitting off and functioning in more than one location at the same time.*

Closing Prayer

Heavenly Father. Thank You. Thank you for the blessings of this day, for the blessings of this evening. Thank you for the blessings of all of the different energies coming through, for the information, for the guidance. For the wisdom. Help us to be able to hold that information in our hearts, and to be able to use that information to the highest in the best, for enlightenment to our lives and those around us. Heavenly Father, we just pray that you shower your love and light and grace and peace upon all of mankind. All entities, all loving beings, all Universal Light Entities, we pray for peace and love and respect towards all.

We ask this in your precious name. Amen

Session 5

Opening Prayer

Heavenly Father, Thank You. Thank You for the blessings of this day. Thank you for the blessings of these souls. Heavenly Father, we lift up the energy in this space to the very highest and the best. Allow for all enlightened beings of the highest and the best to be able to come through and to communicate. Heavenly Father we praise you and we offer respect to our Universe, to our lands and to our Mother Earth. We ask this in your precious name. Amen.

Introduction

THE PLAN FOR THIS SESSION was to request Gatekeeper Baylot to come in and then to provide an open forum. This would allow him to congregate with the various available entities and they could decide who had the most pertinent or pressing information to be shared. I had a deep meditation earlier in the day and anticipated that the God Source would plan to speak during the session.

After the open forum we planned to request to hear from someone in the Star System Sirius. I commented that I had no previous knowledge of Sirius and this star system. We would finish the session by allowing time for Elder Jamar to speak about any subject that he desired.

Open request to Gatekeeper Baylot

We are asking Baylot to find someone who wants to bring their highest and best message, information or guidance for the group.

FIRST INCORPORATION: GATEKEEPER BAYLOT

Okay. Alright. Okay. I'm here. Okay, Baylot we would like you to check and see, ask if there are any, or if there's anyone in particular there with a special message that he or she wants to give to us this evening. *Okay, give me one second here. Let me see who will be the best one. Just give me one minute here.* Okay.

SECOND INCORPORATION: OLIVER

This transition began with excessive throat clearing and body adjustments during the incorporation. A low and slower speaking monotone male voice spoke, introducing himself as Oliver from Sansabar.

I'm going to come through now. I want to go ahead and discuss the heaviness and the trauma, which are affecting the planet at this moment with the changes. May I ask who you are please? *Oliver.* Oliver. *Oliver, is my name.* Would you tell us where you're from please? *Sansabar.* Sansabar. *Sansabar is where I'm from.*

So, I would like to speak about the denseness which is happening right now on the Earth planet. It is a direct result from solar flares which are breaking off and shooting into the Earth's atmosphere. When such high levels of radiation come into the Earth's realm, the physical bodies have a very difficult time dealing with the changes and the chaos and trying to be able to stay balanced. This is also why there begins to be a lot more chaos in governments and when there are bombings and all kinds of other disarray. People find it a confusing time, but this is specifically related to the solar flares. You can anticipate additional solar flares for the next thirteen days, until things will then dissipate and then get back into a normal realm.

During this time, it is important to manage the amount of time that you're outside in the sunlight. You can't necessarily see and feel, but the effects are dramatically impacting each of you anyway, and you need to keep yourself cleared of the excess energy that is impacting your physical selves. Do you understand this? Yes. Yes.

Okay, do you have any additional questions about this? If not, I'll let another come. Thank you. *You're welcome. Peace be with you.* Peace be with you also.

Oliver was very stoic in his presence and speaking patterns. He was factual, informative, and wanted to provide some reasoning for feeling personal changes as well as relating the energy shifts to actions that are concurrently happening around the world as a direct affect.

THIRD INCORPORATION: ANGELINA

As hands rubbed together to assist with energy shift, a high-pitched female voice entered. She was a light-hearted, playful energy and sang her name through her introduction. Angelina came in to speak to us of the Elementals which currently exist upon our planet. We often may encounter their presence but are unsure of our experiences and their actual existence. She was small in stature, elegantly dressed in a beautiful dress, as if a young girl in Easter attire from the sixties.

I'm going to come now. My name is Angelina. Angelina, Angelina, Angelina! I like to be able to do fun light things, and so they're going to let me speak now because that was a rather heavy, dense subject. So, not everything is always heavy and dense, you know.

There's tons of wonderful light and joyful things. The thing that I want talk about right now, is truly taking the time to follow… and to be able to allow your energy to unite with the rainbows. Pauses and smiles broadly… *and to be able to unite with the little star entities… and with the light beams that come down and bounce upon the ocean… and the lakes and the rivers and the streams.*

Light beams are amazing and joyful, and it is fun to be able to follow the different light beams. And what else is really nice and interesting about it? You can actually jump into and out of the different rays of color within the light spectrum. Is that not exciting? You can be in the purple, and the red, and the yellow, and the orange, and the green, and also the lavender. She leans forward to whisper lavender. *The lavender is the in-between colors. When you're following those different light rays, you can actually see things differently, in different colors. This is another way to be able to tap in and see the auras!*

Not everyone can see auras. How many people in the room can see auras? I can. Once or twice. Sometimes. *So, this is something that's exciting, because it seems like more of you don't know yet, but you all can. It's just a matter of practicing and exercising. So, one of the things that's so important to do is to go ahead and to close your eyes when you're looking at an item… and you want to be able to see the color around it. So, what you do is you pay attention to the item with your third eye. Then you're able to open your eyes and you're looking through both the physical and the third eye at the same time.* Angelina is using hand gestures to accentuate the areas of the body that she was describing. *And you just stay looking at that object for a period of time and you'll watch.*

You'll be able to see the energy that's around the outside of the objects. They can be alive, or they don't have to be alive, but everything still has an energetic field around it, and you'll be able to see. The parts that's really exciting about this, is that they all change too! The auras change all the time depending on the temperature, the mood, if it's a person, or if they're fearful. Perhaps it's a deer running, because it's being chased, or a turkey at Thanksgiving time. And if they are running in fear, they are going to have a different color aura than somebody that's having a massage, who's just resting in a peaceful place.

It's the same with different plant entities. If there's a plant that's fighting off all kinds of aphids and disease, it's going to have a darker aura, or you'll be able to see holes in the aura that need to be healed.

Your energies can be used to heal those auras. Did you know that? You don't have to know really how. You just have to have the intention and to pray for... and to pray with for the healing of it. It's a wonderful thing when you're gardening, to pray for and to sing to the different plants and flowers, joyfully. They love music! You'll see them sometimes dancing to the music, when the wind blows, and their leaves and petals are moving. Angelina is dancing in the chair while speaking. *They love company too, and that's why they call in the bees and the butterflies, and all those little winged ones, to come by and to visit and to say, "Hi". So, I think that it's a wonderful idea if you can try to perhaps practice, if it's an interest of yours to learn how to be able to see auras.*

So, this is what you do one more time. You close your eyes, and you concentrate on whatever you're trying to look at. And you see it with your third eye first. Then you open your physical eyes and you continue to concentrate on the item. And you look with your third eye, and your two physical eyes and then you just wait and allow the veil to open, so that you can see the colors of the auras, okay?

Thank you, that sounds lovely. *Alright then, okay that's probably enough for me.* Where are you from Angelina? *Oh, oh... hmmm. I used to be from the Earth plane.* Pause.

Audience Question

I have a question. Can you tell us a little bit about Garden orbs? *Garden orbs... garden orbs are all kinds of things so, is that okay if I continue?* Please do. *Okay, so alright... First of all, there's many different kinds of orbs in gardens. You can actually see the different fairies, and you can see the leprechauns, and you can see the little people and things that are in the gardens. Sometimes you can see them as the actual beings, but oftentimes certainly for ones that are not as experienced they're going to see... um, as orbs first... And so, then you're going to see different colors because of the other thing is, a little fairy moves her wings really, really, really, really fast, and so it almost looks like a blur. So, it's really hard for you to be able to articulate. She had to put herself in an entirely different vibration mode to slow down enough so that you're going to be able to see the actual fairy herself.*

Oh, so garden orbs are created by the fairies. I didn't know that; I see Garden orbs. *Well... um, usually they're of the fairy realm, you know... And of the little gnomes and of the Leprechauns and things, but I'm not going to say that they're not other little beings... that... um..., Okay. The other thing that I'm going to mention to you is that when animals pass away, they can come back as spirits, too. So, that's the same as like butterflies. A butterfly had a beautiful life as a butterfly, and he really wasn't ready to just plain be done. And you know what? And you know what, he ended up becoming dinner for a wasp. So, the butterfly is over there, and he still becomes an orb to fly around for a little while. They have a transitional period that they're able to do that. It's not just the butterflies, sometimes it's the little... um, hummingbirds... and sometimes it's the bees.*

You know what? Sometimes it was a very happy gardener who decides that they were just not ready to leave all of their flowers. So that they come back, and they spend, some time. So, then sometimes, they are actually a person's soul that is around the little garden too. So, there are many different options that are present, but it's really important to... send them blessings of love and light. Does that answer your question? Yes. Thank you. *You're welcome. Does anybody else have another question? I love talking about the fairies, and the gardens and the flowers.*

And unicorns too... I love unicorns. There are unicorns you know. They're just not on your dimension, you can't see them, but they are here. So joyfully speaking and animated with great smiles. *They run through the forests. You just don't know that.*

What dimension are you from? *Oh, I'm from six, six, six, six, six. Ah! She asked me a question and I knew the answer.* Gleefully giggling. Such a sweet light-hearted incorporation. *I like to ride unicorns too.*

I have the most beautiful dress on. I know you can't really see it, but I just want to take a minute to tell you about my little dress, 'cuz it's just so pretty!

So first of all, it's all flowing out, and it's got green, all different strips of all the different colors of the entire rainbow all the way around me. I've got sparkles all in my hair. I have beautiful blond hair and I have bright blue eyes, and it's all wavy. Can you see me? Can you see me? I hope you can see me, too. I know, it's kind of unusual to go ahead and explain what I look like, but it's just... Pause.

Where did I say I was from? From the Earth plane, Dimension Six. You used to be from the Earth. *I think... I think.* She grew overly excited. *I think I graduated to be a fairy. I know an awful lot about fairies, don't I? Yes. I do.*

Perhaps I just haven't put it all together yet. You know we have to learn things while we are here, too, and sometimes we have to put the pieces together to figure it out ourselves. Maybe that's why they let me come to see you today. So very excited and joyful about this new concept. *So that I could know that I'm a fairy too. Oh, I like this! This has been lovely! This has been lovely! Thank you so much!*

Thank you. All right. I guess I better go now. Thank you. Thank you, Angelina. She is joyfully clapping her hands and smiling. *Bye!* Blessings.

Angelina, a slip of a spirit was such an ecstatic and merry visitor. It was wonderful to learn a practice so that we can enhance our ability to see auras that area around us. It was amazing to see and get a first-hand confirmation of the entities' learning process during their personal and spiritual development.

FORTH INCORPORATION: KICKENSTAND

This incorporation began with a loving smile that transformed into a mid-tone musical humming that elevated with a great deal of fan-faire, flamboyance and a grand entrance upon his arrival. It was a jovial male entity that permeated love and happiness, for having the opportunity to come and visit with us. He later stated in jest that he was from Kalamazoo.

Dun-ta-da-dun! Giggling. *I have arrived too! I have arrived too! Let's see. I am from Kalamazoo… And I have arrived too!* Rearranging himself in chair. Big smile and happy. *And my name…* Pause. *Hummm…* Pursed lips and pause. Leaning forward. *Kickenstand. I don't think that's exactly the way it's supposed to sound, but that's what I'm finding. Kickenstand. That's a weird one.* A quizzical look crossed his face.

Anyway. Let's see. So, what am I here to talk about today? I was very excited they let me come through. So, this is good, because I'm here for each of you. So, what we need to talk about right now is … Pause. Pursed lips. *Hmmm…* Whispering to one side. *I was supposed to have a topic ready and I didn't,* pause (chewing bottom lip). *Let's see, let's see, let's see… What do you want to talk about today?* Ummmm… Lifting arms and pulling fingers together, pointer and thumb. Like grasping for a better connection. *Okay, we're going to talk about…*

How to get energy from other things, to be able to utilize it for yourself. Okay. Alright. So first, you all, know that you are energetic beings, and that's just what you are, and that's how you vibrate, and that's the way you work… and you're using energy all the time… and you're using energy that comes from food… and you're using energy that comes from light… and you're using energy that comes from your surrounding area… and that's why actually when you're in the space, where using a whole lot of energy together, but we're also creating a lot of energy. Well, let me take it back. You're really not creating a lot of energy; you're channeling a lot of energy. It's because you are actually opening yourself to be able to receive additional energy to come into this particular room, in this space.

The other thing that is so important, is you're actually able to tap into all kinds of other energy that's happening, that's around you. So, you people living closer to the shoreline, you're able to feed upon the energy of oceans. That's a constant that's gifting you with an influx of other energy that helps to keep your life balanced… This entity uses great hand gestures to reinforce what is being said…, *the same as if you actually go out and you spend time in the moonlight and the stars. The pulsing… of the rays from the star system is very different from that of the sun system. It's of a blue light… and that's why it's important to be able to gift yourself the opportunity to be outside in the darkness and especially in the full moon time, because again, you're going to get the full reflection of the Sun and an influx of this blue light. This blue light directly feeds into your nervous system and to calm things down.* Moonlight is a reflective, negatively charged energy that is necessary to hold balance from all hyper energy surges and also is known for its feminine essence. *That's a wonderful energy that you can tap into.*

Another energy source of course, I think that all of you are familiar with is the mineral world and crystals. Head nodding. *You know, spending time with the different crystals. Allowing your body to fall into alignment with the crystals themselves. Each crystal has a different vibration. You're going to feel a pull to a particular crystal at a particular time. When your body finds itself falling into the same rhythmic pattern as that crystal, then you don't feel the need for it anymore, because you've already then exchanged and fed from that energy source and then you may need to have a different one,... and all of these different crystals help to keep you balanced. It's important not to just go with the colors of the chakras, because you need all different kinds of crystals. You need granite, that's going to help ground you... and again when you have your... your light crystals. Your crystal light white, you know clear crystals, those are the ones obviously that help you around your crown chakra area. But there's so many different rocks and minerals that you need... that includes Mercury.*

I know people get all crazy! Uhhhh... They had it in their teeth. It's okay some of those different minerals are needed within all of your systems to help them work better... and to function and help fight off other disease that's coming in. When the minerals get to be too much and overloaded in the physical body though, the best way to get rid of them is to spend time in the ocean, and allow for your feet to open up, because you are moving all of the time, so you soak your feet in salt water, and it allows those different heavier metals to move out of your body that are not needed anymore. That's an important thing for you to do. It's part of that cleansing. Additional thought, there is a great deal of information about chakras located under your feet and the study of reflexology.

I do want to mention cleansing is important. I understand it's difficult to change your diet for a period of time... and to do particular things, but it does help to reset the physical body once in a while,… and that's an important thing to do. It's like rebooting the computer you know. This one here, she's got a computer. She's got to reboot it, reboot it, and reboot it. Maybe, she needs a cleanse! Probably. Anyhow. Um… I think that's what I really wanted to say. Does that, does that feel like some good information? Yes, it does. *Does anybody have a question that they'd like to ask about it?*

Audience Question

Are you from our dimension or another dimension? *I definitely resonate with the star realms. I resonate with the stars. Ummm… I'm not sure what a dimension is.* Okay. *So, I am not, I'm not sure about that.* Okay.

You recommended us to soak our feet in the ocean to cleanse. If somebody lives up north where they have snow, do you have a recommendation? *Epson salt… Epson salt.* Okay. *Epson salt is wonderful, and that's an old remedy.* Right. *And from where did it come? Ancient wise ones who knew how to do that.* Okay. Thank you. *Okay, alright then.*

Okay, I think that's it for me. So, thank you very much and blessings to each of you. Blessings, thank you. *Bye.*

As Kickenstand continued to speak, his demeanor changed somewhat from the excessive, flamboyant entrance to provide guidance of a more serious nature that would be highly beneficial to our existence and longevity while here in the physical. He wore a long dark green robe that had gold braided trim and was honored to have had the opportunity to visit with this group.

Topic Change

We had decided at the beginning of the session that we would ask to speak to someone from the Star System Sirius, after hearing from several open forum speakers. The group decided it was time to change the topic and invite any entities from the Star System Sirius to provide guidance or speak on any ideas of their choosing.

INCORPORATION: GATEKEEPER BAYLOT

Ask the question please. We need to have someone come forward that can talk to us about the star system Sirius. *Discuss. Discuss. Discuss the star system Sirius. We want to have several speakers from the star system Sirius to come through.* Please. *Please.*

FIFTH INCORPORATION: LIGHT BEING

Hands rubbing together, as he rearranged himself in the chair. He sat up much straighter. A low toned, almost irritated male voice, incorporated. This entity was imposing in stature and had a laborious time fitting into the physical body. Several times he needed to readjust his energy; however, he never provided an actual name to reference, but was a Light Being ray from Sirius.

Well I am being beckoned into the room am I not? Humph! Oh my... humph... Ughh... Ughhh... This is very heavy and uncomfortable here. Hold on a second... Ughhh! Leaning back, stomach extending. Working to get comfortable, deep breathing. Rearranged himself in chair and some grunting, while he attempted to fit into the space.

Alright... okay,... alright, I think I'm settled back in now. That was difficult to get in here! There's just not enough middle room - huh, huh, huh... Huh! Huh! Chuckling into a belly laugh. *That's a funny huh? Okay. Alright then. Alright, we're going to discuss the star system Sirius. Now Star System Sirius is actually one of the lightest largest light entities out there.*

He turns his head to the left in recognition. *Oh, you're a Star Being. I recognize you.* Belly laugh. *Uh-huh, you too! Yeah! Anybody else in here? Hold on... hold on...* He is using his hands to feel the various energies of the people in the room. *You, over here... Yup! It's in your lineage, too! You don't even know what it is? It's okay. Don't worry about it... Don't worry about it, you'll figure it out later on.*

And I think that's the first thing that I want to talk about. I know you want to hear about the actual system, but I want to talk about the way we're able to communicate… and that's what it is. We're able to… we're so interconnected that through the different light vibrations and through our historical, um,… timeline in our lineage. We just resonate and we recognize one another by our own light essences. And that's what all of this is about, is being able to recognize one another and to be able to bring yourself to another space and place. So, there are many things about the star system Sirius…

Gosh, I'm having such trouble with the middle. I don't know what the problem is. It just doesn't fit right! Hold on, I have to try to adjust this again. Deep breathing. Readjusting in the chair. Judi's stomach is protruding greatly. *I guess this is about as good as it is going to get.* Can you tell us your name please? *I didn't already do that.* No sir. *Oh, alright then… Ahhhhhhhhh… Ahhhhhhhh…* Continued long vibrational tone. *Ummmm…* Pause. *I don't think I have one.* Okay. *Ahhhhhhhh… Ummmmmmmmmm…* Okay. *I don't think I have one. Ahhhhhhhhh… I'm not getting it, … It's not coming…*

Do you hear what I was just doing? Okay, I was toning into the different vibrations so that I could get a clear communication back and forth to be able to get the information, because I'm following along the same energetic ray. I am going to call it a ray, but it's not really a ray. It's more of a grid,… and again it's the energy grid, and it goes in all dimensions and it goes in all directions and it goes with into and through all life essences, and it's just an incredibly easy way to go ahead and to communicate, and to discuss things. So, um… I completely forgot where I was going with anything, I am still struggling with this stomach thing. I don't know, what the problem is with the stomach. Huhhhhhhh… Readjusting in chair and moving stomach in and out. *It's very distracting to have to deal with the physical body.*

Because… well right, that's the first thing I'm going to talk about. I don't have to deal with the physical body, and that makes it so much easier to be able to go and to do and to be and to exist! We don't have to even… deal with a physical body. All it requires is a thought. Finger snap… *And there you are… and whatever is going on. You can create anything that you want through the thought process and or you can react to whatever else that's around you.*

110

Our star system is a very joyful place, but we are far advanced educationally than you are, because again, we're not on the same dimension you are. You are at a much lower dimension. We re-res-resonate, resonate… that's the word, move that tongue. Begins to wiggle and stick out tongue. *We resonate in,… in the eighth and ninth dimensions, because all we have to do is think we're there, and create and it will become.* Fingers snapping while speaking. *So, um… things that we do in our system…* Pause for a thought. *Truly it's joyful, peaceful place. We just have a beautiful existence. We don't have to deal with any of the trauma and the drama… the emotion and the craziness. We're just really in a pretty-even keel, and we work very diligently to continue to keep ourselves stimulated, motivated and um,… to grow our own education,… and we do have food items on our planet, and,… um, we don't have physical bodies like I said, so we don't have to deal with houses or anything like that. It's just a light vibration in the way that we are actually able to resonate and to see each other and to be with one another.*

And, um… So, we actually don't have to procreate because we're… we're… we don't. We're not born, and we don't die. We just are. We're always there as Light Beings, so that's… that's just the way it is. Um… let's see. Do you have a specific question? Maybe that might help me to be able to answer something that you might want differently from what I'm giving you? No response. *If not, I can ask somebody else to come in.* That's good. Thank you for your information. *Alright then, okay. You want to hear from somebody else though, right?* Yes.

Please. *Okay.* If someone is available. *If someone is available, okay. Alright, let me see.* Thank you. *Okay, bye. Safe journeys.*

This Light Being had such a difficult time incorporating his energy into the physical body. The physical was very heavy, but after time passed, he seemed to find delight in being able to move things such as the tongue, pointing and progressed to finger snapping. His challenge of fitting within the mid-section was clearly evident by the expanded and protruding stomach. I think he had a very difficult time keeping his thoughts in order, because of the uncomfortable physical impediments that he never got past. Upon his departure there were several large exhale breaths and an overall sense of relief.

SIXTH INCORPORATION: VABRINA

I remained in trance state and began speaking. *What I'm getting right now is a very large pink streak coming straight down through the center of myself and into myself. They're not actually incorporating, they're just sending a beam of light and information through the beam, because it's too difficult to just settle into the physical; however, they are able to go ahead and communicate through the vocal cords, which are here, but the last entity really struggled too much with a physical presence. Therefore, it's not happening now.* Vabrina a female entity began to speak immediately without pause, in the same tone that provided the explanation of the incorporation status. She had a fast, clipped, definitive tone and her posture was very straight, with head arched back as she spoke to us.

Vabrina is my name. And I have been a Star-seed for I don't know how long ... I just have been. Let's see... what do we say about the star system, Sirius.

Sirius is an incredibly beautiful star system. I would say it's the best one out there! The part that's really nice about being just Light Being is, we're able to transport ourselves into any star system at any time, and so we do travel quite a bit. We don't spend a lot of time necessarily in the planet of Sirius, but we do travel in and out of all the other little planets that are around it, and the star systems that are that are nearby. And... and um, we're always gathering information and bringing that back.

What else do I do? One of the things that that I'm actually tasked with is going out, and gathering information from other place, to be able to bring it back to our central location... and so I'm actually, um... I'm a Star Traveler. This is what my... my position is... And everybody does have something that they do for their duties; however, you know, it just depends on where they are, and who they are, and you can change your desire along the way so that you can do something different if you'd like. But um,... so what I do, I go to different places and find out how they're doing things and, and bring back the information to see if I can do it differently, or if it might be an added benefit or interest to the to the system itself. Um... let's see.

We actually do resonate a lot with different crystals but the crystals that are on our system are different from the ones that are on yours. Some are similar, but most of them are different because, actually, we're working with a whole different light system, and… we're a much brighter system than where you are on the Earth plane. And so um,… we have a higher level of clarity in our different mineral systems and um,… that's one of the reasons that we're able to continue to be just Light Beings is because we're able to resonate and to use all of the different light, and the crystals… and the energies from the crystals, to stay in that format and to continue to vibrate at such a higher space,… and along with the different dimension too.

Let's see, do you have any questions for me? Are you sent specific places, or do you just choose where you want to go? *We actually have um… scheduled routines of different places that we go. Sometimes, if there's something specific that's happening, we will go and tap into that location to be able to find out. We also go to places such as the Earth when sometimes things get a little bit too insane, and we're watching things get very, very chaotic. Then we'll send entities down here to try to settle things, and to keep things in a more protected place, but otherwise… Um… we just travel. I travel wherever, you know. I mean it's, um… it takes time to get to the different places, or whatever that realm of time is, you know. I just think one space and then I'm in another space, but I'm bringing it back. And we're just creating it together as one. Does that answer your question?* Yes. I think so.

Is there anything else? No. I don't think so. *Okay. Alright then. Is… is that enough?* Yes. Thank you. *Okay… okay… okay.*

My body remained ridged and arched back during the incorporation, which also included a rapid speech pattern and quite of bit of fidgeting and twitching within the torso. Upon completion, there was a deep cleansing exhale breath, that involved moving entire body through the exit process.

INCORPORATION: GATEKEEPER BAYLOT

Okay… transitioning again… Transitioning again. Time check is 7:25… okay and talk to Jamar. You want to talk to Jamar? And… um… you want to know anything specific from Jamar? No comment. *Let me go get him. Let me go get him.*

You know I am going to tell him this week, he needs to pay attention, because last week, he was he was too distracted,… last week, and there now, we've got plenty of space around here so. Um, and we're okay. So, he should be just fine. He should be just fine.

SEVENTH INCORPORATION: ELDER JAMAR

It was preplanned that the Elder Lemurian Jamar would be provided with time to speak on an open topic of his choosing. After discussions from the group encouraged our weekly visitations with Jamar to increase our knowledge about Telos, the Lemurians as a race and encourage a personal relationship of getting to know him.

Alright, alright, alright… Alright. I'm singly paying attention to you today. Let me get settled in a second. Throat clearing and readjusting the body for a few seconds. The voice tone adjusted lighter.

Okay. There were many different things that were happening last week. I was occupied with that along with being here in this space too. Today I have scheduled myself to be available fully for this time and for this space. So, I understand you want to talk about the different dimensions. I heard that earlier in the discussion, so why don't I go ahead and just tap into that right now.

As I have previously stated, there are many different dimensions which… um, all living entities will function. Different entities in different dimensions… um, all within the same space. And so… um… Let's see how's a good way to describe it. It's almost like… its layers, okay. It's a different speed, frequency speed, that something is operating. If it's a slower motion, it's a lower vibration, and that's where it's operating, but then if it's a higher frequency, it's moving much faster, then that's where it's operating. And so, you almost don't even have to… you don't even have to see and resonate with the other layers because you're staying in what you can see in yours.

I'm going to go ahead and… um, bring it back to an example of watching a fan blade. Fingers spinning. *When you're looking at a fan blade that's parked,* *you can see the three different fan components, but when the fan is going fast, you just see a single object, that's there, because it's continuing to move so quickly that you're just seeing a single object. So that's probably kind of an idea of a... of a dimension... being able to see things. So anyway, the importance of it is that the higher that you go, the less that you have to deal with all the physicals. And so, you did speak with someone from the Sirius Star System, and... when you did. They are of the Light Realm. They don't even have physical bodies that they are with, and that's not just unique to them. That's like with a lot of different entities that are in existence and living Beings. They just operate because they have energetic light existence is what they have. And so,... um, they're able to travel here,... there, everywhere, whenever they want or whatever they want, and sometimes they're traveling in and out of different dimensions to get different information, or to be able to get different guidance... Or,... or they're going to find information that they will then relay to another dimension, to help them through the process, because again, the other thing is, I just really need to go ahead and just say this... is that all life ... is just trying to elevate and to evolve to a greater higher space for the betterment of all... Not just the betterment of mankind, but the betterment of all life... All energy, all existence, all Universes, all Stars, all Suns, ALL! Does that make sense to you?* Yes.*

So, it is so critical that for the people, or whatever we want to call them -- entities, beings, whatever, of the higher different dimensions -- they're charged with the greater level of responsibility to be able to help the lower entities, to be able to feed them and to nourish them and to make sure they don't blow themselves up... to be able to protect them from themselves of just stupidity. They don't necessarily know. So yes, I'll say some of it is ignorance, but some of it is stupidity, and its ego and its greed that gets in the way. That creates all of this different drama and trauma that's happening that's around.

Okay... so, Um... and I guess the other part is you just continue as an entire race, population, planetary system, whatever you want to call it,... to be able to as a whole... to be able to elevate. And again it's very, very interesting to watch all of the diversity which is happening on the human Earth plane, because you've got so many people, who are not just humans,... because obviously you have star-seeds, you have all kinds of,... you have Atlanteans. You have others that are from all kinds of different star systems who have chosen to come back into

115

the Earth plane at this time, in order to help this population to move through the transition of being in the denser, lower planes to be able to move yourselves up, and so they need to be able to allow themselves to open to be able to the vibrations and to the energy surges, to help them through that process... Ummm... Does that help?... With some of the dimensional questions?

Audience Question

I have one Jamar. *Sure.* At what point can a human shed its human form and live in its light form? At what dimension? *That really depends on the human itself, because you can be in more than one dimension at the same time, and so, if you're in more than one dimension at the same time, you can't completely shed your human skin to be a Light Essence. If you're bouncing up and down, generally speaking, by the time you hit the seventh,... um, you really don't have a need for a physical body anymore; however, often times entities will remain to hold on to their physical until really they get to the eighth and ninth and then they let it go.*

There actually are twenty-four different dimensions that are of the primary, that different beings will live on, and as I stated, I'm not on the twenty-fourth by any means. I am working diligently to be able to go up and to visit in other times, and there are other entities who come down. It's again, that's a very large leap for them to be able to come down from twenty-four to nine. That's a very large leap! They cannot possibly spend any time or energy coming back to the third and the fourth realm to help the humans. It's too far down... It's too far down. So, they don't. That's why we're charged with it. We're receiving our additional information from pretty much the thirteen and fourteen realms,... is helping us.

I have a question. *Yes.* Is the goal for everyone to progress through all the dimensions to twenty-four? Is there individual choice involved? *You don't have to.* Is it a common goal? Is there someone who, as you said, you and others will come in and try to help elevate those of us that are in a lower plane? Um... Is it necessary? Is it desirable? Is it the intent of all Beings to progress? *The intent is to be able to be the highest and best you can be for self, whatever that is and wherever that is. You're always continuing to*

116

try to grow to become more. I'm going to ask the God Source to step in. I think that would be a good… um… If you're okay with that. Yes.

Are you okay with that? Yes, very much. *Okay, let me do that. Do you have any other questions for me right now?* No. *I can come back if you need. Okay, I'm going to switch out, because I was hearing earlier too, that the God Source wanted to come in to help tie up some ends.*

Jamar was quite fidgety within this incorporation. Shuffling, rearranging, settled somewhat about half-way through and then was using hand gestures and more comfortable within the body. This was noted most visible with the tone changes of his voice. Historically he was very methodical and had a metallic texture to his speaking. However, during this transmission his voice dramatically changed. He began using vocal fluctuation, plus emotion and passion was shared through his tone. He was emphatic for us to understand this concept and the shared message and began using facial expressions. This was the first time that Jamar truly began using the physical vessel during the incorporation to accentuate the details of his thoughts and message through the use of body language.

EIGHTH INCORPORATION: GOD SOURCE

I had been getting nudges throughout this day that the God Source was planning to come through to provide us with some guidance. Jamar also was able to pick up on this transmission. There was a complete readjustment to the physical body and deep breathing as Jamar stepped out and the God Source incorporated, which took several seconds to complete.

The God Source has such an awesome presence! He is large, peaceful, gentle, all loving and fills the room and our hearts with his inspiring, accepting and humbling presence. The God Source always begins with a huge loving smile upon His face. His voice is soft, speech pattern is slow, and He will often pause to ensure that you have time to absorb his words, which are articulately spoken with an old-style formal accent.

Ahhh, my daughters!

I am so delighted and honored that we are here and working through this process as one. You are smart and asking good questions. Life is life. The essence of all life is to be in love, to share love, to share peace, to be one with joy, to become and to do and to live fulfilled and happy... That is all.

As you work through the various dimensions and the different Universal Beings of all that are in existence, then there is the opportunity to be able to experience and travel to and through each. It is the same as if you decide to get on a boat and go on a cruise to another country. It is the same, to go skiing in the mountains of the Denver... To go and to experience, so that you allow your Soul... to become fulfilled in all that it can be, and that is the essence of all life! You continue to grow to become the best "you"... Soul that you can... And you continue to experience and participate with all of these other life realms as part of your education.

As you continue to grow and expand, then you're allowed to move into and out of the various dimensions, which is again part of the growth. The system of all life continues to grow, to evolve, and to develop far beyond from the single spark seed that was. It just continues to manifest and to multiply over and over, there will never be an end. There can only be more beginnings.

Taking time... Taking time to host circles, such as these, because you are asking the questions and you're providing information that is critical for human development, is such a precious gift. It's such a precious gift to each of you, because it helps you to understand more of what you can be, and how important you are, but how perfect that you are, already as you are. It allows you opportunities to be able to learn and to grow. From what you do not know, but in your hearts seem so familiar, because your Soul does know!

It's about the ability to share love with those who do not remember that they are loved. Every person goes through times in their lives when they just feel alone, and they cannot hear and sometimes they do not hear Me, but they see you... and they see the spark of love of Me inside of you, too.

My daughters, I want you to hear Me. I want you to feel the words that I am saying into your hearts and into your Soul's existence. You can be, anything that you want to be. You can go, anywhere that you want to go. You can become, anything that you want to become, and I encourage you to stretch far beyond the tiny limitations of your mind, that you have crafted to hold yourself back!

The human race has created such boundaries and barriers and bars to hold them back from all the joyfulness that is there, ready and waiting. The key to opening and unlocking is faith... and trust that you know that it will always be okay and provided for. And it is! And it is okay! Humans then will decide at times that they have been upon the Earth long enough and they are ready to go, to wherever they want to go, because they want to explore another solar system. They want to explore another planet. They want to explore another level of existence and perhaps they want to come back as a fairy or as a bumble bee or a butterfly... Or perhaps they are going to continue to work diligently and to be able to be a part of the Angelic Realm. This is a different level of existence.

This is an entirely separate level of existence... Angels have spent their entire essence... many Angels have never been humans before. It is rare to be able to work from humanness through the entire elevation process, to be able to become an Angel... because Angels are all so powerful. They're everywhere at once. They are my eyes and ears and hands and hearts too. You feel their presence surrounding you as I am with you, too. They provide guidance, and love, and hugs of comfort, too!

Do any of you have any specific questions for Me? Pause. Doesn't look like it. What was your name? *I am the God Source and I want you to know that I Am affiliated with all life-- All systems, All entities... because we are all connected to the same grid of energy. There is not one that you can affect that does not touch the other. It may be a small ripple, but it is a direct effect. You need to realize that. Humans need to realize that!*

The importance of what they are doing and the impact that they are making... And the words that they speak... and the impacts of those words, to the others

119

around them. Words are living! They can be the most beautiful gift, and they also can be the harshest enemy, because they,... with a word, it can cut through the Soul and it can cut a chunk out, of the wholeness of a person. That takes great effort to heal again, or they sometimes can never be healed, because the person has to also then choose to allow the healing to take place... to move beyond the words. Words are the most detrimental and the highest and the best that could be. Who would have thought it was just from a chakra? That's why it's up so high, because it shows the importance of... The importance and the value of words and praise... True praise.

I want each of you, daughters, to know that I praise each of you. I am so honored you have chosen... You have chosen with your hearts and with your minds... and chosen to spend your time to make more and to become one of yourself with.

Blessings to each of you. Blessings to each of you. Thank you. Thank you.

The great wisdom and acceptance for each of us and our souls is such a beautiful gift to feel from the God Source. I feel it as a channel and as a recipient both during any channeling of the God Source. It is so beautiful, peaceful, graceful and a soul healing love! The guidance and wisdom provided was truly enlightening and essential for each of our Souls to understand this truth for our existence in this lifetime.

INCORPORATION: GATEKEEPER BAYLOT

Baylot here. Time check, please. 7:50. Okay, time to end. Thank you. Any other questions? I'm good, we're good. Alright. Thank you.

After Discussion

After opening my eyes, I was disorientated in my physical presence (my direction), and my memory (what transpired throughout the incorporations). We discussed the light beings from Sirius and what a difficult time the first incorporation was physically, thereby causing the second visitor to come in as a ray light only. We bantered around the logic of why light energy couldn't fit, but no answers were received. We talked about food and the use of foods by the entities. This conversation morphed into a group discussion of how each of us are affected, as we continue our spiritual growth journey, and our entire diet changes. We eat lighter with more nuts, fruits, and vegetables as our bodies need access to nutrients quicker and we then have difficulty digesting heavy meats, fats and processed foods.

Additional conversations included a great interest that the visitor from Sirius recognized several of the souls within the room. A suggestion for next week was to ask to hear from someone from the future. Then questioned – future of where? What dimension, location, time period, and is that the future as we know it to be?

Another thought for a question next week was how to easily distinguish light and dark energies, frequencies, and intentions of others, so that I can keep clear.

This was an immensely powerful session and message from the God source. Upon editing the video, lighting changes are clearly seen at the end of this session when Baylot left and after my spirit fully settled back into my physical self.

Closing Prayer

Heavenly Father, Thank You. Thank you for the blessings of this day. Thank you for the circle of love. Thank you for energies, the light beings, the wisdom, the knowledge and Heavenly Father, help us to be able to assimilate it into our hearts. Help us to be able to carry forth your wisdom and knowledge and to walk the path that you set before us. Help us to be able to always respect our words and how they're shared with one another. We ask this in your precious name. Amen.

Session 6

Opening Prayer

Heavenly Father. Thank You for the blessings of this day. Thank you for each of the souls who have gathered here together. Heavenly Father, we open our hearts, we open our minds and ourselves to the Universal Light information to come through. Heavenly Father, we are so grateful. We are so grateful! Help us to keep our thoughts clear, open and respectful. Blessings of this Universal Love. We ask this in your precious name. Amen

Introduction

DURING THE OPENING PRAYER WE could all feel the great shifts and influx of energy as we prepared for the evening. It was evident that as our group continued to meet, the group energy was connecting with the ONE. It was scheduled that we would ask two questions and then allow time for Jamar to speak. We would first ask Baylot for his opinion about the future and what we can expect, before moving on to another source.

FIRST INCORPORATION: GATEKEEPER BAYLOT

We called in Baylot so that we could begin the channeling. We are watching Baylot grow and develop each week. He is very excited to have a voice and time to be able to share his guidance and wisdom. He is greatly enjoying having a voice this entire channeling process, and that is evident by the confidence and length of his speaking. He enters with a broad, loving smile.

I am here. I am Baylot. I am delighted that you're choosing to ask me first to come and to speak. Thank you very much for that. I did hear that earlier information and it is very true, and I want to just take a moment if you don't mind to reiterate the importance of getting to know who your spirit guide is.

Your spirit guide chose to become your spirit guide prior to your being born. And it was part of our desire to choose a soul that aligned with what we wanted to learn through our experience of being spirit guides also… and the other part is sometimes things go very differently than what we ever could have imagined, and that's part of our growth too. So therefore, we need to reach out for additional guidance from others to help get you back on track for where we thought you wanted to go in this lifetime. So, it's very interesting and such a… learning situation all the way around.

But um… I am here and I am very honored to have this host as my student and as my partner for this lifetime… and I am ever so excited and grateful that we are journeying into this level of information and exchange of energy… and um,… I will also go ahead and mention how exciting it is to be able to be present with each of your energies. I actually feed upon those energies, too… and they are so vibrant and colorful… and um,… I also have opportunities to speak with your spirit guides when you're here too,… so they also have entered into this space and so we are here as a collective group,… and the more so that we meet together, then again the group will go ahead and get stronger and the information becomes much more personalized for you and the abilities for each of you to be able to tap into and expand from. So, I understand that there's a bit of a tangent, but I do think that that was relevant information, that you may not have thought of and I just thought that it would be important to relay that to each of you, also. Thank you. Question please?

Question

Is it possible for someone from the future to come to us to speak with us? *It is possible for entities to travel through time, because again time is not just a linear thing. It's happening in multiple levels at once; however, I did hear earlier parts of the discussion, and that was true in that you can't necessarily know something that's going to be eons ahead and you can have guidance from what the event may be. It may occur; however, details do become changed. So, we could actually choose to tap into a future self of you, if that's something that ever of interest... Um... and we can do so,... we need to know. What you want to of the future? So, do you want to know something, you have to have a destination. You have to know to bring that, whatever back... Um... maybe I'm not articulating that well enough. Was that confusing to understand? I believe it was. Let me try to do that again. Ask the question once again please?*

Audience Question

Is it possible to have someone from the future come and speak to us? *Yes, it is possible. But what do you want to know?* Can I ask a question Baylot? *Yes.* So, regarding the future I have a question. That as we're moving, and I hear about many places and read many places, that many things will be shifting up until about 2020 through 2033. Can you give us an idea of, as we're moving from third dimension to fifth dimension, is there a time point maybe in 2040 or 2050 with this world, that were living on right now? Will much of the shifting that we're going through politically and sociologically and spiritually and physically? Do you have any information from approximately 2040 to 2050 of what kind of shifting we will have gone through on this world at that point in time?

It's difficult for me to be able to discuss something that's outside of my wheelhouse. Pause, coughing. *Excuse me. Information that I need to move into some of that, but I cannot explain all of that.* I understand. *Okay. I'm going to talk about 2020 is a pivotal year. And I'm not sure if that's something that you are aware of or not. The last seven years have been filled with a great deal of transition which happened, that started in the 2012 timeline and now you're moving out of that 2,000 at the seven-year period after that, and you're going into*

2020. So there has been, the last seven years a great deal of… of transition,… of trauma,… of drama, of,… of cleansing of events, which have been taking place.

You are now reaching a place in your universe where everything is all vibrating extremely high and it's just blowing up all over the place, but it had to. They're not even trying to hide any more politically, the crazy nonsense that they are even doing. They're just doing it and it doesn't even matter, because the public is becoming very disengaged, because of the chaos, and they're allowing that chaos to just be. So now, once we enter the 2020 timeline. And again, up to the 2020 through 2022, you're going to find things truly coming into a much more equalized space again. Okay, you're going to have all the eruptions of all the chaos, but again once for the next three-year period of time. Things are just going to get more organized and they're going to settle out. The reason why is you're having such an incredible shift from materialism back to energy. Okay.

That's one of the major shifts that's happening. You have to be able to release things in to allow yourself to align with the vibrations to rise, because you cannot take things with you, when you're rising. Okay. So… um, let's see. That really didn't answer your question. Yes, it did. It's fine.

Well it didn't take it to the timeline of which you wanted to go. Is her question better for the person from the future? *Let me see who I can find. Who can come in and try to provide you with additional information from the future? Okay. Alright. Thank you and thank you for allowing me to have a voice. I appreciate that. Blessings.*

SECOND INCORPORATION: GOD SOURCE

Hands rubbing together for several seconds, throat clearing and leaning forward during a pause. The God Source softly and lovingly enters with upon a deep inhaling breath.

My daughters,

I am the one to come this eve who needs to speak about the future. I, my child, am the God Source again. Such a loving presence enters the room.

Peaceful, gentle, warm and glowing. *Who better than I, to come into speak of, and to talk about the future, and what can be? I want to say many things about the future, but I need to say that it's very dangerous at times to explain much about the future and events far ahead, because there are others who will go out to try to create larger events and chaotic events, when they know of major shifts and changes which are taking place or anticipated to take place.*

The biggest shift that I want to share with each of you now, is the alignment of communication, which is going to happen, which is free will of the people of this universe along with other universal beings. A long pause with delighted smile of anticipated joy. *There will be opportunities and there will be communications. There will be intergalactic places of exchange of information.*

This will become a world which will accept all races and nationalities not just of the Earth humans but of other Beings too. This is an exciting thing which is already coming to be. But it will all change not just through the fearfulness, but it will change because of the curiosity. It will also be able to change because of the levels of communication and the types of communication, because as you continue to elevate your frequencies and vibrations, you will be able to synchronize with the thought patterns of others in other universes, so that that information can come more easily into yours. Once you have that information and you're able to communicate with them, that alleviates the fear factor.

Smiling, pause. *So, in the 2050. That is but to skip and a jump away... but yes, that is what will be taking place upon those days. Does that help to answer the question?* Yes, thank you. *Is there another part of the question that you would like to have answered?*

Audience Question

Is there any way that we can better prepare ourselves to meet these changes? This major shift? *Well, I think for this particular group it's an interesting question, because you are... opening your hearts. You're opening your minds, and you're allowing different information to come in. You may not understand all of the information that's coming in, but you're allowing it to come in, and that's all that's asked of you, because as you continue to open yourself, to gift yourself with quiet meditative space and time, then again the vibrations in the frequencies shift and change so that you're able to receive and understand things more clearly. Does that make sense?* Yes.

So, I will say for each of you who are here continue your regular daily practices, and continue to understand… and to look for… and to listen for… and to see not just with your two eyes, but with your third eye, too. See the different levels of universal energy which are all happening at the same time on your Earth plane, as it is in other planes. You'll be able to see many different dimensions as you continue to grow. They'll be opened and shown to you to be able to see.

That's very exciting for me too, to know and to understand what each of you are hearing and being one with… and also to be able to share the information through you and those that you come into contact with, too. It's the same as throwing a pebble into a pond and the ripple effect. Right now, we're casting information into this space, but the ripple effect will continue far beyond what your mind could possibly understand. The implications can only continue to grow and to manifest more.

Because it, creates a hunger and a thirst from each of you, too… to want to know more… to study more,… to see more,… to go forth and to do more. Every one of you become those tiny little pebbles that are being tossed into another lake or a pond with new ripples that are going forth. Smiling, pause. *Then all of our ripples will overlap one another… and as a uniform group of chaos, what happens? It becomes complete. Information is whole. Do you have any other questions for me regarding this?* No.

Well blessings dear daughters, blessings to each of you. Blessings. Thank you.

The God Source bows with hands pressed to center of chest upon his exit. His presence envelopes the room with such love, peace, acceptance and purity. You can feel the protection and healing energies long after each session and everyone was grateful for this wisdom and shared knowledge.

INCORPORATION: GATEKEEPER BAYLOT

Did you want to speak to anyone else or is that enough for that question? I think that's good. That was enough. *Okay.*

Next question please?

Question

How can we clearly distinguish between light and dark intentions versus energies?

THIRD INCORPORATION: ARCH ANGEL MICHAEL

Upon incorporation, Arch Angel Michael sits up very straight. Taking several deep breaths. Arch Angel Michael is stately, domineering and in charge! He is fully dressed in his polished armor with his sword meticulously holstered at this waist and ready for battle at any moment as a protector. His energy exudes strength and loving presence fills the room. His voice has a low baritone vibration and speech is articulate and he clearly annunciates each syllable to ensure that we can understand him.

I'm going to come through. One moment please. This is a wonderful question for me. I'm Arch Angel Michael and I'm here to speak with each of the... Ask the question once more please, and I will help to define it for you.

How can we clearly distinguish between light and dark intentions versus light and dark energies?

The reason why I chose to come through is because again, each of you know who I am. And you understand the presence. I am a Warrior Angel. And therefore, it is part of my journey to be able to distinguish... to slice away tendrils which hold one down and can create different levels of,... of chaos and barriers.

So, the first thing that I want to speak about is the human body and the reactions that you're getting. This comes in tune with communication, does it not? Is this what we're starting with? Is how to identify through the communications? Ah, yes. *Let me start there then.*

When you're communicating with another person you step into their presence. And you already have a full indication of who and what they are, by the presence and the energy that's around them. You may not necessarily be paying attention to that energy field, but your energy field is filled all the way around with sensors so that it can feel. When you walk into a room where someone's been having an argument, you walk in, and you feel the anger. You feel the anxiety. You can walk into an insane asylum and you can feel the chaos of it. It's the same as going to a city meeting often times. It's the same level of chaos.

You're able to read the energy that is around and in the space. So, the first thing that I challenge each of you, and bring back to your attention, is when you're in the presence of someone… Now, first you have always done your power protection for self, so that none of their negative energies or whatever energies are going to come in and affect you; however, you're going into that environment fully contained of yourself, but you're able to read what others are.

The other thing that is so important, for you to be able to be looking with your eyes and to be reading and scanning the person not just listening to the words of what's coming out of their mouth. Pause.

The other part is to feel with a heart center. Because your heart center is the same God Spark, which is in any other person that is anywhere. You're God Spark Center can recognize the other God Spark Center. It takes intention and it takes practice. But you're allowed to do that if you choose to allow your spark center to go out to be able to read the other one. This is a wonderful way of being able to clearly and easily identify someone else's intention. People don't know that they actually can do that. Have any of you ever heard of this before? Yes. Okay. *Wonderful. Some yes, some no. It's a wonderful technique to practice. Okay.*

The other thing that I want to make sure is, as you're out there and you're feeling the person's presence. Sometimes you feel a solid, Yes. Snapping fingers. *And sometimes you get a solid, No.* Snapping again. *And very often times you just feel gray. An ambivalence of not necessarily understanding. They're sending mixed signals of what is and what isn't. And do you know what sometimes the best thing to do is? To wait.* Pause. *To wait and to be in a space and to allow them to come back. Doing nothing will oftentimes clarify what the situation is, because if they're in a place of grey and spinning and they don't necessarily understand where their energy source is coming from. Why do you want to get in the mix of it at that moment? Now, if they're coming to you and they're seeking help, you can help to show them guidance towards the light source-- the light source of the Angels, the Light Source of God, the light source of this God Spark that is within each of them.*

Oftentimes humans are so shrouded with guilt, and fear, and terror, and shame. They carry the burdens of others that were not even their own to carry, but all of this feeds as a level of protection around them because it's what they know. They understand the depression. They understand the darkness. They understand the gloom. The light is fearful to them because they don't understand that they're worthy enough in order to draw from that light, and to allow that light into them fully, to accept that they're worthy of all the light. Does that make sense? ...Um-ha...

Ask the question once again, and let me make sure that I have clearly articulated all I wanted you to know on the subject? How can we clearly distinguish between light and dark intentions verses light and dark energies? *Okay, so, I'm going to my... my message. My overall message again is to be able to feel it. You are equipped with all of the sensors you could possibly have in order to be able to feel to be understanding of and know that what you're feeling is the truth even if the words don't match. Okay.* Okay. *Anything else?* Thank you.

Okay, Thank You.

Arch Angel Michael is such a large and protective essence. You feel his power but are also fully aware that power is specifically there to keep you safe, guarded and protected from all. Arch Angel Michael always wears a mighty sword along the side of his royal blue robes. His entire presence showcases this majestic color along with the afterglow that lingers long after his release of the physical.

FORTH INCORPORATION: GREY TONE

There was quite a pause through the incorporation process. Grey Tone entered in a completely neutral and monotone voice as well as all body language. The energy of the room shifted and had an essence of void. It was not positive or negative, just an in-between grey essence. The voice tone was a bit lower which matched his slower, monotone speech pattern.

I'm going to speak on the subject now. Can you ask the question please? Yes. How can we clearly distinguish between light and dark intentions versus light and dark energies? *I'm going to speak as a gray tone.*

This is what you can call me, Gray Tone, because I exist in the between… the between one and the other. There is much energy which is fluctuating all of the time… and there's the between. The between is an opportunity for ambivalence, but it's also the opportunity to change one's mind from one to another. It's very interesting with intentions. They could be thought to be of the light but of dark, and they could thought to be up the dark, but truly end up being of great light, because through the darkness is growth… and change… and development. Through the lightness, you're able to see the shadow side that was hidden between. It is very important… I think the most important message that I want to say is… the judgment aspect of it. Who's one to be judge and jury of?

You came to this world to learn and to learn from. You each are teachers. You each are students. Each experience has highs and lows. It has pain. It has excitement. It has growth through all different types of experiences. You cannot see light and be only in light without knowing the shadow side, and being able to work your way through the shadows of,… and you cannot possibly stay only in the shadows of, without knowing the joys and the love of the light.

Ask the question once again please? How can we clearly distinguish between light and dark intentions versus light and dark energies? *There are both.* Pause… *And there's not good or bad, there, just is both. Blessings to you.* Thank you, Blessings to you.

This energy was totally void of emotion or influx. It was simply a soft neutral existence of energy sharing insight of no judgement – neither good nor bad. It just was. The energy in the room greatly shifted to a lower frequency of neutrality that matched the vibration of Gray Tone.

FIFTH INCORPORATION: DARKNESS

First, a long pause, and then, there was a total physical transformation that took place. Deep breathing and a sinking or crawling down deep into the chair. A low grunting animal noise was heard, which grew from a low frequency vibration which developed into a growl. As the entity continued to move into the incorporation. The growling and moaning ensued, along with ridged body readjustments. The back arched, showing signs of a painful transition.

Voice of Gatekeeper Baylot or other high energy: *"Power of protection for the room: Power Protection for the room: Power Protection for the room: Power production for the room."* Very deep inhale. The low growling, sinister tone continues!

You've asked one of me. Growling type of a roar. Deep darkness and smoke essence clearly entered the room. Gurgling… *ahhhhhhhhh.* My head and back clearly arched way backwards and with lots of growling continued. *Do not think that I am not real, as I am.* Gurgling and deep throat moaning while any speech is a deep raspy growling voice. Body language looks to be in pain. *O-n-l-y those who choose to feed me come to me, but I am always hungry…* Deep breath. *And I feed upon the insecurities… But you can always see me… through the cloak of what I wear… continue to feed against me.*

Gatekeeper Baylot or other high energy invocation *Power of prayer, power of prayer, power of prayer, power of prayer, power of prayer, power of prayer.* Deep inhale and body releasing great energy and weight. *"Love*

light, love light, love light, love light, love light, love light, love light, love light".
Deep breathing once again.

Complete shifting of the body, readjusting itself in all angles and shapes completing with a bowed forward head, labored breathing with many shallow deep breaths to work through the transition. The sort shallow breaths were being used to quickly elevate the energy within the room once again and clear away and residual energy of the darkness.

At the end of the evening, there was extensive discussion about this incorporation, how it came to be and the individual effects as well as the group. Everyone agreed they were not in fear but worked diligently to hold the energy for my personal safety.

After this evening was completed, I later prayed about this with great angst about the possibility of being able to channel such a low vibrational energy. *Why was this allowed? How did he get through? Did God and my Spirit Guides actually allow this happen? How was this in my best interest?*

I was told many things in response to my questions. First and foremost, I, along with everyone in the room, were fully protected and yes, this was allowed this once. The stage had been universally set in motion long before the evening began. I had saged (smoked off) myself, before coming to class. The first incorporation was from the God Source. The first incorporation for this question was by Arch Angel Michael. The Warrior Angel as full protection was set in the room. Next was Grey Tone to begin to lower the vibration to even make an event possible. It was important to allow for a single communication from the lower vibrational soul to validate its presence in the energy world.

An audience member who sees auras told me that while incorporated, mine is generally a bright or brilliant white and sometimes gold. During this session my aura turned to grey smoke. I also know that I was fully protected, and I didn't absorb any residue because of the crystals that are inserted within my body.

I also learned that while the darkness chose to enter my physical space, it was in great pain as if acid was burning his essence all over. It was only allowed for a very brief amount of time and could only tolerate my presence for about ninety seconds. Additional follow-up information is discussed in the next session.

SIXTH INCORPORATION: ANGEL EPHERINA

This incorporation took quite a while to transfer in, as it took great energy to ensure release of all remaining energies of the low energy visitor. Shallow breathing became rhythmic and transformed into longer cleansing inhales. This entity had a higher pitched female tone voice, a peaceful and slow speaking comforting voice. Epherina explained that her purpose is to shower Love and clear away energies.

Angels surround. Angles exemplify all around. Find peace in prayer and protection to this space and to this being before you. This was an incredibly soft spoken, loving entity that came in speaking slowly in a higher pitched female voice. You could feel a dramatic room energy shift and she brought in while and pink love. Calming all energies in each of us and the room too. *All around...*

As you continue to walk and to stay within the highest energies of self and love and light in peace and pure grace. They will always continue to follow around you. It's okay to look at the shadow side of ones. Stay in the peace and the love and the light and the grace, so that it continues to lift and to carry you through.

I'm from the Angelic realm also, and I am Epherina, and my purpose is to always continue to just shower love around... Shower love around and continue to share my love on a much higher level, because I need to be able to dissipate some of the darkness, when it does come in and around. Epherina was rearranging herself, squirming in the chair. Arching her back and seemed uncomfortable, shoulders shifting and body twitching. *That was an interesting experience, that I would not recommend that you do again in this space.*

I understand it was invited, and it was an educational opportunity; however, it's not necessarily in each of your best interest to be able to tap into this energy, because once you become familiar with them, then it also begins to resonate. So, I want to take this time right now to truly send an overwhelming bath of Love into this space. Deep breathing. Hands extended and sending healing love into the room. *Feel the peace into this space... Pure grace into this space... Through every cell... Through every molecule... Through every particle... and atom... Only allow for the purest, lightest and best. Blessings. Blessings of peace.* Blessings.

As Epherina was speaking, all through her visit you could physically feel the room transform to comply with all the healing and loving instructions that were beautifully spoken. I could see all white flowing robes, brilliant white glowing light and sparkles and shimmers of light as it shifted everything and everyone in the space. Her exit was fairly swift with a deep breath in and released on the exhale.

INCORPORATION: GATEKEEPER BAYLOT

Gatekeeper Baylot lovingly stepped back in to inform us that we were done with that question and would be moving forward. He continued to rub hands in a circular motion for quite a while with a slow, soft comforting speech pattern.

I'm going to step back in and I'm going to say that's the end of that question. I know that we've been asking to hear from Jamar, but I'm going to ask the room is there any specific one you want to hear from? Do you want to go to Jamar? Or do you want to allow for an open question from other entities that are waiting to see who else may want to come in with information?

I guess Jamar. Unless someone has a message that they really need to deliver. *Let me ask first, to see if there's someone else who really wants to come in and provide some information. We are in October now. October is a really fun time with the fall in the festivities so let me see. Let me see. We have lots of time, that's good.*

SEVENTH INCORPORATION: ELIMARI

A very quick and soft transition occurred with the neutral voice tone of Elimari from the Sirius Star System incorporated. You could feel the rigid form of this energy as it stepped in. This entity was very stoic. The speech was literal and sounded like artificial intelligence, asexual. Enunciating each letter or syllable.

I'm going to step in once again, and I want to talk again about different universes, the information, and the types of life beings that are on the different star systems. I want to speak about, very briefly, in regard to last time, and the planet system of the star of Sirius, because you tapped into... You received last time, Light Beings of information.

I am not a Light Being, but you did receive light being information. There are many different kinds of beings and subcultures, and so many different living organisms that exist within each and every planet. With each and every state of what you have in your United States and municipalities and within the room that you find yourself in at this moment. There are so many different atoms and micro atoms and bacteria and there's parasites which are living inside of your human bodies along with your... they're other entities that are all around you. So, when you're receiving information from a particular place and or about the system you need to understand that you're only receiving a micro-organism of information about that. Does that make sense? Yes.

Okay, I just needed to mention that, because you're asking information and we're providing you with guidance and some information, but it's also very difficult for you to be able to understand all of it, because you don't have the knowledge and the capacity to be able to understand what you don't know and understand. So that's part of the, the... challenges for us, is to be able to provide you with enough information that makes sense within the parameters of where you are. Yes.

So, I think that's all I wanted to say, and my name is ... Long pause. Trying to find word or sounds. *Alamar... El Lamar,... a-Lamar,... Lamar,... Lamar,... Lamar,... E-l-i-m-a-r-i. Thank you.*

Blessings. Thank you.

Elimari's energy, presence and stature was very ridged throughout the visit. You could not differentiate male or female, but it truly seemed to be almost manufactured as artificial intelligence, precise and non-descript in all mannerisms. In retrospect, it may have been a metallic, fluid energy substance that incorporated.

EIGHTH INCORPORATION: RED HAWK

An exceedingly long pause through this next incorporation. You could feel the energy shifting into a major grounding energy for the room. I am extremely comfortable channeling Native Americans and have a very strong connection as was clearly shown by Red Hawk from the Lenape Tribe. He is an ancient warrior and came to help provide guidance and clarity for us.

Sons and daughters, brothers, sisters, mothers and fathers,

I want to speak. And I... I am. Pause while readjusting during the incorporation. *I am... a Native American and I'm working on the finding the name.... Uh... Red Hawk... Red Hawk is my name and I am from the Lenape tribe... What I need to speak to you about is being able to unite with elder ways once again. I understand you're seeking Universal Knowledge, but I need you also to understand the importance of being able to tap into the native ways. The native way is the mystery and the unification with our Mother Earth. We are the sacred ones, who truly understand how the Mother operates. She operates with the flowing of the water and of the blending of all of the elements in the life... and being one with the life circle... blending yourself with the life circle.* While Red Hawk is speaking, the torso of his body is moving in circular motions. *Allowing your emotions to fall in line with the same light circle and with the beings in the life circle.*

It is the same with the magnificence of this full moon which has just passed upon this harvest time... A great time of pure celebration for the natives to be able to truly honor what we have been able to accomplish with our Mother's cooperation and full partnership, because this is how we live. The Mother Earth needs us too, to be able to help her to grow and change and to be able to continue to evolve herself as a living being that she is. At this point there was a slight pause and Red Hawk began to circle the torso in the opposite direction.

It is so important for each of us as mankind upon this... to be able to work in partnership with the other life entities that are upon this land too. It is just as important to be able to unify yourselves in alignment with all of the different kinds of weather, and with all of the different natural entities that are still alive too, the mountains and the rocks. The great wisdom, which is locked with inside of the different rocks... allow yourselves time to unite with... allow yourself time to emulate the same dancing wheat that's blown across the fields and allow your hearts to sing in synchronicity with that and of that and be that.

Do you pray for the food which feeds your body and nourishes it? Give thanks to all those who sacrifice of their essence, selves and nutrients to be able to feed and to be one with you, to help you to be of your strongest and purest self. See the great value of the animals that are around you. Take time to listen to the chatter of the squirrel, as it flags and shakes its tail at you. What is it trying to tell you? It's time to collect and to prepare for... to prepare for coming times of change. What is the bird who's in... flying around in circles and lands so close to you and looks keenly upon your face for? What is it looking to see? Is it questioning your heart or a decision? Or helping to provide you with guidance and knowledge to go forth and to fly free... to make another decision?

When you light the fire and you sit around it, and you allow the blazes to burn forth, do you look within for the Spirits of the Fire People,... who will show you the magic of inside, and additional wisdom and knowledge for you to tap into? It is the same with the cloud people.... when the storms billow and change and great strength moves across the sky, you see the different shapes and shadows and the piercing lightning that shoots through... But do you take the time to look and learn from that too? These are questions that I have for each of you. It is the same as when you go and look upon the water. Do you look upon only the surface of, or do you take time to look deep within? Do you look at the reflection of a pond to see what is within each of the ripples? There is such wisdom and knowledge, if you allow yourself to step back into the earthen ways... The Earth-keepers, of all wisdom of all knowledge, of grounding of self.

139

This information is critical for each of you and your soul's development because you'll be traveling to and through and spaces of understanding and light vibrations that make you feel out of balance. Your equilibrium is off... and sometimes you find yourself spiraling down into darkness into depressive places and spaces, where truly what you can do is to be one with... one with... Be one with the Earth. Be one with the worms within the Earth. Be one with the Tree people and allow them to show more of who and what you can be. There is so much you can learn from the nature. Coughing. *Excuse me.* Pause and deep breathing. *Sometimes it's difficult to align the vibrations properly within the physical.*

Did you go out and see the moon? Yes. Yes. *Did you feel the pulsing of the moon?* Um-hum. Pausing and smiling. *Each of you felt it because the moon moves the waters within each of you. This is a great time of new beginnings for each of you... and for the celebration of a full year's bounty come to fruition. As the days begin to slow and become shorter and the darkness is longer, this is a time of introspection that I want each of you to think about.*

What seeds do you want to grow? What seeds do you want to become? What do you envision for each and every one of yourselves, not just for the tomorrow but for the tomorrow's of the tomorrow... and the tomorrow's of the tomorrow of the tomorrow? The key to all of this is to understand that the seeds that you were planting for these tomorrows may not always be of the physical, but they are of your Soul's tomorrow, whatever and wherever that shall be, and how it will grow.

What you need to understand is that the lessons in the information that you garner through the Native ways. The old ways, the unification with all of the life essence is the same information within the Soul that's carried forth,... that is carried forth with you, through you, and will always continue to keep you grounded and balanced, wherever you are and wherever your Soul takes you. Do any of you have a question for me? No. *Thank you,*

Thank you for coming. *Aho.* Aho. Thank you.

Red Hawk had a deep baritone voice and was having some difficulty, in the beginning, finding English words to explain his thoughts for this message. He was a tall warrior with bronze weathered skin and very stoic in posture showing honor and respect for being among us. He was gracious but firm in sharing his life message and provoking thoughts to each of us to carry forward and incorporate into our daily lives.

INCORPORATION: GATEKEEPER BAYLOT

On this evening Baylot often decided to step in and out of the incorporations to let us know what he was doing. He asked for a time check and then stated, *I'm going to get Jamar. Get Jamar.*

NINTH INCORPORATION: ELDER JAMAR

Quiet pause, and Jamar the Lemurian Elder, who resides in Telos, gently incorporated. He speaks in a quiet and monotone voice, with little influx or emotion.

Well, this has been an interesting process for me to watch. I am Jamar. I want to speak tonight about this experience for me too. I am learning through each of you. I'm learning through this experience and through the opportunity to tap into your energies and to tap into the wisdom and knowledge of each of your Spirit Guides who have been attending here.

I want you to know that I am trying to reach out to each of you if you're willing, to be able to have personal communication along with relationships with me. I am not a fearful being. I am only of the highest and the best, but I am excited to be able to share information from Lemuria to each of you, if you're interested and willing.

I can only come to you when you are in altered states. This comes from being in a sleep state, in a meditative state. This comes from being in some type of a place where you allow your conscious mind to quiet enough so that the communication can open. You can ask for me to be able to speak to you directly, such as when you're getting ready to go to sleep. Is anyone here interested in growing this relationship? Yes, yes, yes. *Wonderful! I'm so excited.* Jamar breaks into a wide grin to show his enthusiasm.

So, this is exactly what was spoken of earlier, the pebble in the pond. The first pebble goes, then the next pebble… the next pebble, and the next pebble. So, what I am going to do is… I am going to work very diligently this week to work with each and every one of you. So, I'm going to ask you for three nights. You can do it, whichever three nights that you want to do, but I'm going to ask you for three nights prior to you going to sleep that you ask me to be able to come in to provide you information and to show you the City of Telos directly. I would like to be able to do that. Would you like to go and visit the city of Telos? Yes. Yes. Yes. *Wonderful!*

The other thing I want to mention, is more than likely, I will not be by myself. I very rarely come by myself. Generally, I come with at least one other guide to be able to help you down in there to see the city for yourself. So, prior to you going to sleep, you're going to ask. You're going to request that I come in, and then you're going to think about me… right before you go to sleep.

You're going to have to keep a pen and paper by the bed, because you may or may not remember throughout the night, but it is extremely important if you wake up, and you remember where you have been, to jot down a couple of notes. If you have no recollection through the entire night, then you need to take some quiet time first thing in the morning and just start writing. Are you all familiar with the automatic writing? Yes. *Okay, you just start writing, on the three mornings after the three nights. Please give it at least ten to fifteen minutes of writing time and see what comes out. You don't have to think about the words, and which are being written down. You just start writing, or you could type, if you're if you like to type. It does not matter which way the communication goes through. Okay. Does that make sense?* Yes.

Oh, I'm excited about this! So, next week when we get together, I want to be able… I want to be able to come in and I want each of you to be able to share with me what you remember, and I will share with you what I tried to do. Okay, okay. Oh, I'm excited about this!

Is there anything else that you have as a specific question for me? No, we have a plan. I like this. I like this!

Ummm... watch for the stones this week. Stones are very important. We have Lemurian crystals and... um, watch for particular stones that may come into your world, because you may need to clasp them for additional energy. Okay. Um... so just pay attention if you're feeling drawn to one, go ahead and... and collect it. You may not have to buy it, but you may want to buy it, that's up to you. If you have the means and the desire, otherwise, it's okay. We can still communicate without the crystals, but the communication is always easier with the crystals, and it's just because it allows for that attunement of that vibration which it... just it,... It's a telephone line. This is what it allows for, not that we cannot do it without it, but it does help if that's something that you have.

So, um... with that I'm going to say blessings and, I'm very excited about this. This is going to be quite an experiment and I love experiments. So, blessings to each of you and I will be seeing you soon. Blessings. Blessings.

Jamar became very animated about the prospect of connecting with each member of the circle and expressed interest in allowing for additional visitations. He showed great emotion as he used some body language with the hands, and his voice moved out of a monotone to higher pitched influx as well as an increased speech pattern, and he used smiles. As previously stated, this is an experiment for all of us and he was eager to investigate how far this process could be augmented. As Jamar faded out, he was smiling widely and hands clapping together with anticipation.

INCORPORATION: GATEKEEPER BAYLOT

That was all of our entities, are we good with all the entities? Are we good with the timeline? This is Baylot again. Yes, we're good. *We're good. Blessings to each of you and we'll talk next week. Thank you.* Thank you. Blessings.

After Discussion

We discussed the dark visitor, and several sitters spoke about how they had called in Arch Angels, Masters, and love energies to support the room and to keep me safe during the transmission. We spoke about how the evening had transpired beginning with the God Source and Arch Angel Michael. Then the energy lowered with the Gray Tone prior to the Darkness, followed by a great cleansing from Angel Epherina. Everyone appreciated the information that was clearly explained through the Darkness. The group was laughing because so many of us had brought extra crystals and we all had some forethought of the evening.

The sitters were extremely excited about the invitation from Jamar to independently communicate with him. Everyone left with great anticipation of possibly visiting and seeing the city of Telos themselves. We discussed having crystals nearby, engaging in automatic writing, plus they were welcome to reach out with questions as needed during the week.

Closing Prayer

Heavenly Father, Thank you! Oh, Heavenly Father, Jesus Christ, any and all Light Beings, Energy Beings. We give gratitude for Your love, for Your peace for Your presence.

Thank you for Your healing energies. Thank you for Your love. Thank you for all of the gifts that you keep us around in your highest presence of all. Heavenly Father, for any and all residue is emitted, it is disappeared from the space and place and only the highest and the best is allowed to any and all who come into contact with this information, and we just ask for your loving presence around us, and to carry us forward. We ask this in Your precious name. Amen.

Session 7

Opening Prayer

Heavenly Father. Thank You. Thank you for the blessings of this day. Thank you for the blessings of these hearts who have joined together. We pray Heavenly Father that your power of protection will come and enter this room and all those in this room. Heavenly Father we pray that all the highest and the best light beings and entities will be here to carry us forth. Keep our hearts open. Keep our minds open. Keep our ears, eyes, as well as our entire energy systems, open to the enlightenment and opportunities that come forth before us. We ask this in your precious name. Amen.

Introduction

WE BEGAN THIS SESSION WITH a discussion of the visitors from the previous session. This included my personal impressions along with a group discussion after processing what had transpired.

The next portion included reviewing our homework assignments and to share any personal experiences that we may have had. We invited Elder Jamar to incorporate and asked him to provide his opinion about his experience in reaching out to each person during this past week.

Discussion

Judi

One of the first things I wanted to discuss was our unexpected visitor, Darkness that came last week. I thought about this visit, how it came to be and how surprised I was by the visitation. I thought, wait a minute, I'm doing this channeling and Baylot was up there and everything is God led. Everything was directed, guided and of my highest and best.

So, I prayed a lot during meditation about that, because I'm like... You guys are slacking! What's going on here and why would this have come to be? I really needed to get a better understanding of what had transpired, and then concern crept in about residual effects. I had a high level of concern about entering into that kind of an energy force and what may come to be at a later point in time. There were several different things that came to my mind through that reflection.

First of all, I knew was highly protected all the way through, apparently with the different surgeries that I had received with the crystals being inserted. I was operating at a higher vibration, so there cannot be anything unwanted residually attached to me. No entities can attach to me, so that is something new and different that I was not aware of. It was planned and I was a willing participant allowed for this scheduled event, and that's why I believe each of us in our own way knew different things. We prepared for the different puzzle pieces to be given. I had done an extra cleansing ahead of time. What I was specifically told was, "You cannot possibly write a book and show all these different energies without representing that energy, too", because it's true and it's real. I'm just calling it Darkness. I'm not calling it anything else to add any energy to it.

They were very clear that it was only allowed to come in for a very short specific amount of time. Realistically, from start to end, it was ninety seconds. That was from the very first huffing and puffing, to when it was totally done. I had a lot of concerns about this. This was definitely not something I ever had anticipated, ever in my wildest dreams; however, the God Source and divine beings had other ideas.

The other message I received, God Source, the first major entity that came in for the first question, followed by Arch Angel. This was to set the tone and energy level for all of us, to ensure we were all prepared for this spiritual growth process.

Then Gray Tone came in to lower the frequency, because there was no way it was going to be able to come in at all with the level of vibration that we usually operate. When Darkness actually incorporated, it was only allowed for a very short period of time and it was being monitored. This was a scheduled appointment, and so they, knew what they were doing through the lesson. What I found intriguing was that when the entity was in my space and my presence, it was burning and searing, as if it was bathed in acid. That was one of the reasons that it was so painful and growly. It was experiencing its own pain level of being in the presence of this energy level, which was encouraging for my learning. I needed to remember where there is light, there can be no fear or darkness.

Epherina, the angel, came directly afterwards. She was a very specific angel. She followed the dark entity. That is one of her main missions. She follows the dark entity, showers light all around, cleanses, and helps to equalize that vibration, to ensure that everything is clear once again.

I too, was surprised that this experience was permitted and that was my personal lesson, to prepare for the unexpected. I understand that everything was planned and of the highest intention. We all continue to evolve and move forward on this Holy path. My heart is filled with gratitude for the new knowledge and wisdom.

It was important to synthesize the week of experiences to build a foundation of the knowledge and understanding. This session was primarily focused on following up with all participants on their reflections on reaching out to Jamar and what they had experienced with their assignment during the week.

We will begin by discussing if any of the attendees were able to tap into anything with your mind and or what other communications you may have had during the homework exercise. My goal is to go around the room find out what everyone may have experienced or not. Then I want to invite Jamar to incorporate so that he may address each of you, providing clarity anything else that he feels will benefit your spiritual growth. Perhaps he will provide wisdom, knowledge, insights unique to you, that may strengthen communication and relationship building.

Oh, my efforts were rewarded with my own profound visitation. I was invited within once again and was inspired to write the beginning and the conclusion of this book. I wanted Jamar to explain what he experienced and have his perspective recorded on video. I believe it would enhance the learning of all members of this project.

REVIEW OF ATTENDEES EXPERIENCES

The next section is made of recordings of the participants. Each participant took turns speaking and sharing their homework experience. They independently tried on three separate occasions during the week to reach out to Elder Jamar asking for personal communication. Below they shared what transpired through their efforts or other significant events that happened during the week.

Homework Discussion

Annette

I didn't hear from Jamar specifically. I know I tried in meditation and I tried again in the evening over the weekend, and I did not hear from him; however, I think it was last night. I dreamed a dream that was so real, and I saw a light language just pouring out of the sky, or into my room and it was green. It was green! I saw that it seemed like forever! I got up to go to the bathroom and this is the weird part about this. As I went back to sleep, I was back in the same dream!

That's awesome! So, did you try to channel write at all? *Yes, but I got nothing.* Okay, so with your light language what do you think you were seeing? Were you seeing symbols? *It was all in symbols, but I think it was a download for a DNA activation. That's what I think it was.* Okay.

Maybe that's why I am off all day today. So, when we discussed the DNA topic, it said, *...like a blue ultraviolet kind of a light. That doesn't mean that the green isn't also.* So, kind of an emerald green color? *It was emerald green but, it seemed like it was lite up behind it, but it was an emerald green.* That's cool! Green is all healing. Arch Angel Raphael is all green healing.

That's really cool! Did you try to write down any of the symbols that you saw? *No, I couldn't remember them even, if I wanted to.* I've (Judi) got a sheet that I'm going to show you, because I did download some symbols from Lemuria. That's why I was wondering, because I didn't remember them when I saw them, but later I did. What I felt like happened, was that I went back to a space where I could see them from the side. It wasn't a front memory. It was putting myself in this space, so that I could see it on the side. Like a side-awareness memory. That is probably my best description. You may want to try that.

I could try. I do similar to that when I draw. I get half a picture and then fill in the rest. Great, let us know on that. Thank you.

Judy

So, I think at least three nights maybe four, before I would go to sleep, after I've done whatever listening to spiritual stuff, I would converse with Jamar, asking him to come in to my dreams and show me Telos or whatever information that would come from him that night.

Then I'd wake up in the morning. I wouldn't have any memory of dreams, and I would sit at the tablet for about ten minutes and a pen, but nothing ever came to me. Nothing ever came. No dreams, no nothing. Just my normal sleep, dreams, nothing outside of the normal stuff. Nothing outside of what you usually feel. Okay.

<u>Linda</u>

I had a similar experience that she had. I know he came to me, that's about it. How do you know? *Because I knew that part, I do know.* Oh. *I heard that, but what the visit was all about or anything. I don't know and I couldn't write it. It didn't come back to me.*

It may come out today, because he did say that you may be visited by him but not remember. Right. So, it may come out information today. Do you think he was by himself or did you think he was with other? *I only remember him. There may have been someone else there, it was just this brief moment that I remember.* Okay and that was just once? *Yes.* Okay.

<u>Ute</u>

I asked or invited him in at least four nights, as far as I remember. I usually don't remember dreams at all. Very rarely, so it was this time. So, it was Tuesday morning, I did that journaling, writing. What I experienced was just a very deep opening. A very deep insight of infinity… and from the void, so to say, where everything is created. The message which I drew from that is. Okay, so if I'm in a state that I can create whatever I want. So, to me, my task is what I'm working with is like… *Okay, slow down, quiet down, calm down that chatter and the fear and whatever else is there. Bring myself into the present and that is the gateway to that place. Where that was Infinity… It was just dark and vast… Empty… So, clean slate.* That is really cool.

One thing, it is okay to bring myself back into this state. So, you've never done that before? *I think I have had a couple of glimpses.* So, this was informational. *Yeah.* That's really interesting. *Yeah, I thought so too. At first, I thought… hum. I sense it more than that I see it.*

I sense the vastness. So, I get a picture in the back of my mind, a-ha! Of course, the inquisitive mind on the other hand… going back and forth. It's very, comparatively very vivid there. Like I can seem to more easily get in touch with that space, right now. Good. That's good. Growthful! Yeah. *Yeah, that fits in my path.*

You wouldn't be here, if it wasn't on your path. *That's right. That's what I thought.*

Karen

Well, I invited him in, and if he did come, the first night I'm totally unaware completely, and the rest of the time I don't feel like he did. I had dreams, but they were all more or less continuation of what I had.

The only two experiences I had that could possibly relate to being something different, is I did have this, like flash. Debbie said it might have been the thunderstorm. But I didn't go back to explain, it was a very weird. It was almost like a… almost like a burst, but it was like a pin with a head. That came out, but it was brilliant! It's that type of a flash, so it's very weird. Bam! In a split-second, it was gone. I don't know where, what, but somewhere I remember seeing that.

And then the other thing happened last night, after a dream, and everything that I wrote down and what have you. I got "Zircon 752". If anyone can relate to that, that would be awesome. My personal thought, at first, was maybe like a star or something, but I have no idea what it means, and I tried to relate it biblically, and found information to my family, which was cool. But I don't think that was what the message was. It was on the corresponding page number? *Well no.*

I went to my sister, because she does a lot of biblical work with the Bible and everything. I asked, "Does this mean anything to you?" She said she has five different Bibles and I said if you don't mind. She was explaining to me that they don't go by page number and stuff. I understand that. So, I said, "if you don't mind, can you send me a picture of the pages?" I want to read them to see if they correspond with anything that I have previously done or whatever. And in the process, one of the Bibles she opened up, had handwritten papers about my family and it happened to be on page 752! So, I think they just slipped in there as an incidental, an extra, in relation to it, because I honestly don't believe that Zircon 752 relates to that. I think it relates to something else, because of the other things have been going on.

But it's an additional affirmation. *Yeah.* You can't discard it. *Oh, no. I'm definitely not discarding it, but I don't think that was, the first intention. I think that was an extra because I was following this up. It's like, I'll slip in this type of a thing, because I'm still looking, I feel like there's more to this. I just don't know what it is.*

Those were the only two things. Like I said that one flash, I don't know where that came from, and then the fact of the Zircon 752. It just came out of nowhere! It was enough that I got it written down to remember it. So that was pretty cool.

Zircon is a gemstone. It's a drug. *I have come to find out it's a gemstone and it's a drug. I thought of a star, and I haven't followed up on it, but possibly it has some relationship to the Jehovah Witness.*

As for the star reference, whether or not you find a name doesn't mean that it isn't. Obviously, there are so many stars which we have no idea, even if they have them named, but we don't know what they are. *You should always trust your gut and follow your first instinct. It's something relating to a star, and what means. I don't know.*

It may be information that I am to receive and follow up on, because... I find it interesting that first you had a burst of light that came through. *That was several days earlier.* And then you feel like this is a star and you've got a name. So yeah, it definitely feels like those are connected.

Previous work and things that have been coming through to me. One of my messages in my work is, "you are receiving information in pieces not yet to have the whole picture." So, this is just a piece to the puzzle. Yes. *It's what I'm feeling.* Yes. It was able to burst through to break in. *Right, and due to the fact that it came now, I don't know if it relates to Jamar or not. That's why I figured I would share it. Those are the two things that I feel are significant, possibly to this; however, they may have nothing to do with this.* Okay, thank you.

Debbie

This was an adventure! Okay, Monday night I didn't do anything. I had to do some heavy-duty healing and I thought, I'm not going to try to contact anybody. So, Tuesday I thought, okay, I'm not going to necessarily try to get Jamar to come through, I'm going to ask for any Divine Being or an ancestor or maybe one of my family members. I was hoping like maybe my Dad would come, or maybe a Spirit Guide.

All of a sudden, I get "Geronimo", and it was the Native American Geronimo, and his message to me. I was lying in my bed and I have a legal pad next to me. I'm trying to write and I'm in the dark. What he said was, "Reach within yourself, down deep within yourself. Listen with your heart", and then he was gone. I couldn't get anything else. I didn't get to ask any questions. But you got a beautiful message. I said okay, that's really cool!

So, Wednesday night, I tried for Jamar. I thought, okay I was able to get a message. Somebody did come through. And I got this female, Althena, and I was told, "You are not for Jamar. You are for the Stars", and I was like, okay. That was all. They wouldn't answer questions or anything. So, I got ahold of Judi and I was told I was not for Jamar. What's going on? So, she said, it was in the morning. So she said do it again and see what you get. Do some automatic writing and see what you get.

So, in my scribbles of the night before when I first looked at it, I thought the name was Althea. And so, I said can I speak to Althea again? Would Althea come back to me? I heard, Althena! Okay, and I said do you have any messages for me? I got "Darkness, be aware of lurking danger. It hurts". So, I'm like, okay. So, I asked a question. Do I need to avoid Lemurians? I thought, well maybe I'm not supposed to. "Avoid, NO". Very cryptic, then I got a name not sure if I spelled it right, but sounded like "Tetris", "Star-beings". "Home, your home". So, I said okay then. Are Tetris healers? "Yes, they are healers. You

153

*are a healer." and again, "Listen with your heart. Be kind. Be gentle.
Have faith. Trust in the knowledge of who you are, of who you were" ...
And then, "Allow". Then it was like, done. I couldn't get anything else
out of her, or I assume it was a her.*

*So, Friday night I asked for Jamar, and I said Jamar would you please
come in? And I heard,* "No, no, no, no, no!" Laughs. You stubborn
child. You are not paying attention! You're not listening at all!
Group laughs.

*And then I got this, like a female Bethel. I said okay, thank you for
coming Bethel. Can you tell me where you are from? "Albuquerque."*
Laughs. *And I said okay. Something about… I got "Armenian". I said
okay. So maybe it was someone from Armenia, back in the whatever.
So, I said, do you have any messages or anything that you would like
to tell me? I got "oranges, pineapples, pickles". And I thought, okay.
This is going to be one of those funny ones like Judi gets. So, I was like,
okay, let's see what else I can get, please. And all of a sudden, it's like
behind my eyes, it all lit up and there was this beautiful man with the
biggest smile on his face. Smiling at me. And I said, will you please tell
me who you are? And he said "Saint Germaine". The only thing I got
from him was "Pure heart… Focus… Engage," and something about
richness of life. That was all I got from him, and then all of a sudden, I
heard this little voice. Do you remember a song called "Apples, Peaches
Pumpkin Pie", "you were young and so was I".* Laughing. *I said,
oh, no it was Bethel again.* Laughing. *I said, oh no! I just ended it.*

Well Saint Germaine is highly prominent for Lemuria, Mt.
Shasta and the city of Telos. *But I was looking for Jamar.* So,
nothing from Jamar, but you still got incredible messages.

*I don't know what Althenia had to do with Tetris. Did you google
Tetris? Is it a star system? You know what it kept giving me, no
matter how many ways I spelled it? That crazy game! I thought maybe,
Tretus. I tried all different spellings. The only thing I found was a star
system, Tetris and I got something that was a geometric, alga rhythm*

like things that have different cities and said something about the star Tetris. But it was like a place in New York and somewhere else. I don't know. I can't remember what it was. You found something. *But not specifically to do with stars.* There probably is a star named Tetris. We just don't know what all they are named.

I am not sure if Tetris is a star or a person. I just don't know, or if Althenia was telling me, or if Althenia was Lemurian or from Tetris, because they would like, tell me so much, and then it was like, done. Gone. A quick message and then be done with it. This is exceptional. That is a lot of information!

Judi

In my meditations, I had three names come through. I have no idea who they are, but that was interesting. Debra King Brown, Berry Griffin and Warren Hanley. I don't know what they are about, but they were very specific names that were given to me during my meditation. That's unusual to get... those are not like normal names. I don't know. I am very excited about the other information that came through.

What I want to do now is to move forward, tap into Jamar and move through the process, so that everyone can get their messages, and then I want to share mine.

FIRST INCORPORATION: ELDER JAMAR

We invited Elder Jamar, to please come in and to provide each of us with his impressions of what had transpired through our independent attempts in direct communication with him. He stepped in as requested.

It has been a busy week has it not? I am excited to be back here. It has been a busy week for me also. I appreciate each of you taking the time and the energy, to scribe information coming to and through, and in our communicative abilities of contacting one another.

I do want to start off by prefacing that it does take great time and energy for our energies to align to the same level, space and vibration to handle the communication and a visitation. If a person is not vibrating at the correct level, it's not in their best interest to be allowed into the city of Telos, because the vibration rate is so much higher, and it actually can damage the human cells, if they're not prepared ahead of time. Preparation ahead of time comes in many different forms. It comes from different experiences when you've been able to be in contact or different experiences that you had or experiential activities when large waves of energy come in. It also is dependent upon what your spiritual journey is... and if you are meant to have that vibration.

This part that has been a wonderful experiment for us, on our level and being able to communicate with you, and to have the opportunity to have communication with your different Spirit Guides. I know that some of you had better success than others and so I would like to speak to each of you, so that I can clarify some of the information which has taken place, and to help as we're speaking today. It also is allowing for the changing of the vibration of us to build that relationship and to bridge that level of communication better. Don't think that just because it may not have happened this last week, it will not happen. It means it may not have happened this last week, but it's still a process that you're building towards.

So first I'm going to go around the room, such as you actually had spoke... So, I'm going to go over here and speak...

Jamar to Annette

The first thing I want to say to you, Child, is that you are in the process of great downloads of information, but it's because all kinds of things have specifically opened up for you in a very short time. You've had all of this ancient knowledge and you have all of the cellular knowledge which is already within your physical system; however, it hadn't been opened and enlightened enough to be able to tap into. You have now opened it, as if a floodgate's worth of knowledge and wisdom... and then again, the light symbols, such as you just described, are being poured down into you at once. What is happening, is that your vibration was here, and now it's here, and your whole physical body is trying to assimilate it, and to find balance with what's coming into you.

And so, you may not have had the level of communication with me that you had anticipated; however, you are getting such downloads of information… that my coming in and having a specific conversation with you and bringing you into the city of Telos right now, is actually a conflict for what is scheduled to come in. So, I have to actually wait before I can come to you in a higher level of different information.

Does that make sense to you? Yes, it does thank you. *Don't think that I don't want to still have a relationship with you. Okay, but we're just going to have to pace it out a little bit differently than what was. All right. Thank you, daughter.* Thank you.

Jamar to Judy

You, child over here. One of the things I want to speak to you about is because you have such a strong Angelic relationship that's already in existence with Arch Angel Michael. The thing that happens when we are working in our energy fields and coming in and out. It's very important. It's almost like, how do I want to say this?

If you have a prior large entity that's working within your physical self, then they have the priority of being able to communicate with that person first. Does that make sense to you? Umha. *So, when I come in, I can't just come into you. To have a conversation with you is challenging, because Arch Angel Michael is a strong presence, that I actually will end up having a conversation with him, and he's going to allow what to come in. So therefore, it's not that I'm not having information and I want to talk about what was mentioned a few weeks ago.*

It was specifically mentioned… by Baylot. The information from Spirit… maybe it wasn't Baylot. I might have been mistaken on that. Anyway, the entities that are out there and that are providing guidance and information to the various beings, don't necessarily have to be there in the presence to have the message known. Do you remember that being spoken? No. *So, you can have information and guidance from your energy and that can be still filtered through someone else.* Right. *And so, maybe I'm not able to come in and to have a direct relationship with you and I can't. I can't. Arch Angel Michael has housed you, and has, has… um, and it's not a wrong thing, you are just his child. You are his essence and he fills every fiber of who you are, and as you're out doing work and guidance and information, it's just so much an extension of who he is. That is your primary energy source of information.*

So, I can feed information and guidance through Arch Angel Michael, but I cannot have specific contact with you directly. Does that make sense to you? It does. *I appreciate who you are. I think you're an incredibly loving being, and I think you would appreciate being able to visit the city of Telos. Perhaps you could speak with Arch Angel Michael and say, if you don't mind, then we could work on it together, but that would be something that we would have to work with him through.* Okay. *Blessings to you.* Blessings to you.

Jamar to Linda

You, my child… You at least remember… You remember that I came, and you knew that I came, and I'm excited that you knew that I came. So that's a wonderful thing!

I did not come alone, but I did come first and so that's why you remember seeing me first. I think what you remember the most about it, actually is the emotion, and because, what I felt when we touched souls through the energy, was just such a brilliance… and I know you are feeling this energy shift right now. Are you not? Yes, I am. *Yes, Oh, I'm so excited. Yes, because what we were able to do is we're able to go ahead and to start a communication process. Ummmm…*

I'm going to work on building that relationship. What we were able to do though for you, Child, as we actually didn't go down into the city of Telos. We met outside of the Gateway and we're in a different location, because we can be in multiple places at once. We were standing upon the Mt. Shasta, so that you could get yourself vibrationally attuned with the mountain so that we could prepare to go inside later. Does that make sense to you? Yes, it does. *Yes, it does, I know.*

Panther Meadows is a fantastic and a beautiful place that is highly energized. This is where I actually took you. I want you to spend a little bit of time going online and looking at pictures, if you can, of Panthers Meadows. It's already starting to snow, so it's changing. During the summertime, it has beautiful wildflowers and small birds that fly around. It's beautiful, even though the essence of having the snow, that does not change the vibration and the energy and the shifting of it that happens through that process.

But that's where we are starting our relationship. Okay, so if you spend more time... asking for me to come and envision where you are, then we're going to work on being able to have that greater level of communication. Okay.

Did you have anything specific you wanted to ask of me? No. *Thank you blessings.*

Jamar to Karen

I am going to go over here now. Now, you are an interesting one! I'm going to say that right off the bat. The first thing I want to say is thank you so much for all of your energy and your efforts for running the store. I know that it is all encompassing, and it is such an enormous amount of 3D energy that's required for that.

I need you to understand the value of what you are providing to your community, and it's not just the people who were coming into your store, and purchasing the stones, purchasing the sage, and going to the different classes. You have chosen to be a hub of a collector of energy and a distributor of the energy. It is a pulsing vibrating, live, place for energy to emit from. Okay. So, you also have the collection of all of the energy, which is being filtered into all of your different... you know, your crystals and all the energy beings that are coming in. So, you can envision yourself like an hourglass, I think would be a wonderful way.

All the information is being fed down and into you and then it's being expelled again out through you. So, it's not even just the people that are being touched, but it's also the energy that's coming through which also is being emitted out.

Does that make enough sense to you? Yes. *I hope I was clear enough in describing that, because, I need you to understand how critically important you are as an anchor in this area, and in this region of Florida, not just for the people, but for the presence of the space where you're located. There is water nearby that also taps into and emitting through that energy source, too.* Oh, wow. *So, I want to start off with that.*

Now, I want to tap into our relationship. And... um, I have to say this, and that's just what I'm going to say. Okay. *It's difficult to actually work into an individualized relationship with you because there's so many different components that are happening at once. You are already working with different entities for information, and for your specific purpose that you already have. My coming in and starting a relationship with you, creates white noise and chaos. It's not going to help you with growing what you need to do and what's already happening.*

So, when I tried to bridge into that information a little bit, I had a difficult time... I had a difficult time. I was able to help with sparking! I was able to help energize and to help spark in; however, that's as much as I'm able to do with you on a personal level, because you already have a number of different entities that are working with you. Your primary purpose is still to be this light pulsing place and this anchor in this region of Florida. Oh, thank you. *Okay.*

May I ask a question? *You may absolutely.* Can you give me a little more information regarding the water? You said the water source. *Do you not have water near where you are?* Um... *Is there not a river right near there, a canal? A large canal of water that runs right along there.* Somewhat near, but it more like a drainage right near me rather than actual water it's the water is a little farther off. Reed Canal has the ponds and the lakes. *Is Reed Canal not near there?* Yes, it is. I'm on Reed Canal and there are lakes and pond in the nearby parks. Reed Canal is an exchange of Halifax River, which is brackish ocean exchange at the Inlet.

So, there's connectivity. There's a connectivity, because I know that there's water. The water that is near there is absolutely connecting into the energy, which is coming from your space, because it's helping to move it much faster, through the water sources. Okay. *So, it has to be close enough by, unless you're not at the right place, but I think you're at the right place.* Okay. *I think you're at the right place.*

If it can be the lakes and the ponds? *Absolutely! You end up with a lot more surface water for the water particles within the air to be able to absorb from, and to be able to emulate.* Okay. Okay. Now I understand that better. *Any other questions?* I think that's it. Okay. Very interesting. *Alright, blessings to you, blessings to you.*

Jamar for Deb

You my Child. Deep inhale and pause. *Oh, I know we've had an interesting bout, have we not? I think we've both got our hands slapped on this one. Giggling. So, the first thing that I do want to do, is I want to go ahead and talk about your regional experience and what has transpired.*

So, part of me coming in and incorporating, and again, not understanding, the space differential of trying to work our way in. Yes. *What happened very specifically was you were beginning to morph, and your energy was beginning to morph, and so what was happening as you were also being pulled out, because you're not supposed to be a part of this energy and communication and circle of information.*

First of all, let me double check. Are you okay with the feeling right now as I'm speaking with you? It was buzzing, my head pretty hard earlier, but it's settled down now. *Okay. Power of protection. Power of protection. Power of protection. Power of protection. It's not that there's anything wrong with me or there's anything wrong with*

161

you. It's the differences. We are just on such different vibrational levels that it... it... it. Two magnets that go together, they push apart. You understand? Yes. That's what our energy, frequency energies are like. We will not ever be able to have, a direct communication together because it's... it's more like that. That pull apart of.

Okay, so now what I want to talk to you about. We did this experiment of trying for you to tap in. This was a training for you to be able to communicate better with other entities that want to speak to you, and the thing is, the information that you would be drawing from me and from the city of Telos, is just incredible worldly information. You can get that same level of worldly information from other entities that are not me, that you vibrationally attune with much better. Does that make sense to you? Yes. Okay.

So, um.... It's just about the different vibration that's all. It's not a good, bad or otherwise.

Who is Beth... Beth... Bethel? Umha... *Bethel came in. Bethel, she's of the fairy realm and um... she actually pops back in forth. She pops in and out of our entity too, so that's probably why she came to you, so that because, she's a vibration that you can attune with. You always do with all the different fairies and gnomes because that's your level of your energy. So, blessings to you.* Blessings. *Blessings to you, blessings.*

Do you have a message for Ute?

Jamar for Ute

Oh, did I go right by? I went right by! I'm so sorry! I'm so sorry. She keeps her eyes closed to keep it clean, and I just keep right on going is what is going on. Thank you for bringing it back to my attention.

Ute, I did not forget you, but I apologize you're on the backside of this. Okay. So, energies that happen to and through you. We absolutely were able to tap in, and to have beginning level communication; however, one of the things that happens... when you were going into a meditation often times, you really have preconceived ideas of what you already expect it to be. And when we're going in and we're going to have our conversation, it's going to be different than what you anticipate it to be. So, you need to allow yourself to just be in that space of. So, um…

You have the ability to be able to come into the city of Telos. You're already at a vibration that you're able to come in and to visit. That's very important. You have done enough work. You've had enough experiences that you're already vibrating on a level to be able to allow this to transpire. So, what I want you to do is, this one over here (Judi). She's got a picture she's going to go ahead and show you. And what it's a picture of is the Gateway in which she entered into the city of Telos. I want you, and I'm going to mention right off the bat, that there are actually Gatekeepers, which are located at these different gateways, and you have to build a relationship with them also. It's not that the door just plain opens up! Every time that you're going back to these visitations, you have to be allowed to go in. And each of the Gatekeepers, also can monitor what your energy level is, and where you are, and how it feels, so that they allow it to open and they feel like you're in a good space to allow you in.

It's critically important for us within the city of Telos and this is just in any city of wherever you are, that we maintain the health of our community and that can only be done by monitoring and managing the energies that are coming in, that are invited through that space! Does that make sense to you? Sure. Okay. *So, it is very, very important that, you continue to do what you're doing but, you need to meet them, and you need to prepare for that.*

When you're going in, I want to mention to you, is to visualize… Um-hum, *I know you're able to visualize well. You're able to see. You're able to feel. You're able to enter into the space. So, when you're entering into the space of… I want you to envision walking through the tubular tunnels that were made from the lava.* Um-ha-a… okay. *They're dark, but on the edges, there are lights that just will illuminate along the path. So, you're going to be walking along the hard-surfaced areas. Obviously, you're not going to be walking alone, but these are different things that will help you to prepare. So, I don't want you to give up. I want you to continue to work on it.*

The other thing is critically important. You really are more than likely, not going to remember the experience until the next morning when you start to channel write. It's very, very important! I understand you may not be able to read it, but if you can write down a few words during the night, if you have any recollection at all by the next morning time, then you can start to get a broader essence of what had transpired. Okay? Okay. Alright, wonderful. Wonderful.

Jamar and Judi Visitation

The one before you, she did have a visitation and she had quite an experience. I want to explain that on, my part, and I'm not sure if I'm going to be as detailed as she may have been. So, after I leave, she may need to fill in additional pieces… Okay, or you might actually want to have a second opinion from her, as her perspective… Okay.

A majority of this transmission is reflected within The Story Begins, chapter earlier in the book. This profound experiential event provided through this visitation to the city of Telos divinely creates the foundation for the story and guidance to unfold.

So, let me get started.

Okay. So, she had to travel up to Georgia, and this was something that was very important, and it was very, very, very important for her to be able to travel there, because it was going to… She needed to be in a different environmental energy to be able to finish this communication of information. That is something that is real! By going to different locations, you get different feelings of energy and vibrations of energy, that will help you for connectivity. Okay. So that's just something that's an important side note. Okay.

So, Tuesday, she'd driven during the day, to get there. She had her Lemurian crystals and slept. It was a cabin, a small cabin, and she slept upstairs in the triangle part. That was a key part of her being able to have this additional level of information because her physical space was located in a triangle and she was up in the second story of it. All of that helped too. So, her adventure began, because... well alright... I have to go ahead and say.

Her adventure began because she went to the same Gateway that she had entered previously and was met by the same Gatekeeper who allowed her to enter. She went in by herself and along with me. I was the only one to meet her and to greet her. There was no need for anyone else. It's not that we actually had planned what was going to happen. she and I did not have the communication ahead of time; however, because I have had the opportunity to come in and to meet all of you, and to have experiences with each of you. I wanted to invite her down and to be able to meet other Beings besides myself. So, this was the planned intent.

So, it was a scheduled activity on our part of inviting her in that time. We walked through the different lava tunnels, that are specifically lit just inside, because light comes from the different crystals, so it doesn't matter, and so we continued down. We walked quite a way. I don't know how far... yours and mine... I don't know, anyway.

I was taking her to the college. I was very excited that we had this already scheduled! We walked along and the city opened up, and then we went over to where the college was located. And so, the college building itself, is made of white marble, primarily. There are six pillars across the front. We walked up about probably twenty steps or so. There's a large double door. Now our doors... this is a very large structure and they are at least two stories in height for the doors... I'm going to say twenty-five feet tall in your... measuring part of it... Very large,... ahhh, what do you call them... iron,... iron loops to hold, that they would open up, and the top part of the building,... and again this is a very large building, and triangular.

As we step inside, it's primarily white marble, but it's not just white, because it also has speckles of crushed other stones in the marble, so that were able to vibrate all the way around with information that's coming from all these different crushed stones. That helps us with our communication and information and being able to understand things. Now, the hallway is very wide. And... um the plan is to visit this specific gathering that, I've already arranged ahead of time for her to come and visit. So, as we're walking down the hall, there are doors on each side of the hallway. Above each of the different doors is another triangle with different symbols in them. These are the different doors to classrooms, where the students attend, so that they can learn about the various subjects and information that's along the way. We walk until we get to the end of the hallway, which is fairly lengthy... I don't know... I don't know how far it is to the other end of the hall. There are... double doors. They're iridescent, clear glass with... um, you can't see through... opaque... opaque is the word.

This is our meeting room... Auditorium of such. Okay. The thing that you need to understand is... this college is... um. It's not for thousands of people at once. This is a small University, and so there are probably a thousand students in total who attend here. We don't have a large population of youth coming up, because again, repopulation is chosen. We have such very long lifetimes. We don't have large classes coming through at the same time. Does that make sense to you? Yes. Okay.

Alright so let me continue. We enter the room, and there is a large oval table and it has about thirty seats that are around it. It's in a large rectangular-shaped room. Again it opens up and it's two stories high, so it's very high, and there are three rows of seating, which are along the sides and,... um, there's no one in the seats when he first walks in, but there's thirty different people. They're my colleagues. They're my friends. They're who I commune with. They're different educators. They're different important people in our community of Telos, because they want to understand what I've been doing. I've been coming back, and I've been explaining what I've been doing and how I've been meeting each of you, and your Spirit Guides and having the opportunity to listen to the channeling, which is taking place; however, they have not had this opportunity and they are very excited and eager to be able to participate... to become a participant of this particular, um... what we're doing... this experiment, and also, this information which is going to be relayed in book format, which will be distributed out into the world. They all were very eager and excited to become one with.

So, as we're gathering together and starting, the thing that I need to talk about is the communication... Okay, because now that she is in with us. Everyone is wearing formal whites because this is quite an affair... and um,... she's dressed in her formal whites also, because we all understand the importance and significance and the respect of this opportunity for each of us to be there as one. The communication is all done telepathically. No one has to speak; however, we choose to just speak in English, so that it's familiar with her ear, even though her thoughts are being read, and she can also understand our communication. It's a buzz sound. Jamar points to Deb and chuckles. *I had to point that back out, so you could hear that same level of buzz of communication.*

As we're coming in and... and just starting.... and again there's males, females... it doesn't matter, what age they are,... They're all kinds of gathered people of different levels of,... of importance of interest in this. Then the students start to filter in from their instructors, and they fill up the three rows of seating behind. The reason why this is done is, this is our way of training the next level of our leaders, is to invite them in, to be participants of,... important gatherings of information, so they can understand how we are operating,...learning and inviting them to be part of that learning process, first-hand.

What we have decided to... speak in English. First of all, for Judi to be able to understand, and secondly, it's really good practice for all of the students to be able to hear the English firsthand... Everyone can understand any language, all they have to do is vibrate into that language and then they understand what is being said.

So as a group, all got together, and we all sat down. I walked Judi over to the head of the table, and she sat beside me at the head of the table. As we all sat; the room quieted. I stood first, and welcomed everyone there, and explained who she was. The first thing that I did was explain to everyone what we were doing! How, I had actually met Judi when she had come out to California, and I was channeling with her ahead of time and to help call her in her Soul, to be able to come and to start this communication process.

Everyone needs to understand… All of our people, need to understand, that when they start emitting… the calling in, they're going to tap into other entities who will come. They don't necessarily know that. That is something that has to be taught through the process. So, I explained that whole process.

Then I talked about how I was invited in, and the channeling which was taking place as background. Then I had the opportunity to introduce Judi. She was really excited to have the opportunity to be invited in, to meet everyone. She stood up and began speaking in English. She didn't have to speak. She could have just thought, but it's okay, she continued to do what she was doing. She told her story, of her faith and, just growing, and how everything came to be. She spoke about the different surgery that she had experienced visiting John of God in Brazil. The different surgery, when she was invited to the city of Telos in May, and again to be channeling all of these different Entities that are coming through.

She went through her history quite a bit and then… everyone wanted to see and to understand what was happening in the channeling. A large screen came down. Now this is an interesting part… and I am going to say it in the way that she would have explained it. Okay, because, what we're able to do is, we're able to visualize and to feel any and all of whatever has transpired. And it doesn't matter. Time doesn't matter.

We… projected the different sessions, which have been held together with this particular group, and everyone in attendance can actually see and feel the different incorporations which were taking place within her physical body at the same time. I understand that you have met for a number of hours; however, it does not take us a number of hours to go through that information, which was being transferred to each of us who were there. We were able to accept that information very quickly through the process. Every one of the students were able to feel, understand, and experience each of these different incorporations. Her Spirit Guide relayed the information to all of us. We were so excited to be able to feel, to know and to participate with this wisdom and knowledge, first-hand! Jamar was so emphatic and excited about this and clearly relayed this through his speech influx and body language. Pure joy and delight.

So, we were able to gift her with the book of all information. What a better way possibly, of being able to tell the story, is to be able to tell that story of sharing, such that was just done with all of these students? It's not every person who is going to read this book, but a selected student, to learn and garner information, to the betterment of themselves their relationships and, and who they become? So that's how the book came to be into full fruition.

She spoke for her amount of time. Once it was over, everyone was just so delighted and honored to be a firsthand participant of all of the information, which has been gathered from all of the Entities that have come through this visit! After she was done speaking, I thanked her and there really were not many questions, because people really didn't have that much curiosity. They just wanted to be able to understand and to become one with her.

Now, the part that's really spectacular about this whole adventure! We asked her to be a key person to communicate with us on a regular basis. The part that's really funny is that she just thought that was unbelievable that she would've been one who was chosen to be of a representative of mankind, because certainly there are many more that are highly educated and have different information, but it's because of her heart.

It's because of her heart. She is choosing to open herself to whatever adventure will come to be. So, at the end, everyone was just a buzz, but we were not speaking in English anymore and we were just joyfully excited, because it was very interesting that so many of our beings have had different communications with the different entities such as you, but there were so many more that we have not had contact with, and we got a different perspective. They were speaking to the human race instead of to the Lemurians. It was very different from what you are receiving for information than what we receive. Does that make sense to you? Yes.

That is what happened and how the meeting wrapped up. We invited her to come back again at another time. The other thing that I know, she worked diligently to copy the different symbols, which she saw in different places. She was not as fortunate as you to get full downloads of them. She was just looking around and trying to see the different symbols and get some kind of an understanding as to what the various symbols meant in our language, because we do use symbols all over the universe. Symbols are the easiest way to communicate, because generally they pulse like light pulses you know, and vibrate.

So, that is most of her experience. Then she went back. I think she was just super excited to pull the book together. I'm really excited too! I can't thank each of you enough for choosing to come and to support this process and to allow this information to take place! So, does anybody have any specific questions or are we good?

Audience Question

I have a question that I don't know if you can answer. *Okay.*

You said something about Judi having to go to go to Georgia specifically to get the information. There that was a better location. I have a strong urge to go to Montana. Do you know if that's a reason I am to go out there? *This is the thing, when you feel those urges and pulls to go to different locations, once you align with the vibration of that space it's much easier for the communication to take place of whatever it is that needs to transpire.*

Does that make sense? Yes. *It's not that it can't happen where you are, but it's much more difficult for it to happen. If you take action, you have held up your end of the bargain. Why should they continue to reach out to you if you won't even put in anything either?* Um-ha... *Does that make sense to you?*

Well, I'll try to get out there. *And so, when you know you're supposed to, then you open yourself to it, and it will. It will happen. Just allow it to transpire and be prepared to go.* Okay. *Okay.* Fair enough. Thank you. *Yeah, ah… maybe July,… maybe July,… is the timeline on that.*

Anyone else have anything? Okay. I understand this is your last one. I know you're going to catch up next month for two more, just to tie up any loose ends, and receive additional information... Additional things that you feel you may want to have for information is what will transpire. So, thank you. Thank you.

Thank you. Thank you. Blessings. Blessings. *Blessings to each of you.*

Jamar was very enthused to have channeled for such a long period of time, as over an hour had passed. He was amazingly comfortable and during this time his speech became more relaxed. This was noted through his tone. His energy flowed rapidly, and his emotions were clearly visible.

SECOND INCORPORATION: GATEKEEPER BAYLOT

Baylot incorporated in quickly. He was checking in with the group and eager to have an opportunity to speak once again. He wanted to quickly recap where we were as we were completing our primary sessions and would be breaking for a few weeks then return for any necessary follow up.

I want to speak too. This is Baylot. I almost thought I wasn't going to have an opportunity to, and I just want to say thank you to each of you. I really appreciate being able to have an audience or a voice to be heard too.

I also want to remind you, that you were visited by a number of different entities, but the line that still awaits outside that gazebo is enormous, and her line is not any different from your line,... or your line,... or your line. You each have all kinds of guidance waiting to be heard through your different Spirit Guides and through different energy sources that you need to provide you with specific guidance going forward. So, I ask of you to continue to keep your lines of communication open, your hearts open, and your minds open. Certainly, keep your eyes and your third eye open for the information that's coming back from the universe and the guidance.

So, thank you to each of you and blessings, blessings, blessings. Thank you. Blessings.

The channeling session with Jamar and Baylot ended. It was noted that this was the longest period of time that I remained in a single entity trance. The focus and questions were then brought back to me, so that I could take time to explain my impressions and memories of what had transpired for this incredible visitation.

Judi's Visitation

I acclimated myself back to the present and recounted my observations of what transpired. I was blown away when I woke up, I started writing, because all this information was flowing out. I was so energized! Information shared with the group is reflected in The Story Begins, Jamar's rendition of events and available for personal viewing on the video recordings. Additional thoughts are noted below.

I remember that I walked in and Jamar... I had not known I would be going to the University was very gentlemanly, and he opened the door for me. Everyone is taller. Their faces are luminous with color, and had a sheen and a sparkle, almost metallic silver and gold sparkle in their skin and they were beautiful -- drop dead beautiful... Longer arms and all wearing flowing... The women were all wearing flowing... Roman-style robes with satin or silk edging. The women had really beautiful jewelry of large stones and of gold, adorned nicely... with hair jewelry and all were beautifully dressed.

They were all super friendly. I could hear the buzzing. I could hear their thoughts. I could hear their joy. I could hear their curiosity. I could, I could feel their questions while they're watching the video and while the information was being relayed. I could know and understand what they were feeling and thinking and the curiosity, and the excitement. I thought it was so incredibly spectacular that their race would invite in the students to be part of this large collective of leaders so that the students could really learn firsthand about it, and how they operate. I thought that was process was impressive and great planning.

The passage of time was ridiculous, because it was just really fast. It wasn't hours and hours and hours. You know we've had hours and hours of video time and meeting times and it was, it just went through. And when that screen came down and it's playing, they could feel everything from me. They could feel all of my incorporations. They knew my thoughts; they could feel the Entities information. I think they could get more from the incorporation than I had, because they had different knowledge and information of the different Entities than I did. I was like a recorder of sorts by just allowing the essence and information to come through. Where they have different knowledge of them to be able to process what else this means, so that was different.

I remember thinking... look around and try to recall the details of the environment. What was the room like? Were there windows? I still can't figure out if there were really windows or not. It didn't matter. It was just ... they were all just so loving and so accepting and so excited that I was there, and it was something that I, kept thinking about. I couldn't imagine, Jamar coming to America, Earth being treated that way. We never would have treated them that way.

Audience Question

Were there only Telosian people, and you from the upper world? *I was the only person from the upper world in attendance. I was invited to share about this, what we're doing, the importance of what we're doing, and all of these different channelings -- crazy amazing! Never could I have possibly ever have contemplated that, but the part that was amazingly beautiful about it was the book. This story of going down there, teaching and being introduced to all these*

Telosian students has purpose. The channeling is the center of the book and then it closes out with my leaving. So that's the ending of the book.

So, the Telosians were seeking you to come and teach them about our world? Nodding head yes. *Our world and what we're doing, and the channeling that is happening of it. Is that not just crazy?*

So, this has just been such an incredible experience for me, and I know each of you have been part of my experiment. We said when we started this, that it is what it was going to be, an experiment. But it wasn't even ours. This truly was led with the highest of intentions to come to fruition and all of these other Entities have a voice.

I showed the group a sheet of the geometric shapes that I recreated after the visit. I had seen these symbols over the doorways of the various rooms along the hallway in the college. A copy of these symbols can be found in the Resources Section at the end of the book. I also showed the group a copy of the photo that I had taken of the gateway that I had entered through to go and visit the city of Telos.

After Discussion

I knew I had seen the some of the symbols over the doors in the college, but not all of the symbols made sense as doorway markers. I received information each of the four nights while I was visiting the mountains in Georgia. I believed that the reason why I continued to receive information so readily was because of my physical location of being in the mountains, surrounded by a rich mineral base and sleeping upstairs within a triangular space.

We spoke about similarities to other symbols. Some shapes look like runes and other symbols that are identified and documented. An image of these symbols can be found in the Resources & Images. I clearly reminded the group that during this time I had intentionally removed myself from outside influences of reading, online investigations, gatherings or other information to allow myself to remain an open and unbiased channel for this process. I have planned to return after completion of this text and create a resource area. Research was done later to investigate similarities to names, locations and referenced information. This can be found in the Additional Resources section which is located at the end of the book.

Closing prayer

Heavenly Father. Thank you. Thank you for the blessings of this day. Thank you, Heavenly Father, for all the guidance, the information, the wisdom, the knowledge, the strength and the purity that you allow to fill our hearts.

Help us to continue to go forth each and every day, with You guiding us, as well as providing us with wisdom and with peace. Help us to share Your love and light with all. Thank you, Heavenly Father, so much for choosing each of us to participate in this experience --- this incredible, worldwide, universal enlightening experience.

We ask this in your precious name. Amen.

Session 8

Opening Prayer

Heavenly Father Thank You. Thank you for the blessings of this day. Thank you for each of the hearts who have united here together. Heavenly Father we celebrate this angelic day, 11/11. We welcome in the angels. We welcome in the masters. We welcome in all universal light beings into this space. Lift our hearts and open our eyes to all that is and will be. We ask this in your precious name. Amen.

Introduction

AS WE WERE PRAYING DURING the opening, we could all feel a great surge of energy flowing into and through each of us, which created chills throughout the circle. The power of the day was highly evident by the date and enhanced by a full moon, that was rising and seen by many on the drive to our gathering.

We had originally scheduled seven sessions and then decided to add two more so that we could ensure that all necessary information was captured as desired by the Entities and provide closure to the circle participants. Two weeks passed since we last met.

I have reviewed all of the transcripts of the audio recordings and will send copies to each of what you experienced in your Lemurian communication. You also will receive what Jamar provided you for your answers. You will be getting that in writing, as soon as I review them once again. The information communicated and the level of energy that the entities have shared with each of you is amazing!

It is very important to continually monitor and evaluate your spiritual growth. How you are processing, feeling and relating in the world around you? Each person works independently, as well as together as a group. Both activities directly impact your development, which is expanding. Therefore, it is essential to note changes, ask questions about areas you are not familiar, and most importantly, discuss if you are personally experiencing anything unusual or other noteworthy events. I asked each participant: *Did anything different happen? Have you had any additional contact or received any information?*

Linda

Judi asked, I know you were asked to go and to spend some time in Panther Meadows, to try to see what else you could envision. I also know you bought a Lemurian crystal. Do you feel like you have had any additional communication?

I did my first channel writing, because I keep going back and trying to speak with Jamar in the Panther Meadows. I am not ready to go down there yet. Awesome! And yes, I got a Lemurian crystal. I know that he has come back to me. I have been blocked this past week, but I know he has been there. I now just have to work on what I was told or given. It was a big surprise!

Ute

I have called on Jamar. Dreams have become a little bit clearer. I usually forget everything right away. I have felt a lot of confusion again since we talked. I am being guided into more purification.

Do you feel like the weekly classes were helpful to keep you more grounded, and moving along your spiritual path? *I would not say more grounded. I would say – let go of that heaviness.* So that you are more spiritually connected? *Yes, ever since I had that green selenite. It has been more profound. I could feel it more.*

I had some other work done that fit in, and I am moving one day at a time, and willing to open up and to hear what I am told. And believing that is the truth of what you are hearing. That's the other part that is such a challenge. *Yes. It is. Especially with my mind, left brain and the people that are surrounding me.* Quieting your mind, is important.

It is more so about feeling the environment and the energy of the people who are around me. On the mind level, I am usually not aware of that higher energy until afterwards. Here I feel it more while I am here. I feel like the energy is cleansing and shedding all the old stuff. That is good. *I was very happy to see the vivid images of this guided meditation.* That is great news. *You just feel it.* Yes, it is an experiential event. It is the same with these classes.

Karen

I have been journaling and received some messages that I can't understand at all, and others I am still trying to decipher. I'm just trying to figure it out. I have not reached anyone specifically. I have been having very vivid dreams. That is very unusual. Once I even woke up several times and went back to sleep and was able to remember in the morning. So, you have experienced increased communication? They are working very hard to make sure you remember. *Yes.*

Deb

The fairy. Bethel. *You said she must be the fairy. I will be doing things and then I will hear musical ditties. When I bring them up, I realize they have to do with something. When speaking with others, I realize that they are messages of information. The challenge is understanding whether or not the message for me or for someone else. I am hearing songs for messages.* That is great, everyone has their own personal language of communication. *That is all new.* That's great progress. *Yes.*

Open Forum

The plan for the evening was an open forum. I would incorporate and call in Baylot and ask him to see who would like to provide the greatest topic insights. Baylot has so enjoyed having a voice, as have the other entities, and I had not thought of that before. We will call in Jamar also so that he can provide any information that he deems appropriate.

FIRST INCORPORATION: GATEKEEPER BAYLOT

Hello. Hello. Hello everyone. It has been far too long! How are you this evening? Good. Wonderful. Wonderful. We have been busy here too. I know time passes, as you think it does, but we all have got things to do to keep ourselves busy. So how can I help you this evening?*

First, we would like to know if you have anything to share with us, and then when you are finished, would you see if there's anyone else who would like to speak with us please?

I would like to talk about many different things. One of the things I want to speak about is the importance of valuing your Spirit Guides. I want to reiterate to you one more time, that your Spirit Guides chose you. Their mission is aligned with your mission. I cannot begin to tell you how delighted I am that my charge has finally come to this space where we are today, and allows me a voice that can be seen and heard, beyond the spirit world… into the physical world by all men and women… and children… and other entities… and Beings. It also is an opportunity to go into print… and go on that internet,… and then its world,… you know, so people have an opportunity to feel that vibration… and to be introduced to something new… and special… and powerful, too. It is internal knowledge… and wisdom… and insight. We are here to help you to connect the dots. We're here to be your barometers of when you go into rooms to feel things and to understand when a place is safe or not… and to help you understand things that are beyond what your mind understands,… When you come into contact which other human beings with like-minded Spirit Guides, you get a great deal more of information and guidance. It just naturally occurs… and our wisdom can easily be sent to and through each of you at a later time. We now have learned how to interact directly with you, as a Light Being.

Do you understand what I'm saying? Yes. Wonderful… Wonderful… So again, I just want to just say thank you to your Spirit Guide and all those who are working so diligently for you. Okay… let's see… I will look behind me. There are so many that are waiting. I'm not sure what we're going to do afterwards when you stop meeting. I don't know if you can do that! I don't know if she can do that, because the voices still need to be heard. We will have to figure that out. Okay. I'm going to see who has the best message for you this day. I have a feeling it maybe an angel. It's an angel day, don't you know! Blessings to you, blessings to you. I'll be back later.

SECOND INCORPORATION: ARCH ANGEL AZRAEL

A soft gentle cloud like female entity slowly settled in and shifted the energy for this incorporation. Her presence filled the room with golden, white and sparkles, her face and broad smile beamed with love and happiness. She spoke in almost a whisper with her loving words cascading around each of us, providing peace, love and great joy within her entire presence.

I'm stepping in. Good evening. Azrael is who I am. Have you each heard of me? Yes. *I am so glad that you would have. I want you to feel my presence. Take a moment and notice the different shifting that's happening in the energy, all around you. Can you feel the sparkles that are glowing to and through all of you, and within this space? Wonderful!* During this portion, Azrael was slowly and gently waving her arms to build the energy for exchange as if preparing for flight.

181

I want to talk about the Angels and our missions in life. I want you to know that I never was a human person. I have always been of the Angelic Realm. I want you to know the joy and peace that I get each and every day for working with and talking to and being a part of each of your lives. I can never be asked of too much. The more that is asked of us, the more we grow to become. Do you understand what I am saying? Yes. The more that you ask of us, the more that we grow and become! During this portion, she opened her arms very wide in a circular expanding motion as if sending out great waves of love and embracing all life.

It is the same with the Universe-- all universes, all life, all entities. The more that you allow your heart to grow the larger the love can only be! The face beamed with pure rapture. *There are no limits, only eternity! Is that not such a glorious thing to learn of? Yes. I know. Let me think. I would like to gift each of you with a message upon this day, too. This is a very special 11/11 angelic day. Do you often see the one ones?* Um-ha,... *Ahhh! Know this is our way of communicating. It is like ringing the bell... Ding-dong, Avon calling!* Laughing at joke. *Ding-dong, Angels calling!... 11/11. It is to remind your heart and soul that you're not alone... That we are always around and showering love to and through each of you. Welcome us in. Ask us to join you. Allow us to carry your burdens and provide you with opportunities and new abilities to master any challenge that may be facing you. Ask! Ask us for the wisdom and the knowledge to educate you... and for joy to carry your heart, too.*

So, upon this day, my message to each of you... is to dance! When was the last time that you allowed your heart and your feet to unite as one? Dancing is glorious gift, when the mind gets shut off and you allow the music and pure grace to unite the two... to carry you into a completely joyful space. When have you ever seen an unhappy dancer? I don't think it is even possible, because one must release that whole portion of thinking of worry and hurry, to truly allow your body to go with the flow. The vibrations of the music go in complete synchronicity with the self. It's a beautiful blending of unity. So, I challenge each of you to go forth, and to allow your hearts and souls to dance. Blessings to each of you. I must allow the next one to come in. Blessings. Goodbye. Blessings.

Azrael spoke with a formal dialect, perhaps with a European accent, where the long "o" sounds were easily detected. The presence was just so bright and glowing. She used many hand gestures to accentuate her thoughts and to softly clarify the feeling that was enveloped with her message. The room vibrated with acceptance and such great love for each of us as she spoke to us and then gently floated away with her exit.

THIRD INCORPORATION: GOD SOURCE

Azrael had elevated the energies to a very high frequency. The energy in the room remained highly charged, therefore with a few short hand rubbings and a deep inhale the God Source swiftly moved in and incorporated with a large and loving smile that illuminated his presence.

Ahhh,… my daughters,

My sons and daughters and mothers and fathers and children and brothers and sisters too… It is the I… It is the I AM. It is the mighty. The ALL Mighty… the God Source. Whatever you want to call me… Abba… It does not matter… It is I.

I have laid it upon the heart to talk about some things in the human experience you may not understand. When you are getting ready to go to sleep, and your mind begins to quiet, you will often see, feel and experience many different things which are taking place. You may not understand what these are, but they are very universal to all humankind. It does absolutely change and grow as does your spiritualism… and the growth of your faith and your belief… and your personal commitment to understanding more.

Things will begin when one may see the white brilliant light that is within the Third Eye. Some will see this brilliant white light and they will follow the light to help them find the space of peace and sleep. They do not know that they are actually traveling down this white light of enlightenment… and information… and education. That is where the white light leads. It's always safe, and it always will bring you back, to the perfect self of who you are. You may not remember all that transpires within the dream time sleep. You do not need to. This is the busiest time of your life.

So much happens during your nighttime hours, when you allow your consciousness to rest... so that the sub-consciousness can come to its full life... and growth... and potential,... and expansion. This is why... when you are getting ready to go to sleep... if you're thinking, concerned and worried about a situation. Then the next morning, you happen to wake up with a brilliant idea on how to think about the situation differently. It's because We,... Me,... as the God Source... and all other Entities are working together to unite... and to bring information... and guidance to you... that will be of your highest and best good.

The other things people see, when they are getting ready to go to sleep,... is they will see many sparkles of light,... that may be silver,... it may be gold,... it may be white... and perhaps they are shooting in and all around. This is actually when you're traveling to another dimension. You're traveling through the light rays and the beams of consciousness to the next space and place. This is almost like a glorified light show which takes place,... and it allows you to be able to relax,... moving through and seeing all of these brilliant lights,... just helps to shower and to settle any unease and rest,... and allows for the soul to elevate.

Often people will see faces and images and shadows. They are such a fleeting second. Sometimes, they're brilliant and bold and directly before them and then they wonder, who is that soul? Other times, they are just clips, and shadows and perhaps just a corner portion of a face. The nose and an eye or the mouth and a chin... or perhaps it's the side... or the hair that goes with just an eye. I want you to know that these images are of the soul families who you each are affiliated. These are the energy entities who you have spent many lifetimes, that help you to grow and to develop to become the very best that you can be. This includes ancestors. This includes Beings, who will become and be born into your life circle once again. This includes animal spirits who have gifted you with such love during your lifetime, who come back again to you... in another form of an additional four-legged or two-legged.

It is the same with the great loved ones in your lives. Watch for them to return again, once again, in another form to you. You must understand, the reason why sometimes they look so fragmented, is because a portion of their Soul has already been reincorporated somewhere else. Again, a portion of the Soul can also be in the ethers. It is the same with each of your Souls. You have each come and gone many times, and therefore, there are many fragments of your Soul. You can see the fragments of your own Soul, within those faces that come. They are not to be feared. They are there to gift you with guidance and love... peace,... wisdom,... knowledge... and acceptance. Sometimes you will see the faces of those who will be coming into your life, soon. They will be providing new and something that you need within you too.

You can ask to see the faces. You can ask to see the loved ones who have passed. If you request information and guidance from them, they will come through your nighttime dreams. Other times, they are just checking in on you, just to send you love... and peace. What a beautiful gift from your Soul family!

Another thing that you may see when you are getting ready to go to sleep are mandalas. You will see very intricate symbols. Some are very complex geometric shapes and designs. They are designed perfectly. They are always in existence. The difference is, you, my child, are changing your vibrational attunement and alignment to be able to understand intricacies of these different symbols.

This is where the monks have spent much time, creating these mandalas. It does take time to create them; however, great wisdom and knowledge are gifted to each of the creators, too. As you take the time to draw what you're seeing, then you are calling in that alignment, that attunement, and that vibration of the higher elevation. This will help to lift you up in your soul journey in this lifetime. They come in all colors, all shapes all sizes, all designs. Sometimes it looks as if it were a kaleidoscope. You know, the thing you turn with the different colors and all the different shapes that come to be. Yes.

Where do you think that idea came from? It was others, far from the beginning of time, have known about. These incredibly beautiful designs. You're able to look into them and see the universal designs of all life -- the light grids, and how life is formed. Everything is created through geometric patterns... through DNA coordination... calculation and vibration. Everything is! When you allow your consciousness to quiet, your sub-consciousness will emerge and be birthed, and to truly grasp and to call in, then you are able to see things differently. There are many things that can happen during the nighttime hours of peace and sleep.

You can travel. You can astrally project your spiritual body from the physical body, and you can go anywhere. You are safely tethered, so you will never be disconnected from where you go; however, you're allowed to visit all entities, and planets. You can visit Heaven. You can visit the angels. You can visit loved ones who are many miles away, to check in on them. Some people learn to do this during the day hours, not just during the night, because, they've been able to train their physical body and their consciousness to go into an altered place, therefore allowing for the sub-consciousness to be able to travel this way.

Each of you who are sitting here are growing and expanding, as you are choosing to. Learn and to be and to feel. You can develop far beyond what you really could ever imagined, because you cannot imagine what will come to be. We can't ever know it either, because it is continually changing, expanding and growing! Is that just not the most glorious gift of all?

The gift of knowing that you cannot know. It is all a surprise! It is all love, peace, grace and perfectness, and more of what your limited mind can possibly imagine, if you allow it to become. Stop being the guardian of gloom and doom within your lives. Let the barriers fall away, and only allow for pure grace, and peace to light your way… and to all those around you!

Well, my sons and daughters, I think this is good information for each of you. You can practice by taking notes beside the bedside too and praying for more wisdom and knowledge. Learning from the cycles too.

So, blessings sons and daughters. Blessings, blessings. Did anyone have a question before I go? No. Wonderful, blessings, blessings to each of you. Blessings.

Words cannot adequately describe this beautiful transmission of great wisdom and specific techniques that we each can practice to intentionally expand our own level of consciousness and life purpose. It was such a gentle, peaceful message and the God Source specifically mentioned sons and daughters to allow for those who would later be watching or reading and were not currently present within the room.

INCORPORATION: GATEKEEPER BAYLOT

Time check. Okay, so I will go. Time passes so quickly there. It does pass so quickly there. Okay. We barely get started and we must keep going. Okay, Jamar. Correct? Yes.

Did you want anything specific of Jamar this evening? Just whatever he feels is important for us to hear. *Okay. I feel the Lemurian crystals in the room.*

I had preset four Lemurian crystals in the center of the floor to assist in aligning the energies. Crystals are well known to allow for changes to the surrounding energies and elevating the frequency. This was set to support whatever would transpire. Baylot was gleeful, bouncing, and he could feel their vibrations and was smiling and chuckling with delight upon his departure.

FOURTH INCORPORATION: ELDER JAMAR

The energy settled as I inhaled deeply. Lemurian Elder Jamar from Telos incorporated. His tone of voice was more fluid and the emotional dialect adjustments made last session were still audible. Both of our energies were developing through our frequent visits.

Hello daughters! Hello. Hello. *Hello. Oh my! Oh my, I love the feel of our crystals in the room!* Jamar, shrugging his shoulders as if experiencing an energy shiver. *Oh, the vibration… You do notice the difference, do you not?… Maybe, maybe not. It might not be in your conscious level, and still your subconscious.*

You over here. A wave of hand towards Deb. *Are you feeling okay?*

You're good? Good. I know I worry about you. I worry about my vibration and you. No. No. No. They say no! It's really okay. It's just because you are working with different Beings besides me. And they are concerned about the conflict of energy. It's just a different vibrational rate, that's all. Okay. It's not good or bad. It's a different vibrational rate and if I interfere, then that is going to cause chaos for them and they're working very diligently with you first. So, I need to wait my turn, or I guess I'm not even allowed this life. That's okay. You still are here. Thank you. You're welcome.

I think I want to follow up with each of you about what I have been doing the last two weeks with each of you, too. Would you like that? Yes please. *Wonderful!*

Jamar to Deb:

Well, I guess I already started over here. So, I'll keep going this way. Miss Deb, I greatly appreciate the woman that you are and the work that you're doing. I may not be able to directly influence you, but as we've discussed before, I am allowed to work with other Beings, and Etherina,... Epherina,... no,... Althenia,... uh oh... She's going to yell at me. Althenia. Yes. Althenia, that's what it is.

So, she is from the Star System Alkazeria, and that is the star system that is working with you at this time. Thank you. *I can communicate with her, and that star system is a very interesting star system. Blue is their primary light, and most everything operates off of that blue vibrational light. Okay. Okay. So, blessings to you.* Thank you.

Jamar to Karen:

Okay, you over here. I know you're a do, do, do, do, go, go, go, go... and you're having a hard time! I have been working with you, but I have been working more so with your store.

What I am doing is, I am pulling my vibrational energy into that space, to help accentuate the energy that's beaconing out into the world.

You may not necessarily see and feel me, but I am absolutely there and working with you. Thank you. *You're welcome.*

I think the one before you are going to come and start doing some classes there within the next year and perhaps, I can speak there too. That would be good, would it not? Sure. *I think so too. Alright.*

Did you have any specific questions for me? No, you caught me off guard. *Oh, alright then. Okay.* This was great. *Do you have Lemurian crystals?* Absolutely. *You do have Lemurian Crystals at the store. Yes. I know you do. And I just want you to know that what we're doing,… is we are actually energizing them much more directly, and so people who want to know and to feel are going to be called to your crystals.* Okay. Thank you. *Okay. Blessings to you daughter.*

Jamar to Ute:

You my child. I am not going to pass by. Chuckling. *We have been working diligently in your consciousness, not your sub-consciousness. Your awareness is where I'm to work with you, child. So, have you spent any time really thinking about the city of Telos? Read any books… or have you done any research at all?* Not much. *Okay.*

This is an opportunity for you to better understand. Do you feel like this is a time in your life that you would like to learn more about this? Yes. *Wonderful. Wonderful. There is a great series of books that are about the City of Telos. And so um… it does share a lot of good information, that just helps you to think beyond and a little bit differently,… and more than what you may have before. The internet also is a good place. There's a lot of different people who do channel various Lemurians, and therefore, you may want to go to that YouTube video and or just do the Google search and you can do "Channel messages from Lemuria", and see what comes up.*

You may be able to find a better connection with some of those too. Just to help. Once you start tapping in, it is all about gathering light balls of information, and you're going to gather it from many different places, and all of those different places help to grow your knowledge base and your light essence. Therefore, it helps to change your vibrational rate, so we can communicate on a better basis. Sounds good. *Wonderful. Do you have any questions specifically for me?*

I think with what you've said you have already answered my question. How to open more or more directly? Yeah, I guess my consciousness and, in my heart, to get in touch to get connected with the invisible realm. *I also want you to remember the green selenite. You were invited into that selenite. Allow yourself to go back to that space to unite with that vibration and help it to be able to open your heart.* Okay. *Okay. Blessings daughter blessings to you.* Thank you.

Jamar to Linda:

You, child, over there. We are making great progress are we not? Yes. Yes, we are! *I want you to know it's just not me alone who is working on building this relationship. It is also your Spirit Guide. It is also the God Source which is helping to prepare you, through the use of my information and my energy to grow you. Do you understand this?* Yes. *Wonderful, wonderful!*

So, the Panthers Meadows… Have you taken time to look at that upon the line, that online thing? Yes. Giggle. *Wonderful.* Yes, I have. *Wonderful! Have you envisioned yourself going and visiting there yet?* Yes, I have. *Wonderful. Where did you sit?* I can't tell you the exact spot. I know I sat on a slate stone with the mountains behind me and looking into the meadow. *Wonderful. Wonderful! Oh, I got such chills right then, because I knew exactly where you were.* Very excited demeanor. Clapping hands. *I knew exactly where you were!*

So now, the season is changing and there is snow that is falling upon the land. Great peace comes with that, too. So… you do not have to feel the temperature of the weather, when you're traveling there within your mind. Your heart always keeps you warm and safe within that space. When you are there, you need to listen with more than your ears but with your heart…, to hear the whispers of the words of wisdom. The wisdom of the land, and the wisdom and the knowledge of the sacred people that are of that land.

The other thing that I need to mention, is that there are more than Lemurians that are on that land, it being of such a high vibrational space. Many different kinds of Entities are all gathering to this place. So, you do need to be cautious of all the different entities that are coming into play that may be wanting to come and to communicate with you. Just always pray for the power of protection beforehand, to ensure that you are prepared and guided all along the way. That's all I have to say.

Do you have any questions for me this day? No, not really. *Wonderful. Then continue to go ahead and to write and to journal and to go back to that place. Plan to visit before sleep. This is a great time and more shall come soon.* Thank you. *Blessings, blessings to you.*

Jamar to Group

So, what I want to say upon this day, is thank you. Thank you to each of you, for truly opening your hearts and your minds to more than what you understood. There is always so much more than what we know of... The world is round, not what it was thought to be. There is always more to be learned, and to grow and to do that's new, and I am just so grateful to have had the opportunity to work with each of you. This includes the visual audience too.

Blessings dear children, blessings to you.

Jamar was very loving and gentle in his speech tone and vibration. Soft, joyful and delighted to have visited once again. It is very evident that as time passes, his comfort level increases with the use of the physical body and the vocal vibrational control that he can manipulate. When he first visited, he was stoic and had a computer resonance while speaking and now he emits emotion and love through his thoughts and words.

INCORPORATION BAYLOT

Baylot entered once again at the conclusion of the session. His energy is incredibly supportive, and he works diligently to balance mine through the many incorporations. *Baylot here, once again. I just want to say thank you. Is there anything that is left remaining that we need to clarify or clear up on this evening?* I don't think so. *Wonderful.*

Wonderful! Well blessings to each of you.

After Discussion

After all incorporations departed, I commented on my feeling of elation. Relaxed, joyful and loving. I have grown exponentially through the incorporations, and this evening I felt as if I were still glowing with residual energy afterwards. I could feel a very large aura around me that was just spectacular. I also commented on my ears popping, because of the pressure changes I had experienced with the incorporations.

We talked through the various visitors and spoke of Azrael's message that the more we ask of the angels, the more they will grow and the importance of asking for assistance at any time. One participant knows Azrael as their Angel and confirmed the essence was the same. We all found it fascinating to hear from the God Source about our activities during the night hours, sparkles of light, mandalas, faces and family soul connections. Another similarity we observed was an orbing, pulsing visualization. We need not worry when traveling as long as we remain with a loving intent. We will always be accompanied and safe from harmful influences.

Closing Prayer

Heavenly Father. Thank you. Thank you for the blessings of this day. Thank you so much for the blessings of each of the spirits, the wisdom, the knowledge, and the grace that has been showered into this room and all those who are listening. Heavenly Father, we ask that you hold our love up, and allow it to emulate out into the universe, far beyond, for all Lights Beings. Heavenly Father, we pray for peace around this planet. We pray for healing to our Mother Earth. We pray for personal guidance always within our hearts. Help us to go forth and to walk your path. We ask this in your precious name, amen. Amen.

Session 9

Opening Prayer

Heavenly Father, Thank You. Thank you for the blessings of this day. Thank you, for the magic that swirls in the air. Thank you, for the love that showers down, upon and into each and every one of our hearts. Open our hearts, our minds and our energies to all of the opportunities from beyond our knowledge, beyond our wisdom and into and through all energies of life. Heavenly Father, we welcome all to this sacred circle. We ask this in your precious name. Amen.

Introduction

THE MEMBERS OF THE CIRCLE expressed the desire to connect with each of Spirit Guides as a focus for this session. It was decided that personal messages to the participants would not be included within the manuscript; however, all group messages or guidance would be. The guided mediation was unique in that it allowed personal time for everyone to look deep within their hearts, to meet or to see their special spirit guide. Everyone had more than one spirit guide, one who has chosen to be with you for this lifetime and then others who will accompany you at various times. We inquired who had identified their guides names or not.

This was our last scheduled session and as time allowed, we opened the remaining time to Baylot for whomever had the greatest message to share. We would complete the session with allowing Elder Jamar to provide any closing thoughts or guidance.

FIRST INCORPORATION: GATEKEEPER BAYLOT

I spoke about Baylot just prior to incorporation explaining who he was in my life. Baylot is my Gatekeeper and not my Spirt Guide. He has a specific job and a duty as my protector of energy. Baylot has waited many years for me to develop into this role; however, he was not the only one guiding me to get there. We have seen great transformation with Baylot through this process. He began ridged, timid and matter of fact in his tone and only showed up occasionally. Now, as our relationships developed, he has become vibrant, jubilant, animated, loves having a voice, and relishes being the center of attention. We have now referred to him as "Bob Barker", the game show host. Presently he has enjoyed visiting before and after each of the incorporations. Baylot has NOT been eager for the sessions to end, as there are so many still waiting in line with knowledge and guidance.

Hello, Hello. Baylot here. Baylot here. How are you tonight? Good. How are you? *How am I? This is my day.* Belly laugh. *This is my day. I get to be in charge today, so I'm very excited!*

We're going to be speaking with Spirit Guides tonight are we not? Yes, we are! *We are, and I have to tell you, I am a little bit sad that the other ones aren't here tonight to be able to get their messages, because we've been working with so many of their Spirit Guides throughout, and now, their Spirit Guides are a little bit bummed, that they're not going to have the opportunity to have their messages herd, or to be able to understand the true meaning of their relationships.*

We have spoken of Spirit Guides several different times throughout this series of classes and it's very important. It is truly the most important relationship you can have with an Entity besides the God Source, because they're with you from the beginning until the end. They only wish for the highest and best for you. They always are available to help... provide... and to guide you towards your betterment of life... all that you can be, all that you might be, and allow you to think beyond yourselves... so that you can become.

They are always your biggest cheerleaders of all time! The other thing I want you to understand is that they feel what you do. I know that may sound odd, but when people are very sad and they're in a depressive place and space in their life, their Spirit Guides are also in that emotion. They're not as joyful, because they're working so hard to help lift their energy and to pull them up. They're working so much harder to help them get anything done during that time... When you're asking for, listening for, and allowing the dreamtime activation and downloads of information to come into your lives. So that's a very important thing for each of you to know.

So, let's see which Spirit Guide do I want to get first? You may be surprised tonight, because I'm going to reach out... to provide you with information that's different than what you already knew. Okay. So, it's not what you have already mentioned. What you now know is not wrong by any means. This is just an opportunity to expand and to increase... to add to for each of you... For your own personal development.

Well... let me see who's going to come in first. Okay... so let me see who is going to come in. Goodbye.

SECOND INCORPORATION: SOUL STAR

The shift began with some body stretching and then the Spirit Guide Essence, Soul Star sat straight up in the chair. This is a male voice that is very monotone and structured in his speech pattern. The gentle essence filled with great wisdom began to speak.

I'm going to step in first... First, I will mention my name shortly. This is different. I am not a Spirit Guide for anyone in particular, but I am a Spirit Guide Essence. I want you to know how Spirit Guides come to be. What my position in the Universe is to help to train and to educate Spirit Guides and prepare them to be able to come into the Universe, so that then they are affiliated with a specific soul energy.

I want you to know, that the Being before you is now channeling me. There is great purple and violet light, which is transmuting through her essence, and I would not be surprised if each of you aren't seeing her. It's that orbing, pulsing violet light that's happening... and I want to mention that so that you have record of it, because there will not be memory later on. I exist in an entirely different place.

So, when different entities pass, humans can work their way through many levels and many lifetimes, to train to become a Spirit Guide for another human later on. It takes many lifetimes to train for this to transpire. I want you to know that what... a spirit needs to do, is to truly get to a place where they have no want of self. It is complete selfless gift of all! They spend their time exploring what is out in the universe, and then they understand what the soul of the person is looking for, because that's what the soul chose to be able to do within the universe. The Soul Spirit Guide is then decided upon, based on whatever the person's desire is that they want to come back and to accomplish in their lifetime.

I don't know if I want to say... What happens sometimes is that some Spirit Guides will choose to stay with the same soul's development for many different lifetimes. This is not something that you may be aware of, but this is a karmic agreement... that they will help them from the time of inception, to work through all the lifetimes that are necessary, if they're working towards going into the Angelic Realm. Do you understand that? Yes. Okay. Wonderful. Okay.

I want to take a few minutes to step in first, so that you can have a different level of understanding of how souls come to be,... and the soul of each person is made up of many different particles of other souls. They can take the very best of what is, of so many different souls and choose to create a new soul from that.

Today as the world continues to change so rapidly, there has to be a greater level of new souls that are created instead of just a single reincarnation, because these souls are too dense to manage and to live on this Earth as they are,... so they need to be changed, such as what was discussed before with the DNA bank and changing the DNA within the person. That's the same process that needs to happen with the souls. The souls have to be adjusted, to be able to come back and to be able to deal with the physical changes... along with the changes of energy vibrations, which are happening. The impacts of those energy vibrations, which are so electromagnetically made by mankind, are impacting and damaging the cells... and also the communication level within the Spirit Guides. Does that make sense to you? Yes.

Thank you. I appreciate that. This is very interesting. I've not had an opportunity to incorporate before... oh, my name! He stops speaking, smiles widely and faces each of the participants to share the smile. *You like those names. I don't have one of those. Um... You can call me Soul Star!* He sat up straighter and could tell he was proud to have a created a name and smiles broadly once again.

Sounds good. *Thank you. Thank you. Thank you for the opportunity to speak and I will go now.*

Soul Star was fairly monotone in voice quality and influx. He had a data quality to the essence of information that was relayed to the group. We were provided with highly valuable background information as an introduction to the subject prior to each of the spirit guide visitations.

Individual Messages

Several different spirit guides incorporated to provide personal guidance messages, which were specifically gifted to the various participants in this session: Bethel, Red Hawk, Blue Feather and Pricilla. Not all messages are written within this text and therefore are omitted if it was of personal nature to the circle participant.

Two of the transmissions spoke in other languages. Speaking in another language, whether the person can understand it or not isn't necessary, as the tone, vibration and frequency that is spoken through the verbal exchange will directly affect each of the participants. This energetic exchange can initiate new neurological pathways of communication or understanding that can be conscious, subconscious or both simultaneously.

THIRD INCORPORATION: RED HAWK

This incorporation began with great strength from a male entity. He stated that he too, was from a First Nation Native Tribe and began to speak in Native American language. His persona was an authoritative, warrior essence. About two minutes into his dialogue he opened his eyes, raising his hands and pointing toward the recipient for a direct transmission of energy. The energy was such a powerful shift in the room and exchange to the recipient. He then transitioned into English and explained the reason why he spoke in his native tongue was to open a new language level of understanding as part of her development.

After he stepped out, I was left with the residual of a mighty essence from this concentrated transference of energy. After discussion with the recipient, she reiterated the intensity of the energy that was received. She explained that her eyes became wide as saucers and she was truly taken back by the experience and what was initiated through this interaction.

FOURTH INCORPORATION: BLUE FEATHER

Audible deep breathing ensured as palms heated while rubbing together and a second powerfully strong, male Native American Spirit Guide stepped in. He also began speaking in Native America language. This was a different language from the previous guide. This was a tall warrior, dressed in full regalia including two red stripes across his cheek bones and you could see a battle scare over his right eye. An impressive spiritual entity who came to share ancient knowledge. Blue Feather spoke with a broken type of English and barely took in air while speaking. It was evident that he had not incorporated often or if ever.

Everyone in this group needs to understand the power and the connection of Mother Earth. As each of your Native Guides… come into this space… it is to help each of you to tap into the Earthen Roots as you're continuing your journeys to elevate. You need to be able to have true… connection with Mother Earth. That means you need to allow your roots which grow through the bottoms of your feet. Energy must be emitted through the soles of each of your feet to unite… around the different roots of the trees, through the microfibers of all of the living microorganisms, which are under the ground. It's the minerals… beyond the rocks. It's the minerals. Travel even deeper down into the core of the Mother Earth.

The energy that each of you are calling upon is coming from the highest God Source entity; however, it has to balance itself with the center core energy of the Universe, because it must be in a complete and total alignment. This is why sometimes you find yourself being pulled in two directions at once and it's because that's exactly what is happening you. Your growth and your energy is dependent upon the same as above as below to be able to help each of you with your growth process.

At this point Blue Feather completely shifted his energy and targeted one of the recipients and provided an individual message. During the message, he referenced the sacred gifts of animal parts and how their spirits are always attached, and we need to always remain respectful of each item. He also discussed the importance of walking barefoot on the land, as this naturally balances and grounds your energies. There is great wisdom when you spend time with the elements of life, Earth, wind, water, and air.

INCORPORATION: GATEKEEPER BAYLOT

After the four Spirit Guide message incorporations, Baylot stepped back in. He smoothly, rubbed hands together as a gentle and relaxed energy shifted through the circle.

Was that good? Yes, that was amazing! *Wonderful! Do you have any specific questions? No. Okay, we still have some time… let me see who is in the front of the line and thinks that they need to come in to provide some guidance.*

FIFTH INCORPORATION: GOD SOURCE

As palms were rubbing together for about fifteen seconds. My body bent forward with a deep inhale, I arched my back to a full upright position with a large and loving smile. A feeling of Infinite energy filled the room, the walls barely containing it – as the soft and loving presence incorporated. The temperature in the room increased and my face turned flush.

Daughters,

It is I… You need to understand the love that I feel for each of you. I need you to understand… and to feel the full presence… of the impacts of what each of you is doing.

I want each of you to understand what your energies are creating into the Universe, not just in this room, this space and of this world, but within and around the Universe! As you heard earlier today, it was spoken by, Soul Star. You need to reach deep within the center of Mother Earth and to balance the energies… it's not just into the center of Earth, it is through all of the Earth and all of the other energies.

Energies are very specific mathematical, geometric shapes, which travel along specific lines and unite. They come together in a circular form and they cross over. Each of your energies is traveling along those lines. What you may not understand is that because of the strength and the personal development of each of you, you're creating new energy lines that are emulating out from you, so that others are going forth and creating new intersection lines. Does that make sense? Yes.

You are each Star-Beings, with many points. Not just of the top and bottom and each side, but you have light emulating from all directions of each of you as a center essence of life. Each one of those light beams coming out are creating that same single spiraling motion and straight into and through each of you. You each are the beginning of a new life. New lives and new Universes are being created through the energies of what you are doing. The energy that is being emitted through each of you, your knowledge and wisdom are supporting that development too.

Humans have no way to comprehend what that means, but I want each of you to understand the incredible value of what you are doing. All of that energy, where does it come from... the beginning of it... the God Spark of love that is within the center of Self, because you're choosing to go out and to live beyond the mental mind of just a single person. It is for the betterment of mankind. It is for the love and the peace of this world. It is for the love and the peace of all men and woman... also, all of the Earth.

The elements of the earth... the grass... trees, water, and air... cleaning the air... by planting more trees and allowing once again... the balance once again to flow into and through. The positive impacts of your energy and the expressing of your energy into the Universe are transforming Mother Earth. I want... to try to explain that to each of you, so that you could understand the enormity of the beauty... and the pure essence of each of you,... and the universes you're creating too.

I thank you, daughters, for being... Being perfect... Being open... Being willing... Most especially for being a loving person... Choosing to look beyond yourself and allowing for your heart to lead you upon this way... allowing the energies of all to heal as it flows.

I also want to remind you, that you are here to experience life... all the flavors... all the colors... all the emotions. Please do so! Break outside of the limitations that you choose to create and barriers. Just allow yourself to be! Open yourself to new. Allow all of the blessings to shower down upon you.

There is so much to be seen and experienced, not just on this Earth Plane... Each of you has expanded yourself into new levels of knowledge and wisdom... to work with and to travel to these places. So, I want you to have faith, and to have no fear, because there is nothing to fear... only opportunities of more. The more people that you choose to get to know in life, the broader your blanket of love becomes. So, go forth and share. Share your heart... Share your wisdom... Share your knowledge... Share your peace... So many look upon you every day and are so gloriously joyful for what you bring to their lives. They may not tell you, but I'm here to let you know, what a glorious and beautiful being you are... and just how proud I am of each of you, for what you are doing in your lives and choosing to be.

So again, I remind you to go forth -- dance and celebrate! Be joyful and happy. Live each moment to the fullest... because you can! Blessings my children. Blessing to you. Blessings to you also.

The God Source always fills the room with such joy, peace, and love. The presence is omnipotent. Any concern or stress residual energy evaporates immediately, and we are embraced with comfort. He gracefully exits as an ocean wave upon the shore, with a large smile and exhale. A sigh from the group follows.

SIXTH INCORPORATION: ARCH ANGEL ARIEL

As My hands rubbed together, the familiar female essence gently joined the circle. Her purpose was to blanket everyone in healing love energy and the room filled with a soft pink glow.

I want to speak once more to add something quickly. Thank you to everyone for all that you have been doing and sharing your love into this space. I want you to feel the peace and the love that is around you. Pause.

I want you to feel the pink bubble of love, which I am infusing with all that can be, all that shall be and all that is. I want to offer you this opportunity to place in the center of this love bubble any worries or concerns for any loved one that you have in your life... or anyone that you know of... or any illness... or concerns you have in your own lives. Please place that in the center of this love bubble right now. Pause. *Allow for the healing energies just to carry it away... up into the ethers, into the Angelic Realm to heal it.*

Now just remember, you must let it go. If you hold on to it, we cannot fix it. Allow us to make that transition and that change. Blessings of love all around. Blessings of love and light to each of you.

Peace be with you. And with you.

Arch Angel Ariel very specifically came in to elevate healing energies of a large pink bubble that we could choose to place any worry or fearful thought within, so it could be carried to the heaven and be healed by all Entities within the universe. She closed the session with her hands in a prayerful pose and a slight bow of the head. She raised her arms toward the sky and floated up and away.

INCORPORATION: GATEKEEPER BAYLOT

Baylot here once again, to say thank you again to everyone. It was a very good night. I want you to know that the line of entities up here, is getting shorter. They know that you are going to stop for a few weeks, so they are not going to drive this one before you crazy. They are going to be a little bit mellow about that. Thank you. This has been a beautiful, beautiful experience! Thank you for giving me a voice. Blessings to you until we meet again. Blessings to you also.

Baylot was very gentle and at peace with this last incorporation. The entire circle's hearts were filled with gratitude and abiding devotion for the progress that had been made on this journey and accomplishments gleaned from this project.

After Discussion

The temperature of the room was calescent and we knew this was because of the high level of energies and the visiting Entities. I spoke about Soul Star's visit, and how I could see purple pulsing and vibrating light during the entire encounter. We all found it fascinating as none of us had ever heard previously that a spirit guide could go through multiple lifetimes with a soul. We then discussed the God Source message that our energies are creating new universes. Everyone commented on feeling different energies in the room, vivid colors, itching, heat waves and tingling throughout the evening. I commented on the importance of receiving guidance in the Native American language was to directly open a new level of communication with each who listened to the verbiage. Even though they did not understand the words, their Souls heard the divine messages imparted.

I reminded the group that they would be receiving written transcripts of the messages they received from the past few sessions for their personal growth and understanding. Everyone expressed their personal satisfaction with their participation in this outstanding event!

Closing Prayer

Heavenly Father, Thank you. Thank you, for the blessings of this day. Thank you, for the blessings of these souls. Thank you so much Heavenly Father, for the incredible wisdom, knowledge and guidance that you're providing into and through each of us. Help us to be able to carry forth this information to all those that we encounter. Heavenly Father, we are so very grateful that you lead the path which we follow. We ask this in your precious name. Amen. Amen.

THE JOURNEY CONTINUES

THE CHANNELINGS HAVE ENDED, AND the recordings are saved for posterity. I observe the classroom located in the college of Telos once again. Many hours have passed, but no one is tired. Everyone is still in complete attention and fully invested in learning all that they can from this meeting. I know that the perception time is different in an altered state, and all that has transpired did so in such a minuscule amount of time as I know it be. Jamar stands once again beside me and thanks me for participating in this valiant and loving adventure.

I feel the glow of gratitude of the other beings in attendance. I can feel their thoughts and curiosities as a slight background buzz, but it isn't distracting. The rhythmic hum only enhances my overall experience. The thrill of each of us who shared this spiritual journey unites our spirits, and we are better for it.

I really had not thought much about being brave. In retrospect, stepping out into the unknown, and listening to words beyond my understanding took extreme courage. My thirst for greater wisdom beyond my knowing, a desire to expand my personal journey, a willingness to reach beyond myself and then act upon that guidance truly was a leap of faith. I believe this is a trait that the entities find most appealing and inspiring. Believing in something beyond what is safe, having the courage to surrender to your higher Self, and allowing the journey to unfold before you, one brilliant step at a time, transforms how you see your world. It is so worth the effort!

I am incredibly honored to be a seeker and to have chosen to share this information released from the Universe, to be but one of the many who has opened her heart to receive this sacred guidance. For many months, I have reflected on the events which have transpired, while writing this book, and will continue to unwrap the details and meaning of this adventure. The words which filtered through me, have resonated in my soul. The lingering effects of the transmissions, their meaning, emotions, healing energies, love, wisdom and eternal truths imparted, extend far beyond human limitations of thought, time and space. I remember it all with such gratitude and joy. It is the *Truth Beyond*!

It was time to leave the lecture auditorium and I stood to do so. The room erupted in delight along with a thunderous applause for my visit. Everyone was a-buzz with thought chatter and excitement for what had transpired. I was introduced to so many incredible Lemurians. I was overwhelmed with the love, appreciation, and acceptance for my presence. An invitation was extended to return at any time by Jamar and the congregation. As I tearfully scanned the room for a final time, I photographed every detail in my mind for posterity. And so, we continue our individual journeys as both teacher and student simultaneously. The Lemurians hoped that I would return at a later time and why would I not? I see no ending to my thirst for knowledge for the remaining years of my life.

AS FOR THE OTHERS

THERE ARE NO CHANCE ENCOUNTERS in Spirit's Divine Plan. When I opened the invitation to a meditation circle online and in a local publication, I had no idea of who, if anyone, would join this enlightening sojourn. To my delight, God Source provided six consistent and courageous women!

Before you read their perceptions of the journey to Telos, it is important to share one more testimonial. When Su and I traveled to Harrisburg, Pennsylvania, to conduct a Shamanic workshop, you will remember from the chapter, "Prophesy," that I conducted a soul-retrieval session with a client. I reached out after returning to Florida by email to ensure all was well. It had been an extremely dramatic healing, and I wanted to inquire if any follow-up healing was needed. I received the following affirmation:

> *Thanks for checking in on me. It's lovely to hear from you. I am doing well. I went a week without meat and now that I am back eating it, I find I have less desire for it. Particularly red meat. The salt bath also helped. I feel that I am less critical of my past now and at least one friend has remarked that I seem "lighter". Tonight, at a Meditation workshop I drew a card that said, "Treat yourself with gentleness" reminding me of a major theme of our private session. I'm working on it!*

> *I really enjoyed both the class and the session and hope that you will return to Reiki Space in the future. I also hope that your time in New York State was wonderful.*

> Marie M.

The Meditation team was an integral part of the success of this endeavor. They contributed their energies like batteries, lifting and sustaining the transmission. In turn, their faithful participation ensured the authenticity of the channeled messages. Please read how they were affected by the sessions:

> *Judi is such a wonderful soul! Her beauty, love and warmth radiate from her. The work she does with crystals, healing, channeling and class instruction are phenomenal. I have worked beside Judi for a while now, doing healing services. She has been a light for me, as a counselor and a friend.*

> *I have truly enjoyed being a part of the Channeled Spirit Circle series. As Judi opens herself to be a vessel for many forms of light beings to come through and answer direct questions as well as provide other information, you feel the energy, see their personalities and realize the joy that these entities have to be able to have a voice. The ability to communicate with Light Beings that exist beyond our mindset and beliefs is such an enlightening personal experience. This experience has allowed me to grow. Thank you, Judi. I look forward to working with you further.*

> Linda

★★★★★★★★★★★★★★★★★★★★★★★

> *I have known Judi Weaver to be a gifted shaman and healer of great compassion and integrity. This class, however, challenged my thinking in ways unexpected. My understanding of the world we are part of has shifted and clarified because of the*

messages received through her channeling of entities near and far. What an honor to be witness to this experience!

Joan

★★★★★★★★★★★★★★★★★★★★★★

In the words of David A.R. White, "Life isn't about finding yourself; it is about discovering who God created you to be." Fortunately for me, meeting Judi kick-started my discovery process.

I met Judi one Sunday as she was leaving a church service. She was so friendly and open that I asked her about the church. We spoke for quite some time, and she invited me to attend their services. She was a co-pastor at the time, and later became the full-time pastor.

Judi was always encouraging, positive, giving of her time and knowledge. She helped me believe in myself and to love myself. Because of this, I began to realize my soul's purpose; and for that, I will always be truly grateful.

Although our church group no longer meets for regular services, we have kept in contact. I was excited to hear about the channeling circle Judi was forming. I was already aware of Judi's channeling abilities but this proved to be a different and unique experience for all of us. There was so much powerful, loving energy within the room each time we met. I believe we were all enriched in one way or another. Some of the information we received was new to us, and some affirmed what we already knew and believed.

I am so grateful that Judi invited me to join her on this mind and soul expanding adventure. I feel truly blessed.

Debbie

★★★★★★★★★★★★★★★★★★★★★★

A truly sacred experience for me! As Judi prepared and opened herself to allow for the energy of Universal Light Beings to come in and answer the stated questions through her voice, I felt their energy and the energy in the room throughout my own energy field. This stayed with me up to two days afterwards and felt very transformative. An amazing experience for me, as I have not explored Psychic Channeling before much and especially not in person. It is way different from watching it on YouTube! The personal group questions were responded to in a clear, understandable way to give guidance for our lives. Imagine, having an actual conversation with the Being speaking through Judi at that moment! The tapping in beyond our knowing for universal exploration to receive divine messages and guidance from Universal Light Beings was a fascinating personal experience that lingers, and my Soul from deep inside asks for more. Thank you, Judi!

I thank you very much for all that you've given us, your service, and your love.

Namaste, Ute

****

With no expectations other than to see what type of experience this would be, I agreed to go to my first channeling. After the first night, I left knowing that I wanted to attend every session! I definitely was not disappointed. I learned things that enhanced what I already knew and got confirmation on things I wasn't really sure of. I was overwhelmed with great joy of all the experiences that took place during these channelings, and would do it again in a heartbeat, to continue learning, as I know this is but a mere fragment of the many wondrous things to be done, explored, and learned.

Great thanks for the opportunity to participate in such a magnificent venture.

Many thanks, Karen

★★★★★★★★★★★★★★★★★★★★★★

I am grateful to have participated in the Channeled Spirit Circle. It was interesting to hear from the different entities on their perspective of the spiritual shift occurring on the earth at this time.

Hearing what the other participants in our group had to say or were experiencing, was also helpful and comforting. I thank each of them for their thoughts and input. I believe that our combined energies focused on healing our earth does make a difference.

I thank the Rev. Judi Weaver for her guidance, energy and talent in bringing Jamar, from Telos, and all the other entities into our presence to impart their wisdom on us. It was truly an amazing experience.

Annette S.

★★★★★★★★★★★★★★★★★★★★★★

It is certain that each of the participant's spirituality was ignited, and they will continue to seek their way on their individual paths on the spiral circle. I know they are forever transformed by their experiences. My heart overflows with joy with thoughts of their endeavors and service to other seekers they encounter.

UNTIL WE MEET AGAIN

I HOPE THAT YOU HAVE enjoyed my story of this amazing life adventure that I have shared within these pages and moments of time. I pray the energies exchanged by these words, the power, wisdom, peace, and love which have been gifted, will permeate any barriers, allowing for your acceptance and personal growth. May these words inspire your acceptance of your divine Self. May your willingness to open your heart to the unknown and celebration for this incredible life journey that you find yourself on at this time.

The Entities continue to congregate to provide additional guidance and wisdom. I continue to channel their information through hosted circles, gatherings, online and book tours. I invite each of you to reach out and stay connected. Please visit me at the following touchstones:

> Websites **Heart4Souls.com, SpiritualServices.online**;
> YouTube Channel **Rev. Judi Weaver**; or
> Facebook **Heart4Souls**.

Without exception, this spiritual journey has been led by God, Source and Universal Light Beings, including the timing of its occurrence. When I began the project, I fully understood the importance of the 222 messages that I had received during October of 2017 and related it to my desire to have this book published by February 22, 2020. I had not remembered all the details and how the plan was actually prophesized during that transmission. It became evident through the editing process, which added great depth to its validity and purpose to mankind. According to Tania Gabrielle, 22:22:20:20, astrologically speaking, in January was a quadruple conjunction not seen in 500 years, which is impacting us all year long. Now Mars has joined Pluto and Jupiter which all culminate on April 4th, 2020. "We are going to be the sacred warriors that Mars represents through this healing process!"

I had booked a few speaking engagements early and was looking forward to having the book ready to launch. It became evident that my timing was off and asked for a delay, which was granted. Little could I have ever anticipated the crippling affects from the Coronavirus 19 and the world moving into a state of pause during this same time. My scheduled slot was filled from the prior month's cancelations. I am so honored that due to unforeseen publication issues the book is being republished through Balboa Press, just as Spirit had intended. 2020 is the year of complete clarity and truth to be seen for all. This book was born through the ashes and great awakening of our world such as the birth of a phoenix!

Life is such an amazing adventure and now we are blessed that your path has intertwined with mine. We will be forever changed for the better through this encounter. I invite you to join me at an event, class or personal session to allow yourself to learn more. May you become what you soul has called out for your personal destiny.

Blessings of Love & Light

Judi

ADDITIONAL RESOURCES & IMAGES

ALKEZIA STAR SYSTEM: Information was found on star system search. For five hundred years, the city of Alkezia has stood for peace and has worked for the reunification of a splintered world. It alone breaks the continuous Wall that stretches around the globe, separating the people of the world into those with powers and those without. What made them separate in the first place is something no one really knows, although the Gifted blame it on the Non-Gifted and vice versa, each having their own versions of the story that has been so embellished and twisted over time that no one really knows the truth of what happened anymore. Alkezia alone stands between these two warring nations, providing a haven for all those who wish to work for a better, brighter future. https://faadv2.proboards.com/thread/356/alkezia.

ALTHENIA: Spirit Guide name. Althenia is a genus of aquatic plants of the family Potamogetonaceae. Wikipedia.

ANGELS:

Arch Angel Ariel: Ariel's literal name means "lion or lioness of God" as referenced in the Hebrew Bible. According to ask-angels.com, she is known for overseeing nature, healing, magic and manifestation. Ask-angels.com.

Arch Angel Azrael: Arch Angel Azrael's name means 'Whom God helps," and his primary function is to assist people in making the transition from this world to the afterlife. Though often known as the Angel of Death, Azrael actually uses his compassion and healing energy to assist everyone during the death process. Ask-angels.com.

Arch Angel Michael: His name in Hebrew literally means: "Who is as God" is an incredible being of Cosmic Intelligence. When we're in his presence we naturally question the truth of our nature and what is required to further progress and to "be as God" more in our individual lives. Ask-angels.com.

Angle Realm, Jerilla: Knowing the Angelic Realm: Angels are the bridge between the spirit and the physical realm. They are the messengers of God and vibrate in God Source light. There are fifteen or so Arch Angels who are holy angels and protect both, the spirit and the physical realms. Speakingtree.in.

Angel in Training, Gerome: To understand an angel "in training," it may be helpful to have knowledge of a hierarchy of angels. The idea that there are different types and ranks of angels is not a new one. This concept comes from Christian esotericism where there are seen to be nine ranks or orders of angels, also called the Angelic Hierarchies.

Each of the angel ranks refers to that group of angelic beings who have evolved to a particular level of consciousness, and it also refers to the activities and the work and service they perform. Ask-angels.com.

ARCHAEA STAR SYSTEM: Refers to a stellar system of starts that orbit each other, bound by gravitational attraction, not to be confused with planetary systems.

ARCAEA: Jerome stated that we do not have a clue that it exists. Arcaea's Star System is in the Galaxion Orpha Myasis System. Research found video game references, but no-star related information was found.

ATLANTIS: Is the Lost Island Kingdom of Greek Legend. ATLANTIS was a legendary island realm of the far west which was sunk beneath the ocean by the gods to punish its people for their immorality. The term "Atlanteans" was also applied by the Greeks to the Phoenician colonies along the Barbary Coast of North Africa--i.e. those living near the Atlas Mountains. www.theoi.com › Phylos › Atlantes.

AURAS: We are energy and it is our frequency that creates an energetic field around us. This field around our physical body is known as the "aura." The auric field generally radiates six to eighteen inches around the physical body. To be able to see auras, we need to develop our ability to understand how energy feels in our bodies. Close your eyes, align your breath, and ask the colors to show themselves to you. As we achieve a state of relaxed awareness, softening our gaze, we allow the colors to come to us. https://www.gaia.com/article/how-to-see-auras.

BETHEL: (Ugaritic meaning "House of El" or "House of God", Hebrew: בֵּית אֵל bêṯ'êl, also transliterated Beth El, Beth-El, Beit El; Greek: Βαιθηλ; Latin: Bethel) is a toponym often used in the Hebrew Bible. Wikipedia.

CHAKRAS: There are seven main chakras, starting from the base of the spine through to the crown of the head. The Sanskrit word, Chakra literally translates to wheel or disk. To visualize a chakra in the body, imagine a swirling wheel of energy where matter and consciousness meet. This invisible healing energy, called Prana, is vital life force, which keeps us vibrant, healthy, and alive. Centerchopra.com.

DARKNESS: The polar opposite of brightness, is understood as a lack of illumination or an absence of visible light. Human vision is unable to distinguish color in conditions of either high brightness or high darkness. The emotional response to darkness has generated metaphorical usages of the term in many cultures.

As a poetic term in the Western world, darkness is used to connote the presence of low vibration shadows, evil, and foreboding, or in modern parlance, to connote that a story is grim, heavy, and/or depressing. Wikipedia.

ELEMENTALS (Fairies): The Elemental Kingdom of Humans, Fairies, Elves, Gnomes, and Earth Spirits, Nature Angels. There are many different types of beings in the Elemental Kingdom, including 'mythical creatures' such as leprechauns, sylphs, mermaids, brownies and tree-people. There are four basic essentials of the Elemental Kingdom, with each of the four elements holding the nature spirits which are their spiritual essence of Fire, Air, Earth and Water. Air spirits such as Fairies, can be found wherever there are plants or animals. They may often appear as tiny, twinkly colored lights or swirling mists. Fairies are the Elementals who are primarily involved with animals and pets, but also with healing humans. Animals have fairies as their guardian angels and those who live in or upon water have 'sylphs' as their guardian angels. Fairies can also act as guardian angels for people whose life purpose involves nature, ecology and land conservation as well as animal welfare.

Some of their characteristics: love of nature, mischievous and fun-loving, very sensitive and not usually ones to listen to authority. www.7thsensepsychics.com.

GATEKEEPER BAYLOT: Judi's Spirit Gatekeeper organizes, monitors and acts as a guardian in preparation and during incorporation channeling.

GERMANIA: the Roman term for the historical region in north-central Europe initially inhabited mainly by Germanic tribes. Wikepedia.com

GOD SOURCE: God is the Infinite Intelligence that creates all things. It is not a man in the sky or a woman for that matter. It is an energy that pervades all things and is part of it all. It does not judge, condemn or think like we do. It is simply a vibration of love, of wholeness, of completion. In that energy you feel complete and at peace. There is nothing you have to do or prove or become. It is just a state of peace that you relax into when you connect with it. www.jodiannemsmith.com/2015/08/08/what-is-god/.

GOD SPARK: In Gnosticism and other Western mystical traditions, the Divine Spark is the portion of God that resides within each human being. In these theologies, the purpose of life is to enable the Divine Spark to be released from its captivity in matter and reestablish its connection with God who is perceived as being the source of the Divine Light. In the Gnostic Christian tradition, Christ is seen as a wholly divine being, which has taken human form in order to lead humanity back to the God Source. Wikipedia.

GRID: A network of uniformly spaced horizontal and perpendicular energy lines, specifically used for locating points by means of a system of coordinates. Webster's dictionary.

Their findings were published in '*Khimiya i Zhizn*', the popular science journal of the Academy of Sciences, entitled 'Is the Earth a Giant Crystal?' They decided that there was nothing in theory to prevent a lattice-working pattern – a 'matrix of cosmic energy' as they put it – being built into the structure of the earth at the time when it was being formed, whose shape could still be dimly perceived today.

INTERGALACTIC DNA BANK: Is the New Divine. Your DNA and your cellular consciousness are changing. The Information stored in The Coding of Your DNA is evolving as you immerse your cellular consciousness in the God Source frequency your cells and DNA vibrate in harmony with the fifth dimension. Humanitythenewdivinehumanity. com › 2012/09/16 › dna-and-the-5th-dimension.

KRYON (place): Unable to find location for Kryon.
My name isn't really Kryon, and I am not a man. I wish I could impart to you what it is like to be the entity that I am, but at this time, because of basic human implants of psychological restriction, you simply are unable to understand. I am KRYON of *"magnetic service"*. I have created the magnetic grid system of your planet. This took eons of Earth time.

221

It was balanced and re-balanced to match the physical vibrations of your evolving planet. Earth polarity was altered many times. Your science can prove this; look for soil strata that will show multiple "*flips*" of north and south polarity of the Earth during its development. (The Earth did not flip; only the polarity). http://www.ascensionnow.co.uk/kryon--who-is-kryon--and-who-are-we.html.

LABYRINTH: A Labyrinth is a place constructed of or full of intricate passageways and blind alleys a complex labyrinth of tunnels and chambers or a maze (as in a garden) formed by paths separated by high hedges.

LAW OF ATTRACTION: The Law of Attraction is the ability to attract into our lives whatever we are focusing on. ... It is the Law of Attraction which uses the power of the mind to translate whatever is in our thoughts and materialize them into reality. In basic terms, all thoughts turn into things eventually. www.lawofattraction.com.

LEY LINES: Straight alignments drawn between various historic structures and prominent landmarks. The idea was developed in early 20th century Europe, with ley line believers that these alignments were recognized by ancient European societies which deliberately erected structures along them. Since the 1960s, members of the Earth Mysteries movement and other esoteric traditions have commonly believed that such ley lines demarcate "earth energies" and serve as guides for alien spacecraft. Wikipedia.

LEMURIA: Spiritual messages are transmitted from Ascended Masters and Telos, the Lemurian City of Light. The Lemurian Age took place approximately between the years 4,500,000 BC to about 12,000 years ago. Until the sinking of the continents of Lemuria and later of Atlantis, there were seven major continents on Earth. The lands belonging to the gigantic continent of Lemuria included lands now under the Pacific Ocean as well as Hawaii, the Easter Islands, the Fiji Islands, Australia, New Zealand, as well as lands in the Indian Ocean and Madagascar. The Eastern coast of Lemuria also extended to California and part of

British Columbia in Canada. For a very long time before the fall in consciousness, the Lemurians lived in a fifth dimensional frequency or dimension and were able to switch back and forth from fifth to third dimension at will. It could be done whenever it was desired, by intension and the energies of the heart.

The Lemurian race was a mixture of beings that came mainly from Sirius, Alpha Centauri and a smaller number of them from other planets as well. Eventually, as these races mixed together on Earth, they formed the Lemurian civilization. Lemuria was really the cradle of civilization on this planet, the "Motherland" that assisted in the eventual birth of many other civilizations. Atlantis came about at a later time.

The continent of Lemuria thrived in a state of paradise and magic for a few millions of years. Eventually, as a result of wars between the two major continents, great devastations took place on Lemuria and on Atlantis. Twenty-five thousand years ago, Atlantis and Lemuria, the two highest civilizations of the time were battling each other over "ideologies". They had two very different ideas about how the direction of other civilizations on this planet should be. The Lemurians believed that the other less evolved cultures should be left alone to continue their own evolution at their own pace according to their own understandings and pathway. In the time of Lemuria, California was part of the Lemurian land. When the Lemurians realized that their land was destined to perish, they petitioned the Shamballa-the-Lesser, the head of the Agartha Network, for permission to build a city beneath Mount Shasta in order to preserve their culture and their records. https://www.lemurianconnection.com/lemuria-and-telos/ The Lemurian Connection; https://www.unariunwisdom.com/mount-shasta-telos-and-lemuria/.

LEMURIAN ELDER, JAMAR: Jamar identified himself as an Elder Lemurian who had lived in Lemuria when it existed off the coast of California. He currently resides in the City of Telos where he is a regarded Elder, teacher and leader in his community. He is the Entity that telepathically reached out to Judi and channeled guidance, information and initiated the sessions and the creation of this book. Jamar told us he was approximately 25,000 years old, widowed, and truly wants to help mankind through our evolutionary process. Judi is the first and only channel that he has chosen to work with.

LIGHT RAYS: A light ray is a line (straight or curved) that is perpendicular to the light's wave fronts; its tangent is collinear with the wave vector. Light rays in homogeneous media are straight. They bend at the interface between two dissimilar media and may be curved in a medium in which the refractive index changes. Wikipedia.

MANDALAS: Sanskrit मण्डल, mandala – literally "circle", is a geometric configuration of symbols with a very different application. In modern, typically American and European use, "mandala" has become a generic term for any circle ornament which can be used as a relaxing tool, for diagnostic MARI card test or in art therapy. In various spiritual traditions, mandalas may be employed for focusing attention of practitioners and adepts, as a spiritual guidance tool, for establishing a sacred space and as an aid to meditation and trance induction. Wikipedia.

MINI CHAKRA'S: There are over 114 chakras in the human body. You thought it was just the seven? We are complex bodies with up to 7200 meridians, too. Out of the total chakras, major, minor and micro, 112 are within the human body and two are outside the human body. Moreover, mini, minor or secondary chakras in the human body are even described differently. Atperry's.com.

NATIVE AMERICANS:

Blue Feather and Red Hawk of Lenape Tribe: Historically, there have been many Native Americans with names that reference Blue Feather and Red Hawk, and this includes the Lenape Tribe. As Native Americans age, they will change their names based on traditional milestones during their lifetime. There are specific animal totem meanings behind chosen names such as noted: a feather from a bluebird symbolizes happiness and fulfilment; a feather from a hawk symbolizes guardianship, strength and far-sightedness. www.warpaths. peachpipes.com.

REDWOOD TREE IN CALIFORNIA, GRANDFATHER REDWING (Sequoia): These giants of the forest grow to heights of 300 feet or more above the forest floor. They are among the Elder spirits of the earth plane, who grow together in a community. Many Light Workers and sensitives who walk these groves feel the sacredness from the roots below to the towering evergreens overhead... The Sequoia Tree symbolize wellness and safety in that they have a natural ability to withstand fires and many types of decay. www.buildbeautifulsouls.com.

Grandfather Redwing was physically located outside of the window where Judi stayed in Mt. Shasta, California and channeled guidance to her during the visit and again later during session to the group.

REFLEXOLOGY: The underlying theory behind reflexology is that there are certain points or reflex areas on the feet and hands that are connected energetically to specific organs and body parts through energy channels in the body.

By applying pressure to reflex areas, a reflexologist is said to remove energy blockages and promote health in the related body area. https:// www.verywellhealth.com/reflexology.

SANSABAR: Nothing found for Sansabar; however, it could be a decedent from Zanzibar. Zanzibar is a Tanzanian archipelago off the coast of East Africa. On its main island, Unguja, familiarly called Zanzibar, is Stone Town, a historic trade center with Swahili and Islamic influences. It's winding lanes present minarets, carved doorways and 19th Century landmarks such as the House of Wonders, a former sultan's palace. Wikipedia.

SACRED GEOMETRY: Ascribes symbolic and sacred meanings to certain geometric shapes and certain geometric proportions. It is associated with the belief that a God is the geometer of the world. Wikipedia.

SIRIUS STAR SYSTEM: Sirius is the brightest star in the night sky. Its name is derived from the Greek word Σείριος Seirios "glowing" or "scorching", with a visual apparent magnitude of −1.46, Sirius is almost twice as bright as Canopus, the next brightest star in our galaxy. Wikipedia.

SPIRIT GUIDE: Each person is the leader of a team assembled to achieve tasks. You organize your team prior to each lifetime. Some of your teammates are also currently inhabiting human life forms--other people. The rest are not. These non-incarnate essences are sometimes referred to as spirit guides or helpers. Most of your guides are not working exclusively with you. However, everyone has at least one primary guide. https://www.michaelteachings.com/spirit-guides.html.

SOUL STAR: According to author Liz Oakes, the soul star chakra is associated with the origin of enlightenment and with the principle of ascension, and to the ideal, 'I transcend'. This chakra is situated above the highest point of the physical body, and is approximately a hand width above the head, or around six inches, and up to two feet in some people.

It is the first transpersonal chakra. It is sometimes called the seat of the soul, as it is the point where spiritual energy, and Divine Love, enters the body. https://www.healing-crystals-for-you.com/soul-star-chakra.html.

TELOS: Lemurian City located inside of Mount Shasta in California. See Lumeria references.

TELEPORTATION (Astro-Travel): By definition, it is the instantaneous or near instantaneous transmission of energy from one set of space-time coordinates to another. Time travel involves a similar process except that you travel to a different time coordinate as well as, or instead of, different spatial coordinates. It is very possible to create or increase your 'reality depth' in another location or dimension so that this can rival or exceed the experiential lucidity of your physical reality.

Remember that everything starts with your imagination, intention, and creative willpower.

There are several techniques for teleportation including focused meditation, lucid dreaming, spiritual journeying, astral projection, and bilocation. These methods often require significant time and effort before tangible results arise and don't require long development timescales and expensive technology. Many are internal methods and depend on internal spiritual and esoteric cultivation. There are also external technologies for teleportation like those seen in **Star Trek** and Doctor Who, which really do exist! https://www.starmagichealing.com/teleportation-techniques/.

THIRD EYE: The third eye chakra is the space between the eyes, which perceives the more subtle qualities of reality. It goes beyond the more physical senses into the realm of subtle energies. Awakening your third eye allows you to open up to an intuitive sensibility and inner perception. https://www.chakras.info/third-eye-chakra/.

TONING (SOUND VIBRATION): Vocal Toning is a powerful sound healing technique which uses the vibration of your voice for stress relief and relaxation by creating a real body and mind massage from the inside out. Vocal Toning is a boost for your physical and mental health. https://www.udemy.com/course/vocal-toning-sound-healing-through-your-own-voice/.

UBANIA: Jerome told us this was a country in the star system of Alkezia. Unable to find additional information for this.

VENUS: Venus is the second planet from the Sun. It is named after the Roman goddess of love and beauty. As the second-brightest natural object in the night sky after the Moon, Venus can cast shadows and, rarely, is visible to the naked eye in broad daylight. Wikipedia.

Gateway Entrance

Lemurian Sacred Geometric Symbols

Channeled by Rev. Judi Weaver, 10/2019

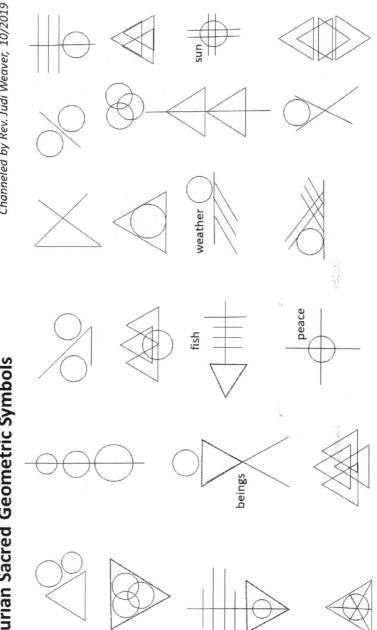

Lemurian Symbols

ABOUT THE AUTHOR

REVEREND JUDI STETSON WEAVER IS a gifted psychic trance channel and healer who has many sacred energies flowing through her. Judi walks a path which is open to growth and change each day. She is both teacher and student, receiving information in unique ways so that learning is meaningful. With willingness and a pure heart, she grows facing the sun as the sunflower.

Judi is an Ordained Minister, Psychic Channel, and international professional Certified Healer with twenty-five years of experience. She is the founder of Heart 4 Souls, a non-profit organization, dedicated to spiritual development. She is a published author and Shamanic Practitioner, being the dedicated Grandmother Sun Spirit of the Talking Stick Circle in the Southern Cassadaga Spiritualist Camp in Florida.

She has studied with internationally recognized teachers and has been spiritually healing for decades. Her services include remote and hands-on healing, with the ability to move a person into deep unconsciousness and unite the hand of God or Source Energies to alter the physical, mental, emotional and spiritual conditions that are not of the highest and purest intent. As a trance channel, she allows for various light beings through the God Source to filter into the physical plane so that information and guidance can be relayed to mankind. This information can be used to answer personal questions or can allow for clarification of an unsettling life situation. You will feel her works, but more importantly, your soul will connect with the Universal that permeates through her heart and into yours. Love, peace, joy, patience and perfectness of Self -- all of who you truly are.

Reverend Judi provides group and private sessions, both in person and virtually. For more information or to schedule a session please visit the website: www.Heart4Souls.com; www.SpiritualServices.online.

Blessings of Love & Light

Testimony

Judi Stetson Weaver is a true gifted Spiritual Counselor and Healer. She connects with her clients with extraordinary and loving insight, which helps them to shed the mysterious veil surrounding their problems. Thus, with this assistance, healing rapidly begins. Upon meeting her, you will feel her transcending Love.

Nancy Jo R.

In early 2019, I felt guided to create a ceremony space at my house. It was a slow and intuitive process, leading me deeper into connecting with Mother Earth. Judi helped me along the way with guidance and encouragement.

She opened the space in July of 2019, in a ceremony together. She called in Native American Spirits who provided messages of love and gratitude for the space. Then she led our first ceremony with six people during a full moon on September 13th, 2019. It was powerful! We had an owl greet us as we called in the east and a hawk flew near us as the winds shifted as invited. She channeled messages from the spirit world and also gave an individual message to each of us.

Judi also created a stunningly beautiful Native American garment for me for the occasion. Judi is a powerful healer of love and light and I am filled with gratitude for her help to initiate my ceremony space!

Judy S.

Grandmother Sun Spirit, Thank you so much for the monthly Talking Stick Circle. I leave feeling up-lifted and more positive. The like-minded people I've met there are kindred souls and they love nature, too. I've made many new friends.

April. W.

Printed in the United States
By Bookmasters